Parliament Under Pressure

By the same author

THE THATCHER GOVERNMENT

THE THATCHER DECADE

HONEST OPPORTUNISM

Parliament Under Pressure

PETER RIDDELL

VICTOR GOLLANCZ

LONDON

First published in Great Britain 1998
by Victor Gollancz
An imprint of the Cassell Group
Wellington House, 125 Strand, London WC2R OBB

© Peter Riddell 1998

The right of Peter Riddell to be identified as author of
this work has been asserted by him in accordance with
the Copyright, Designs and Patents Act, 1988.

A catalogue record for this book is
available from the British Library.

ISBN 0 575 06435 8

Typeset by Rowland Phototypesetting Ltd,
Bury St Edmunds, Suffolk
Printed in Great Britain by
St Edmundsbury Press Ltd, Bury St Edmunds, Suffolk

98 99 5 4 3 2 1

To the ladies who have transformed
my life, Avril and Emily, this book is
dedicated with all my love.

Contents

Author's Note

To avoid cluttering the book with footnotes or notes at the end of chapters, I have given page numbers of quotations in the text and refer readers to the bibliography at the end of the book for details of the works cited. Where a committee or inquiry is normally known by the name of its chairman, such as the Nolan committee or the Scott inquiry, the reference in the bibliography is to the chairman's name. To avoid cumbersome his/her references in the text, I have used the masculine form as generic, not least because most chairmen in politics are still men.

Acknowledgements

This book is the result of the twenty years that I have spent observing and reporting on Parliament in various ways, first for the *Financial Times*, and then, after nearly three years in Washington, for *The Times* since 1991. During the 1990s I have increasingly felt that much is wrong with the House of Commons and that this view is shared not just by the public but by MPs as well as fellow journalists and academic observers of Westminster. I also believe that the real character of these challenges has been insufficiently appreciated in existing books about constitutional reform or more detailed studies of Parliament. The first tend to be too broad, and often underplay the significance of Parliament, while the latter are usually too narrow in their focus on improvements in procedure.

My aim in this book is to put Parliament into a broader context of political and constitutional changes. But it is not a textbook nor a reformer's tract. Rather, it is an analysis of the new challenges to Parliament coupled with some specific proposals about how the House of Commons, in particular, should respond. In part, the book grows out of my earlier discussion of the changing nature of political careers in Britain, in my 1993 book, *Honest Opportunism – The Rise of the Career Politician*. In the final two chapters of this book I develop some of the ideas that I more tentatively outlined in the first edition of *Honest Opportunism*, but these now form only a small part of a much wider analysis and more far-reaching programme of suggested reform of Parliament. This covers not just the careers of MPs but also the broader role of Parliament within the political system.

My debt is therefore primarily to the dozens of MPs and peers, as well as to my colleagues on *The Times* team at Westminster, with whom I have discussed these issues over the years. Many will recognize their views, though often in very different forms from the way they originally expressed them to me. Most are anonymous, except where they have made their views public. I would, however, note the influence on the development of my thinking of two notable recent commentators on the constitution, Ferdinand Mount in his book *The British Constitution Now*, and Lord Nolan in his Radcliffe lectures of November 1996. In the latter Lord Nolan offered a challenge to the Whitehall conventions which was more telling because of its carefully restrained language.

I have also been fortunate to have been able to debate several of the themes with academic commentators on politics, notably David Butler, Tony King, Peter Hennessy, Philip Norton, Vernon Bogdanor and Andrew Adonis. Michael Ryle, a distinguished former member of the Clerk's department, made valuable comments on Chapter Six and helped me understand the arguments over self-regulation, though he would not agree with all my conclusions. Naturally, the responsibility for what follows, and for any errors and misunderstandings, is entirely mine.

For the past three years I have also been closely involved with the Hansard Society for Parliamentary Government and have learnt much from members of its council. I also owe much to the insights of old friends such as Helene, now Baroness, Hayman, her husband Martin and their opinionated sons; Jim and Ellie Naughtie; Roger Liddle and Caroline Thomson; and Tony Halmos.

Sean Magee of Victor Gollancz has, always, been a delight in spurring me to action and delivery. We worked together in the 1980s on a book I wrote on the policies of the Thatcher governments and then, more recently, on the paperback version of *Honest Opportunism*. It has been a pleasure to be reunited with him again on this book.

My main thanks are to my wife Avril and to my daughter Emily, the lights and inspirations of my life. It would be idle to pretend that this book was completed always as a result of their help and support, rather than, sometimes, despite the happy distractions they both offered. But both because and despite, my gratitude to them is expressed in the dedication.

Peter Riddell
July 1997

Preface

Sir Politic Would-Be wakes up to the *Today* programme to hear a cabinet minister interviewed about a government policy initiative due to be announced later in the day, a Green or White Paper, or a new bill. Later, the main opposition spokesman is also questioned, together with a Liberal Democrat and someone from an affected pressure group if the issue is really important. Sir Politic then looks at his morning paper, where details of the announcement have been widely leaked by advisers to the minister ('an exclusive story to every paper in town', as the immortal Lina Lamont said in 'Singin' in the Rain'). The agenda has been set for the day – to be followed by the *Evening Standard* and the lunchtime news programmes. The formal statement in the House of Commons comes almost as an anti-climax, and Sir Politic wonders if it is worth turning up since he knows what is going to be said and his own comments will not be reported in the press.

In his morning paper, Sir Politic – though he is thinking of calling himself just Pol in the more informal Blair era – also reads of a ruling in the High Court challenging a decision by the Home Secretary (a much rarer event than before the election); of a proposal from the European Commission in Brussels that will affect a large number of his constituents and of which he has barely heard before, and a decision by a utilities' regulator that will change prices for all households, and force suppliers to implement redundancies. The Bank of England has also used its recently won independence to raise interest rates, despite some tut-tutting from ministers and government backbenchers. These decisions, all important to his constituents' everyday lives, have been taken outside Parliament by people who are not directly accountable to MPs for their specific actions.

Parliament, and in particular the House of Commons, appears, and is, marginal to many key decisions. No wonder MPs themselves often

feel frustrated about their lives at Westminster. Nevertheless, while
the number of MPs leaving the Commons voluntarily at the 1997
general election (excluding those either rejected by their local parties
or squeezed out by boundary changes) was 100, up from 75 in 1992,
just fifteen in both cases were aged under sixty. MPs may moan about
the Commons, but most are still reluctant to leave the place that they
have sought so long to enter. Their frustration is in part because Parliament is held in low esteem by the public, notably following allegations
of 'sleaze'. According to MORI polls for the Joseph Rowntree Reform
Trust, the proportion of the public who thought that Parliament works
well fell from 59 to 43 per cent between 1991 and 1995, while those
who thought it works badly had almost doubled from 16 to 30 per cent.
The 1995 poll was taken after the 'cash-for-questions' affair erupted and
just before the first report of the Nolan inquiry into standards of conduct in public life. But the same poll shows that people's satisfaction
with the job their local MP is doing for their local constituency
remained constant between 1991 and 1995 at 43 per cent, against 23
per cent dissatisfied on both dates.

These are symptoms. The real malaise at Westminster is a sense of
exclusion, a belief that the real political debate and decision-making
are elsewhere – in European institutions, in the courts, the media, the
Bank of England and financial markets, and in the decisions of regulators and those who run quangos. Moreover, the Labour government
elected in May 1997 has brought forward proposals for constitutional
changes that would further challenge the position of the Westminster
Parliament with the creation of a parliament in Edinburgh, with tax-
raising powers, and an assembly in Cardiff, as well as through the
incorporation of the European Convention of Human Rights into
British law.

This book is about how Parliament is increasingly being bypassed,
about its failure to cope with these alternative sources of power and
what it should do to find a new, and probably more modest, role within
a more pluralistic political system. I want to put Parliament in the
context of the many constitutional and other changes affecting it. Some
I support. I am more sceptical about the desirability of others. But they
are occurring, like it or not, and Parliament has to adapt, rather than
turn its back or complain about being ignored, as MPs too often do.
Short of leaving the European Union, which I would regard as disas-

trous, British politicians and the House of Commons have to find a way of living more harmoniously with European institutions and trying to influence their proposals before they become law. Similarly, successive governments have devolved powers to quasi-independent bodies, whether utility regulators or the Bank of England, and Parliament has to make them more accountable. The growth of judicial activism has also presented a challenge to elected politicians that will only increase if Britain has, in effect, its own bill of rights following incorporation of the European Convention. A new balance is needed between the judiciary and the legislature. Above all, Parliament needs to show that it is still central to the political debate. The debate also needs to recognize how these changes relate to each other: how, in practice, they involve rethinking the role and powers of Parliament within a new constitutional settlement. What this implies is, in part, a reinvention of Parliament. Of course, it is impossible to consider Parliament as being somehow separate from government or from the ties and loyalties of the party system that are necessary for coherent and successful government. But even within these constraints, there is scope for a substantial strengthening of Parliament's scrutiny role. A revitalized Commons, and possibly Lords, would no longer be merely what Tony Wright and David Marquand have described (1996) as an extension of 'Government and Opposition locked into a permanent election campaign on the floor and in the committee rooms of the House of Commons'.

Strong support now exists across the political spectrum for reform of Parliament, reinforced by the demands of the big influx of new MPs in May 1997, particularly the record number of female members. Complaints about what is wrong were made within a few months of each other in 1996 by distinguished former members like Bernard Weatherill, Speaker of the Commons from 1983 until 1992; the veteran Tory Sir Patrick Cormack; and long-standing advocates of reform like David Marquand, a former MP and professor, and Tony Wright, a political scientist turned MP. They all accept the need for action, and there is wide agreement on many of the detailed remedies. The right-wing Centre for Policy Studies proposed, in its agenda for a fifth term (Keswick and Heathcoat Amory, 1996), giving more powers to select committees and streamlining the consideration of legislation. These are similar to the suggestions made by the centre-left pressure group

Charter 88 in a pamphlet by Greg Power on reforming the Commons. (I do not discuss in this book the calls, especially by new MPs, for changes in the way the Commons works, its hours of sitting, methods of voting, organization and the like. I concentrate on political and constitutional issues.)

Disagreement exists on the broader context of change. Some Tory reformers regard parliamentary reform almost as an alternative to wider constitutional change – for instance, a strengthened Scottish Grand Committee as an alternative to devolution. But Tony Wright and David Marquand have questioned (1996) whether 'reform [of Parliament] is possible without a much wider set of political reforms. The Commons is like it is because our political system is like it is. Reforms have to connect.' However, they argued that 'it cannot be said too strongly that an effective Parliament has to be central to any new constitutional settlement. A more robust Parliament would even make some elements of constitutional reform less pressing.' Yet, in their criticisms of current structures, they seem almost to regard Parliament as the problem rather than the solution. Marquand has frequently questioned the doctrine of parliamentary supremacy. He has argued (1988, p. 175) that the 'Westminster Model' of absolute parliamentary sovereignty inhibits the desirable objective of 'open and explicit power-sharing'. Will Hutton, who has in the 1990s become an influential popularizer and propagandist of this thesis, argued in his best-selling *The State We're In* (1995) that the doctrine of parliamentary sovereignty and executive discretion were at the heart of Britain's institutional problems. He described (p. 287) Britain's official culture as having no complaint about centralization and the mushrooming of unaccountable quangos, and colluding 'in the notion that the majority party in the House of Commons, in effect, is the state'. The Marquand–Hutton view, shared by constitutional reformers in the influential network embracing Charter 88, Democratic Audit and the Liberal Democrats, favours what Will Hutton has called a 'republican' attitude. This does not necessarily, or even probably, mean getting rid of the monarchy but it does involve a wholesale change in attitude, a replacement of subjects by citizens (as we all already are of the European Union) and a formal separation of powers not just between executive, legislature and judiciary but also between national, regional and local (and European) tiers of government. This would be defined in a written constitution.

This approach has the merit of thinking out the implications more explicitly than the piecemeal approach offered by the Labour leadership. But the Marquand–Hutton case has two flaws. First, the radical reformers exaggerate the significance and impact of their agenda. Many changes are desirable in their own right but they are not as important for the overall well-being of the nation as they pretend. Second, the reformers' dislike of the theory and practice of parliamentary supremacy leads them to underrate the continued importance of Westminster as the central body with democratic legitimacy. I believe a more pluralist structure is desirable: European institutions and devolved elected bodies, both regional and local, should have their own role and authority. But the national Parliament at Westminster should remain the core of the system, the ultimate source of sovereignty on behalf of the people. The question is how to relate the Westminster Parliament to these other sources of power.

The discussion has been bedevilled by the concept of parliamentary sovereignty, in particular the version argued so forcefully by A. V. Dicey which has been the starting point for constitutional textbooks over the past century. In the first chapter, I discuss various myths about Parliament and look at its real roles. Then over the following seven chapters I discuss the various new challenges and how Parliament is handling them – Europe, the judiciary, ministerial accountability, constitutional reform, self-regulation, the media and the relevance of conventional politics. In Chapter Nine, I pull these themes together to look at the current state of Parliament and at recent attempts at reform, such as the extension of the select-committee system, and at its impact. In Chapter Ten, I argue that a piecemeal approach will no longer work and that the changes to procedure now being considered have to be seen within the broader context of these constitutional, political and social changes. In the final chapter, I put forward ten specific proposals for reform. Most of this book is focused on the House of Commons and I only discuss the House of Lords in Chapter Five as part of a general discussion of constitutional reform. This is not because the Lords is unimportant. It is not. But it is secondary to the broader themes of the challenges to Parliament, which are the subject of the book.

The Labour government formed in May 1997 has put forward far-reaching proposals for changing the procedures of the Commons and has moved rapidly to set up a Select Committee on the Modernization of the House of Commons. The detailed suggestions made by Ann Taylor, the Leader of the Commons, are in the right direction. During the debate in the Commons on 22 May 1997, discussing the modernization of procedure, she set out four priorities: producing better legislation through publishing more draft bills and more extensive consultation; holding ministers to account including the hourly afternoon sessions for questioning the Prime Minister and other ministers; improvements to scrutiny of delegated legislation, whether statutory instruments or European measures; and 'the style and symbolism associated with Parliament'. The new committee decided at its first meeting on 11 June 1997 to embark 'immediately on examination of ways in which the procedure for examining legislative proposals could be improved'. Its first report, produced just seven weeks later, made a number of desirable and sensible suggestions for improving consultation, scrutiny and the programming of legislation.

But these ideas, while welcome and certainly necessary, do not really address the extent to which Parliament is now being bypassed by the emergence of other centres of power, which is the main theme of this book. They reflect the gradualist, Fabian approach of the Labour leadership, the belief that the weaknesses of Parliament can be corrected in an incremental, piecemeal way. The lack of an overall framework for reform brings the risk that the changes may benefit the executive as much as, if not more than, the legislature. There are always tensions between even cautious advocates of reform like Mrs Taylor and the desire of the party whips not to surrender control. Parliamentary reform has always turned on the balance between procedure changes that make it easier for MPs to call ministers to account, like the introduction of the select-committee system in 1979, and those that enable the Government to conduct its business more smoothly and predictably, like Morrison's changes to the handling of legislation in 1945–6. These tensions were seen, for instance, in the debate of the early 1990s over changes to sitting hours and the timetabling of bills. The executive has seldom been willing to concede influence, let alone power, to the legislature.

None of the other twelve speakers in the half-day debate on 22 May really addressed the seriousness of these challenges either, apart from some sensible discussion of how to improve scrutiny of European legislation. Alastair Goodlad, speaking from the opposition front bench, argued that 'Conservative members are determined that Parliament, and particularly the House of Commons, should retain its central role in our political and national life.' But he failed to discuss how actions taken, or permitted, by the previous Conservative government had undermined that central role. The sole exception was Robert Jackson, the former Tory minister who has devoted much thought to these issues. He argued that the Jopling reforms to the hours of the Commons, eventually introduced in 1995, had 'dismantled one admittedly obsolete system of parliamentary influence – that which was based on the struggle for parliamentary time – but failed to erect an alternative system. The net effect is that Parliament is now even weaker *vis-à-vis* the executive than before. The challenge to us in this Parliament is surely to build that alternative system for which Jopling created the space.' Mr Jackson maintained – rather in political science jargon – that: 'In a modern legislature, the main source of parliamentary influence over the executive is to be found in the structures of institutionalized pluralism and a diversity of centres of influence which have to be negotiated with and operated by a well-informed and professionally disciplined cadre of members.' Against this background of an intensive debate over reform and continuing work by the select committee, this book is an analysis of the extent of the largely unappreciated challenges facing Parliament, a progress report on reform so far and a guide to future changes that are needed if Parliament is to regain influence at the centre of the political system.

CHAPTER ONE

Myths about Parliament

Under all the formality, the antiquarianism, the shams of the British constitution, there lies an element of power which has been the true source of its life and growth. This secret source of strength is the absolute omnipotence, the sovereignty of Parliament.

A. V. Dicey, *England's Case against Home Rule*, 1886

The main task of Parliament is still what it was when first summoned, not to legislate or govern, but to secure full discussion and ventilation of all matters, legislative or administrative.

L. S. Amery, *Thoughts on the Constitution*, 1947

The doctrine of parliamentary sovereignty is one of the greatest threats to the health of Parliament. The sovereignty of Parliament – or more properly the Crown/executive in parliament – has been the cornerstone of British constitutional debate for more than three centuries. What Parliament decides cannot be challenged by the courts or by any other elected body in Britain. But, in practice, the absolutism with which this doctrine is usually presented confuses more than it clarifies. Taken at the extreme, it denies a constitutionally legitimate role for any other institutions, which are viewed almost as grace-and-favour bodies allowed to exist solely by the decision of Parliament but otherwise without their own legitimacy or authority. This view is nonsense, both constitutionally and historically. It prevents any understanding of the role of Parliament within the political system and in relation to other institutions. Parliament is ultimately sovereign in the constitutional and legal sense but that does not mean it has not agreed to share power with other institutions, and cannot do so again.

It will be already clear that I do not take the opposite view and regard Parliament as the root cause of all our constitutional ills. Far from it. I believe Parliament should be at the centre of our political system but in a stable and creative relationship with other political institutions with their own legitimacy and authority. MPs should not always be whingeing about threats to some absolute notion of sovereignty. I respect Parliament's history: the battles of the seventeenth century with the Crown that established our liberties and the great debates of the eighteenth and nineteenth centuries over, for example, the American Revolution, the extension of the franchise and Irish Home Rule. I believe there is a place for the rituals that are a reminder of this past but in no way interfere with Parliament's current role, like the slamming of the door of the Commons chamber to Black Rod and the 'dragging' of the Speaker to the Chair (though in May 1997 Betty Boothroyd seemed, rather, to be dragging her two sponsors). The danger lies, of course, in becoming over-romantic about an institution whose members are seldom romantic or selfless about their own behaviour or ambitions. Talk of the Mother of Parliaments (more accurately, and tellingly, in John Bright's original phrase 'England is the mother of Parliaments'), or 'the grand inquest of the nation' (Sir Henry Campbell-Bannerman's only known pithy phrase) or 'this little room is the shrine of the world's liberties' (Winston Churchill during the First World War) risks creating a rosy-eyed attitude that obscures the real position of Parliament.

Those who view sovereignty as absolute tend to see other political organizations as threats to be resisted at all costs. There is no sense of checks and balances, of sharing power with other institutions, whether the judiciary or local authorities, or with international bodies such as Nato, the International Monetary Fund and, above all, the European Union. No wonder Lord Hailsham famously talked of an 'elective dictatorship' in his Dimbleby lecture in October 1976 when he called for a written constitution and a bill of rights. He had second, or was it third or fourth, thoughts in 1991 when, after his own eight years as Lord Chancellor and more than a decade of Conservative rule, he took the opposite view in proclaiming the virtues of an unwritten constitution. It depends, as so often, whose hands are on the levers of power. For the advocates of this absolutist view, a government with the clear backing of a majority in the House of Commons can do whatever it wishes. This is inconsistent with any belief in a pluralist structure, let alone with international obligations – or, at the extreme, with the rule of law.

Claims that Parliament is, and always has been, supreme in enjoying absolute sovereignty do not really stand up to historical analysis. Even A. V. Dicey, the great propagandist and myth-maker of sovereignty, qualified his beliefs in his later years when he became obsessed with the dangers of Irish Home Rule. This led him, first, to embrace the unparliamentary device of the referendum and, then, in 1913–14 to urge the King to dismiss his ministers. He even wrote in support of armed resistance by Ulster to a Home Rule law passed by Parliament. At this stage, the sovereignty of Parliament had turned into the sovereignty of the people. In *The British Constitution Now* (1992), by far the most thoughtful and original recent book on the issue, Ferdinand Mount elegantly dissected the pretensions and inconsistencies of Dicey. In concentrating upon the centrality and omnipotence of Parliament, Dicey ignored other features of the constitutional system. Mount noted (p. 52) that Dicey denied 'the possibility of overlapping consents to different authorities or of a subordinate national loyalty coexisting with a sovereign allegiance'. Moreover, Dicey's assertion of the sovereignty of Parliament was contradicted by his support for referendums: 'Far from buttressing the more modest and entirely correct claim of Parliament to be the supreme law-making body in the land, it immediately undermines the authority of Parliament.' The sovereign will of the people was seen by Dicey as superior to that of Parliament. Mount intriguingly linked Dicey's absorption with Home Rule with the argument made by some recent historians that the growth of parliamentary supremacy and sovereignty may have been an assertion of national unity over the Scots, Welsh and Irish.

This argument has exact echoes now in the debates over the maintenance of the Union and over Britain's relations with the European Union. There is a similar absolutist definition of sovereignty. As Mount argued (p. 61), Dicey's orthodoxy still mesmerizes an influential group of politicians and political commentators in Britain: 'the fear of the internal crack-up of the United Kingdom, reinforced in recent years by the fear of alien incursion from and eventual take-over by the European Community'. There is a confusion about sovereignty and self-government. Sovereignty means constitutional independence, the ultimate authority to reclaim powers that have been granted to supra-national or other bodies. It is a relative, not an absolute question. But the Dicey doctrine rules out a pluralist state.

Moreover, in a further parallel with Dicey's contortions, those Conservative Eurosceptics who have most frequently invoked parliamentary sovereignty to fight off the claims of European institutions – as during the battles over the Maastricht treaty in 1992–3 – have themselves been happy to propose a referendum as a check on Parliament. That led Tory constitutionalists, like Nicholas Budgen, reluctantly and with reservations, to take a first step down a road that ended up in the dismissive comments of the late Sir James Goldsmith about the mediocrity and uselessness of the whole bunch of elected politicians. There is a case for a referendum on major constitutional changes, but it can only be convincingly argued by those who accept that parliamentary sovereignty should, in practice, be qualified. As with Dicey, the popular will is presented as more legitimate, even more sovereign, than Parliament. But the authority of Parliament derives from the regular election of its members to the House of Commons. Therefore, parliamentary sovereignty is necessarily conditional on the popular will.

The conventional focus on sovereignty also obscures a sharing of power that has always occurred. There was, for instance, Grattan's Parliament in Ireland in the last two decades of the eighteenth century; and, in this century, Stormont, which ruled Northern Ireland for fifty years until the imposition of direct rule in 1972. No one then said that the sovereignty of the Westminster Parliament was being undermined. As Andrew Adonis has argued (1993), parliamentary sovereignty is a legal fiction: 'the relationship between people, parties, pressure groups, power and Parliament is complex and multi-faceted, with each subject to a matrix of pressures and counter-pressures. It cannot be reduced to one neat doctrine about parliamentary supremacy.'

Even in the case of Europe, discussed in detail in the next chapter, the cries of protest about the threat to sovereignty miss the point. As Lord Nolan pointed out in the first of his Radcliffe lectures (1996), the Westminster Parliament remains sovereign in the sense that the legislation of 1972 authorizing British membership of the then European Economic Community could always be repealed. 'Parliament has not been reduced to the status of an offshore assembly, and will not reach that stage, so long as it retains the fundamental criterion of national sovereignty, which is the ultimate ability to repeal the 1972 Act and to withdraw from the Union, however unlikely this may seem in practice.' Britain could leave the European Union by the decision of its elected representatives – in the sense that people living in Cornwall could not legally and constitutionally declare unilateral independence. This point is, however, questioned by those seeking Scottish devolution, let alone independence. Their assertion – in, for example, the Claim of Right backed by the Labour and Liberal Democrat parties in the Scottish Constitutional Convention – is that the people of Scotland are sovereign and have the right to demand their own parliament. But that view is specifically, if controversially, rejected by Tony Blair in his vivid, if tactless, reference to a Scottish Parliament being a creation of the Westminster Parliament, and of English MPs, with powers like a parish council. In the Blair view, not shared by many of his Scottish colleagues, sovereignty remains at Westminster, even if substantial powers are devolved.

The focus on absolute sovereignty, either in the context of devolution or the European Union, obscures the real arguments about where power lies. Even if sovereignty still lies in theory at Westminster, no one would dispute that some power has shifted to Brussels, or will shift to Edinburgh when a Scottish Parliament is established. Britain's membership of the European Union has, of course, led to a far-reaching challenge to the supremacy of Parliament and of British laws, but it is one we have voluntarily accepted as a result of the treaty of accession, an act, if you like, of a sovereign Parliament.

The real challenges to Parliament are, therefore, more about power, rather than over an absolute notion of unqualified sovereignty. Of course, some take a legal and constitutional form via the growing role and competence of European institutions, the rise of judicial activism and the Blair government's proposals for devolving and decentralizing power to other institutions. Parliament is also under pressure from the media, from global economic forces and from changes in the way that government itself is run. All these changes have made Parliament less important and less central to where power is exercised. Parliament is failing to adjust. MPs are puzzled and unhappy when the media and others do not treat them with the respect they feel they deserve. This is partly because they, the Westminster politicians, are less central to ordinary people's lives.

Before going on to consider the nature of these challenges in detail in later chapters, I want to discuss other myths about Parliament which can produce exaggerated and unreal ideas about what it can do. For instance, Norman St John Stevas, the then Leader of the Commons, said in June 1979 when setting out the plans for the new system of departmental select committees: 'The proposals that the Government are placing before the House of Commons are intended to redress the balance of power to enable the House of Commons to do more effectively the job it has been elected to do.' But, as Peter Hennessy has argued (1995), Lord St John of Fawsley, as he now is, oversold his proposals since his phrase about redressing 'the balance of power' not only inflated expectations but was also misleading. Balance of influence would have been a better term. It is often forgotten that Parliament itself does not govern. Ministers govern, or try to do so. Parliament's role is to create, sustain and hold government to account, but not to govern itself. It is therefore idle to compare British select committees and their powers of scrutiny with congressional committees on Capitol Hill in Washington. The latter have a completely different constitutional status as a formal branch of government. The point was elegantly put by Bernard Crick in his classic study of parliamentary reform in 1964, when he argued (p. 273) that parliamentary control was effective not because of the division lobbies but because debates are aimed at the electorate. 'The British Parliament is not – and has not been for almost a century – a direct restraint upon the Government, but rather the focus and the prime (but not sole) disseminator of political opinion and information to the electorate. The voter does not expect his MP to turn out the government he has elected; but he expects him to ask the right kind of questions and to help him know what is happening.'

Some reformers, however, tend to view Parliament as an entity distinct from the Government, which could somehow have its own separate life. In its most naïve form, the enemy is party ties and the power of the whips, so MPs could somehow be liberated and become independent as in some past golden age. This, of course, never existed, and anyway grossly exaggerates the power of whips over members. Parliament without party would be unpredictable chaos, as was recognized by Bagehot, writing right at the end of the era when groups in the Commons were fluid and did make and break ministries. In *The English Constitution*, published in 1867 (p. 158), he said party was of the essence of the House of Commons. The alternative was, he wrote, 'impotence. It is not that you will not be able to do any good, but you will not be able to do anything at all. If everybody does what he thinks right, there will be 657 amendments to every motion, and none of them will be carried or the motion either.' Throughout the previous twenty years, leading politicians had warned about the dire results of the weakness of party and looked back to earlier 'glorious' days, that is before the split of 1846, when parties had been stronger. The future late Victorian prime minister and third Marquess of Salisbury complained in 1857 that over the previous decade votes had been given for 'selfish or sectional ends. Private gratitudes or grudges, the promotion of some sectional interest, or the glorification of some parochial notability, have replaced the old fidelity to a party banner.' So party is essential and, indeed, the whole life of British politics remains, as Bagehot described, 'the action and reaction between the Ministry and the Parliament'. Virtually all MPs are elected to the House of Commons under a party label with the aim of forming, or opposing, a government. That is their primary loyalty. Any reforms have to be seen in that context. It is muddled and idle to try to define Parliament separately and, in some way, opposed to the Government. At present, however, there is an imbalance. Parliament is focused almost entirely on its role in forming, supporting or opposing the executive, and not on its long-standing other roles, especially those of scrutiny and holding the executive to account.

Many attempts have been made to list the differing roles of Parliament. The most elegant description remains that of Bagehot: the provision and maintenance of the executive; the expressive function (reflecting the mind of 'the English people in all matters that come before it'); the teaching function (teaching 'the nation what it does not know'; the informing function (expressing the grievances of the governed to government); and the legislative function. Peter Hennessy (1995) noted that Bagehot was curiously ambivalent about a sixth function, the granting of supply to the executive by approving spending and tax proposals. Contemporary constitutional writers would use different language but would accept the thrust of this list, while adding the scrutiny of European legislation.

My own list would start with the creation of governments, followed by the provision of ministers, approval of the Government's expenditure and tax proposals, legislation in its various forms, scrutiny of the actions of the executive and its agencies, relations with the European Union, and raising grievances on behalf of constituents and other outside bodies. Some functions, particularly the first and the last, are performed well; others much less well.

By far the most important role of Parliament in the twentieth century has been in translating the votes of the public at general elections into clear-cut decisions about which party should form a government, and sustaining it in office. Apart from the formation of the wartime coalitions in 1915, 1916 and 1940 and their break-up in 1922 and 1945, there have been only two brief occasions this century when a change of party in government has not been the direct result of a general election. In 1905, Balfour resigned in the hope that Campbell-Bannerman could not form a workable administration. Not only did he but the Liberals went on to win a landslide victory in the subsequent general election in the following month. In 1931, the disintegration of the Labour cabinet led to the formation of a Conservative-dominated National Government under Ramsay MacDonald, the outgoing prime minister, which, against its original intentions, went to the country two months later. The other ten changes of party in power this century have all occurred after general elections, without exception in the seven cases since the Second World War. The verdict of the people is absolute in determining, via the balance of MPs, which party forms the Government. Since 1923, no party defeated at an election has waited more than a few days before resigning. This is in contrast to the nineteenth-century practice, especially before the Second Reform Act in 1867 when ministries were formed in response to often shifting groups in the Commons and often at the initiative of the Crown.

The coherence and party discipline of the Commons ensures that the popular will expressed at an election is usually sustained throughout the parliament. No government this century has been defeated by a revolt from its own MPs – even though in the exceptional circumstances of May 1940 a sizeable Tory revolt substantially reduced the Government's majority and forced the resignation of Neville Chamberlain as prime minister. So, within the terms of the first-past-the-post electoral system, the Commons can be said to perform its function of creating and sustaining the executive efficiently. Even parties with very small majorities, or in a minority, have been able to survive for a long time, as the Callaghan government showed in the late 1970s and the Major government between 1992 and 1997.

The related function is to supply the members of an administration. As I argued in my book on political careers (1993), the House of Commons acts, in effect, as a closed shop from whose members the Government is chosen. The sole exceptions are members of the House of Lords. There is no law requiring members of the administration to be members of either House and since 1987 the Solicitor General for Scotland has not been, under either Conservative or Labour governments. But it is the practice that virtually everyone else is a member of the Commons or Lords, notably to ensure ministerial accountability. However, this need not mean every minister in a department being answerable on the floor of one or other House since he or she could still give evidence to a select committee. Even when outsiders are appointed ministers they are made peers, as happened in May 1997, when Sir David Simon became Minister for Trade and Competitiveness in Europe, Charles Faulkner became Solicitor General, Andrew Hardie became Lord Advocate, and John Gilbert (admittedly, a just retired MP) became Minister of State for Defence Procurement. It is striking that several of the Lords ministers in the Blair government had been made peers only in the previous few years so, in that sense, were outsiders to Westminster. But this is so far only a minor qualification to the criticisms I have previously made about the narrowness of the group from which ministers are picked – reinforced in Labour's case by its ludicrous rule that members of an incoming cabinet have to be picked from the Shadow Cabinet in place before the election. Tony Blair observed the spirit of that rule with the result that a number of obvious duds were appointed to his first cabinet. In Chapter Ten, I discuss the case for reducing the number of ministers. This could be balanced by bringing in more outsiders in semi-ministerial roles (as super-advisers). This would be to ensure a high-quality executive as well as a legislature that is not solely dominated by the ambitions of MPs to become frontbenchers.

From the viewpoint of the executive, Parliament performs its role in approving the Government's expenditure and tax proposals smoothly. With rare exceptions, they go through without a hitch. When the Chancellor gets up on Budget day and announces tax and expenditure changes, that is largely the end of the matter. Any subsequent changes during the passage of the Finance Bill are usually not because of parliamentary pressure as such but as a result of complaints and arguments raised by interested bodies outside. In some cases, these points are taken up by the opposition parties or by government back-benchers, but the decision whether to make concessions or adjustments is taken by the Treasury rather than by the Commons. The only recent exception was in December 1994 when a combination of opposition MPs and Conservative Euro-sceptics who had just lost the party whip forced the abandonment of the second stage of the imposition of VAT on domestic fuel. The gap was quickly, and easily, filled with small tax increases elsewhere. There are no recent instances of the Commons having changed the Government's spending proposals.

So Parliament has largely given up its detailed financial role to the executive. But there are two important caveats. First, the work of the Public Accounts Committee and the National Audit Office (as it has been known since 1983) has expanded to cover not just whether public money has been properly spent but whether the expenditure has been effective. This has been important in identifying mistakes but it has inevitably dealt with past decisions rather than useful proposals for future spending. Second, the expanded select-committee system has become a useful forum for discussing longer-term expenditure trends and in highlighting inconsistencies and contradictions between com-mitments and resources in government plans. This has applied both at the macro level in the work of the Treasury Committee in its reports on the Budget and at a micro departmental level in the work, for example, of the Defence and Social Security Committees. But not all committees are as assiduous and these committee reports have the same role and impact as outside specialist and press commentators. They have no specific impact on the way that the Government takes decisions in these areas. They inform, rather than change, the public debate on spending. The suggestion by Gordon Brown that, in future, there will be Green Papers setting out the economic options six months before a Budget may help, but only if any suggestions by committees on an alternative mix of spending or taxes are taken seriously. The Treasury has always been reluctant to share power.

The record of Parliament in handling legislation is even worse. The shortcomings of the traditional, adversarial system are now accepted by almost all MPs, apart from a few more blinkered traditionalists, especially in the whips' offices. The system has been geared entirely to getting bills through, regardless of whether they are properly scrutinized. During the standing-committee stage of line-by-line scrutiny, government backbenchers are actively discouraged from participating lest their speeches delay progress on a bill, so they can be seen doing their constituency correspondence and, depending on the season, their Christmas cards. If a formal guillotine is imposed, this stage can be even worse since large parts of a bill may not be properly considered at all. Attempts by the opposition to put forward amendments are almost invariably rebuffed on partisan grounds. Moreover, the more important, and controversial, the bill, the less likely is Parliament to play a creative part in its scrutiny. The result is a mass of hastily considered and badly drafted bills, which often later have to be revised. Anyone doubting the weight of these criticisms should read the authoritative report of the Hansard Society Commission into the legislative process chaired by the late Lord Rippon of Hexham and entitled 'Making the Law' (1992). This report concluded (p. 138) that: 'The legislative process in this country has been unsatisfactory for a long time and ministers have not, up till now, shown a willingness to change it. We believe a change of heart and of attitude is required on the part of ministers, of the Opposition, and of backbench Members of Parliament on both sides – and indeed of Parliament itself – if things are to be put right.'

Some progress has been made since then under Tony Newton, Leader of the Commons between 1992 and 1997, whose achievements were obscured by his consensual, low-key style. He introduced more consultation on legislation with the publication of more draft bills, although there was too little use of existing mechanisms such as special standing committees that can take evidence before the usual line-by-line consideration of a bill. Improvements in the way legislation is considered have also been the top priority of the Select Committee on Modernization of the House of Commons. Among the ideas put forward in its first report, in July 1997, are: publishing more bills in draft and having pre-legislative committees to examine draft bills or White Papers, as well as proper programming of legislation without resorting to government-imposed guillotines, and provision for the occasional carry-over of bills from one session to the next. Ann Taylor, Newton's successor in May 1997, was careful to say that not every bill should be considered in draft and by a pre-legislative committee. What she had in mind was bills where there might be differences of approach across the party divide but where there was agreement on an objective or at any rate that a certain problem needed to be tackled. Before the select committee was set up, Taylor announced that the Government intended to publish a record number of draft bills in the 1997–8 session: on a food standards agency, freedom of information, tobacco advertising, regulation of financial services, limited-liability partnerships and the control of communicable diseases. These are all important matters, but they are mainly second order in terms of the main political debate.

But Labour ministers do not believe that the main controversial bills should be subject to such extensive consultation. This is a mistake. Of course there will be fierce disagreement between the parties about such bills, but there is still scope for the Commons to make sure that even a hotly contested plan is workable in practice. The classic study of the poll tax by David Butler, Andrew Adonis and Tony Travers (1994) shows how Parliament never properly looked at how the tax, more properly the community charge, might work in practice or how it might be improved – apart from during the final stages when the legislation was going through. The Environment Committee never looked at the issue of local-government finance during the period of several years when it was a matter of intense debate within government, and then of public debate. The authors quote (p. 230) Sir Hugh Rossi, the committee's long-serving chairman: 'We decided, as an act of conscious policy, not to become involved in topics which are the subject of major political controversy or which are likely to be debated fully on the floor of the House in any event.' It is anyway doubtful whether any topic is 'debated fully' on the floor of the House, as opposed to the detailed scrutiny it can be given by a select committee. The Rossi doctrine, as the authors call it, is flawed. Of course MPs from opposing parties were never going to agree on the merits of such a controversial measure as the poll tax, but if a detailed examination had been undertaken of the cost of its introduction and its impact on various groups, there might – and I emphasize might – have been scope to produce a more workable tax. As it is, the Rossi doctrine involves an acceptance of an entirely executive-driven view of policymaking and legislation. Select committees cannot make policy or initiate legislation, but they can advise on how both might be improved.

These criticisms also apply, to a lesser extent, to another of Parliament's main roles, that of holding ministers to account. The main public focus tends to be on questions on the floor of the House, and, in particular, on Prime Minister's Questions, especially since sound broadcasting began in 1978 and the television cameras arrived in 1989. How much the actual behaviour of MPs has become more raucous and partisan over this period and how much it has simply been highlighted by the arrival of microphones and cameras is less important than the hostile public reaction. As the postbag of successive Speakers of the Commons shows, the public does not like its politicians shouting at each other. The prime ministers and opposition leaders of the broadcast age have used the opportunity to convey a message to the broader public via catchy sound-bites in their answers. While Prime Minister's Questions is a crude way of holding the occupant of 10 Downing Street to account, it does ensure that he or she is pressed on the issue of the day.

There was a lengthy debate during the 1992–7 parliament about possible reforms, and in July 1995 the Procedure Committee recommended (Seventh Report, 1994–95) an experiment whereby on one of the two days for Prime Minister's Questions, members would have to table a substantive question on the day before, rather than the present open-ended question which does not ask about a specific subject. The hope was that this would provide more structure and coherence, in effect creating a mini-debate. But Tony Blair, the then leader of the opposition, was quoted in the Procedure Committee's report as being reluctant to give up his ability 'to raise immediate and critical issues' (p. xv). So nothing happened before the 1997 general election. However, immediately afterwards, and before the Queen's Speech, Ann Taylor, the new Leader of the Commons, announced that the twice-weekly sessions on Tuesdays and Thursdays would be replaced by a single thirty-minute session on Wednesdays. This suggestion had been specifically rejected by the Procedure Committee in its 1995 report. The Conservative opposition protested both at the lack of consultation and at the reduction in the number of opportunities to question the Prime Minister. There was a further twist in that the halving in the number of Tory MPs to their lowest since 1906 and the rise in Liberal Democrats to the largest third party since the Liberals in 1929, had shifted the balance on the opposition side, and therefore in the rights of the leader of the opposition and of the Liberal Democrat leader. Further changes are possible as a result of the review by the Select Committee on the Modernization of the House of Commons: for instance, looking at the balance between open (unspecific) and closed (substantive) questions and over the period of notice for tabling them. If the thirty-minute session is to be permanent, then there is a case for allowing at least half the time to be concentrated on one or two issues rather than to ramble from one matter to another.

Of much more importance in ensuring ministerial accountability is the existence of the select-committee system. The extension to a departmental basis in 1979 has had a big impact in ensuring that ministers and civil servants have to explain their actions in public. As I argued earlier, this has not given the committees power – the St John Stevas fallacy – but it has given them influence and has, most important of all, been a major factor in the opening up of the workings of government over the past twenty years. This is still imperfect, as the Scott Report of February 1996 on the supply of arms-related equipment to Iraq amply showed. Ministers and civil servants can still be evasive. But there have been real gains, and there is big potential here.

My worry – and it is a central theme of this book – is that Parliament has failed to cope with the growth of alternative centres of power. The formation of Next Steps executive agencies, the creation of regulators for the privatized utilities and the devolution of key decisions over, for example, the setting of interest rates to the Bank of England all have far-reaching implications for accountability. The official line that these bodies are still accountable, via ministers, to Parliament is an unconvincing and inadequate description of the real position, as the Public Service Committee argued in its excellent report on 'Ministerial Accountability and Responsibility' in July 1996. The lines of accountability need to be strengthened while in no way undermining the operational advantages of greater independence. This involves changes in the existing, somewhat rusty, constitutional conventions about lines of accountability and in the behaviour of the House of Commons.

The record of Parliament in scrutinizing Britain's relations with the European Union is mixed. This is partly because a sizeable minority of the political class – at least, that section represented in the House of Commons – has never properly come to terms with Britain's membership. There has been a continuing resentment at the encroachment of European institutions and, in particular, a dismissive attitude towards the European Parliament as a lesser institution and not really a parliament at all. Consequently, as I discuss in the next chapter, the Commons has failed to play its proper role in examining proposed new European directives and holding British ministers to account for their actions in the Council of Ministers. The problem is only partly procedural since, during the 1990s, scrutiny committees have existed and have churned out reports. But they have been outside the political mainstream and there has been little consistent follow-up. The inadequacies of Westminster's relations with European institutions are one, admittedly big, example of a broader argument about Parliament's failure to cope with the emergence of alternative centres of power.

The final main role of the House of Commons is in representing the grievances of constituents and outside bodies. On the former, at least, individual MPs are much more assiduous than before and, in their role as local ombudsmen, can obtain redress from local offices of various central-government agencies. MPs still have status and standing, reinforced by the threat of going public and making a fuss. Demand for MPs' services has risen as a result of a combination of higher unemployment, a more discretionary (and therefore apparently more arbitrary) social-security system, more housing problems and a less deferential attitude by constituents towards their member. At the same time, the younger generation of MPs is temperamentally and by experience more attuned to constituency work since many were previously local councillors (the proportion of former and current councillors among new MPs has risen sharply since the 1960s). Many MPs say they gain most satisfaction from dealing with constituents' problems. And, as noted in the Preface, the same polls that show that Parliament and politicians generally are held in low repute by the public also indicate that people respect and value their individual local MP. The worry is the opposite: that MPs spend too much time on routine constituency service and welfare cases as opposed to their national responsibilities at Westminster. Philip Norton and David Wood (1993) have noted how the 'pressures requiring the member's attention to constituency work are matched by pressures from other sources requiring him to devote more time to Westminster activities'. However, improved secretarial services and the belated use of information technology by MPs have enabled them to cope better than their predecessors could have done. But if there is a genuine devolution of central government powers to regional and local bodies, maybe MPs should transfer some of this role back to locally elected people.

The role of MPs in raising the grievances and concerns of outside bodies is inevitably more controversial in the wake of the cash-for-questions affair. It is no longer a matter, say, of an MP for a predominantly rural constituency raising the problems of agriculture or the like. Such outside groups are now well organized to lobby, often employing professional public-affairs consultants. In most cases, their activities are better directed at Whitehall, at ministers and civil servants, rather than at backbench MPs. The new rules introduced in the wake of the Nolan report of May 1995 have anyway restricted what members can do, and forced them to disclose their earnings from consultancies (as I discuss in Chapter Six).

The overall picture is mixed. Parliament – by which I mean primarily the House of Commons – performs some roles well: notably by creating and sustaining governments and handling the grievances of constituents (though advocates of electoral reform would argue that the first-past-the-post system produces a distorted outcome). Parliament's record in examining legislation and in holding ministers to account is patchy at best. It is tempting to write about the decline of Parliament. This has been a common complaint at regular intervals over the past century or more, as Ronald Butt argued in *The Power of Parliament*, published in 1967 during a previous reform phase. This is still among the most illuminating books on Parliament, even if some of his instinctively conservative worries about the increasing role of select committees are exaggerated. Butt noted (p. 5) how 'Criticism of Parliament has a long history. In this century it has been almost incessant since parliamentarians were depressed, after the First World War, by a sense of lost independence and by the encroachment of bureaucracy and government action. Such criticisms have become particularly strong in recent years.' Recurrent complaints, he recorded, have been the impotence and low calibre of members, the frustration of life at Westminster, the failure of the press to report adequately on the proceedings of Parliament, and the inadequacy of Parliament as a modern instrument of government without drastic reform of procedure. In the 1920s, Parliament came under fierce attack: at a time when central government was taking on more economic and social responsibilities, there was a widespread belief that the House of Commons was no longer able to exercise adequate influence over the executive. There were frequent complaints then about the low standing of Parliament. Political scientists and politicians alike saw Parliament as ineffective compared with bureaucracy and party machines. This led in the 1930s to demands on the left for an even stronger executive to tackle the problems of mass unemployment with Parliament being relegated to a secondary, almost rubber-stamp, role approving enabling legislation conferring wide general powers.

In so far as there was a high point of the power of the executive and a low point for the influence of the legislature, it was probably during the Second World War and its immediate aftermath, when central government vastly extended its role. That was, after all, the period when there were no private members' bills for the first three sessions after the end of the war because of the pressure of government bills. Herbert Morrison proudly claimed (in Donoughue and Jones, p. 357) that, 'the Labour Governments of 1945–51 organised their legislative programme and parliamentary business more thoroughly than any previous administration ... it demonstrated that Parliament could be a work-shop as well as discharging its necessary functions as a talking shop'. Backbenchers generally accepted this more passive role and both Labour and Conservative governments easily saw off pressures for select committees to be established to scrutinize the activities of ministers. The House of Commons became more active during the 1960s, largely as a result of the arrival of the first generation of more committed career politicians. They wanted to do things, whether as ministers or as backbenchers. This was linked with a more general mood of national introspection. Typically, the Penguin Special series on *What's Wrong with* ... in Britain included one on Parliament, written pseudonymously by two members of the Clerks' department (Hill and Whichelow, 1964). There was also a whole series of pamphlets urging reform written by political scientists and younger Labour MPs. These bemoaned the decline in Parliament's popular esteem and in its influence over government. Most urged an extension of select committees and streamlining of the consideration of legislation, as well as improved working hours and conditions. This pressure culminated in the much discussed but ultimately disappointing period when Richard Crossman was Leader of the Commons from 1966 until 1968, which produced few lasting results of importance. His frustrations in face of the conservatism of the

Whitehall and Westminster establishment, and his own prime minister, Harold Wilson, are vividly conveyed in the second volume of his diaries, when he repeatedly refers to the lack of support for his plans.

The change in attitudes among younger MPs was also reflected in a greater willingness to rebel, which has continued, and also a desire for more influence, through select committees. Much of the talk about the power of the whips is exaggerated and out of date. Contemporary backbenchers are more willing to defy their party's whips than their predecessors twenty or thirty years ago. As Conservative Chief Whip in the early 1990s, Richard Ryder had more difficulties containing the Tory Euro-sceptics over the Maastricht bill in 1992–3 than Francis Pym, his predecessor in the Heath administration, with the opponents of entry in 1971–2. Similarly, the expansion of the select-committee system since 1973 has given the legislature more influence and forced the executive to explain itself, albeit in an imperfect form. However, as Butt argued throughout his book, MPs have always influenced ministers in more informal and subtle ways than by outright revolts, through party committees and the like. Even parties with big majorities have disliked alienating their own supporters and have been engaged in a continuous dialogue with their MPs. Butt's well-documented case about the informal influence of government backbenchers on ministers is too often ignored, though it undermines simplistic arguments about the over-mighty executive and all-powerful whips.

So talk of the decline of Parliament is a misleading over-simplification, as these arguments usually are. But there has been a big change since the debate over parliamentary reform in the 1960s. That was mainly expressed in terms of the balance between the executive and the legislature. But the issue now is much more the growing irrelevance of Parliament to the main decisions affecting people's lives – to which I turn over the following seven chapters.

CHAPTER TWO

Europe

'Under the terms of the European Communities Act of 1972 it has always been clear that it was the duty of a United Kingdom Court, when delivering final judgment, to override any rule of national law found to be in conflict with any directly enforceable rule of community law.'

> Lord Bridge, in the House of Lords ruling on the
> Factortame case, 1991

European law accounts for a large and growing proportion of the law of each member state, yet it increasingly seems to be made in a private club. . . . National Parliaments are, and should remain, the primary focus of democratic legitimacy in the European Union. . . . They are closer to the citizen [than the European Parliament], and are uniquely qualified to provide an element of responsiveness and democratic control that the Union needs.

> Select Committee on European Legislation,
> Twenty-fourth Report, Session 1994–5

Parliament has always had an uneasy relationship with the European Community, now Union, ever since the United Kingdom formally entered on 1 January 1973. A substantial minority of MPs and the press have never been reconciled to the implications of Britain's membership, while the challenge to Britain's long-standing constitutional conventions has been greater than in other countries, and the Westminster Parliament has had no formal role in the decisions and laws made by European institutions. As a result, a quarter of a century later, there is still suspicion among MPs of the bureaucracy in the European Commission and of the Parliament, whose UK members remain outsiders at the Palace of Westminster. In many ways, business, the professions, trade unions and local government have adjusted far better to the implications of Britain's membership and to working in a harmonious and practical way with Brussels institutions than have Westminster politicians.

Both the House of Commons and the House of Lords have set up committees to scrutinize new legislative proposals produced by European institutions. These structures are more thorough and effective than I had realized when I started writing this book – and than the vast majority of the public and many MPs appreciate. However, these scrutiny committees remain outside the political mainstream; their public meetings and frequent reports are largely ignored by fellow MPs and by the press. Many British politicians complain about the interference of the European Community and Union, and are constantly suspicious of further encroachments yet, with few exceptions, unwilling to make use of the committees that exist for monitoring its day-to-day activities. Many MPs make a great fuss about any new treaty negotiations but ignore the specific consequences. Philip Norton (1995) has commented on the paradox that 'in dealing with European secondary legislation both Houses of Parliament have introduced important mechanisms of scrutiny – at least as and generally more extensive than those introduced by other national parliaments – yet appear reluctant to integrate UK members of the European Parliament in that process and, furthermore, in responding to primary legislation [treaty amendments], Parliament, primarily the House of Commons, has conveyed the impression of being a reluctant partner.' In this chapter, I want to examine why, despite good intentions, the Westminster Parliament has so little real influence on European developments and what can be done to improve accountability within the structure of European decision-making.

The full constitutional implications of joining the Community were not appreciated at the time of entry. To 1990s' Euro-sceptics this was a deliberate act of deception by Sir Edward Heath. An alternative view is that there was confusion at the time about the implications for Parliament, while the nature and scope of the Community, now Union, especially over the rulings of the European Court of Justice, have changed and broadened since then. My own view is that the Heath government did not deliberately deceive people, though its language was ambiguous and understated the constitutional implications of entry. As Professor John Young has argued (in Ball and Seldon, 1996, p. 274),

the Heath government's 1971 White Paper on entry 'had the weaknesses of other major declarations by ministers on the European Community at the time. It did not explain exactly how the EC would improve
Britain's economic prospects, it fudged the issue of greater supra-
nationalism in the Community in future and, while trying in some ways
to present membership as a great opportunity and visionary step, it
blurred the impact of this by arguing that Britain would not be forced
to change past policies.' As so often, much of the confusion has turned
on the word sovereignty, and the Heath government's subsequently
much contested claim in the White Paper that British membership
meant there would be 'no question of any erosion of essential national
sovereignty'. As Professor Young has noted, the White Paper talked
of a 'sharing and an enlarging of individual national sovereignties' in
the European Community and 'thereby reflected Heath's belief that a
narrow definition of sovereignty [as the ability of a country to have
a "final" say over its own future] was impossible in an increasingly
interdependent world'. In the absolute sense, the Heath view is true
since the Westminster Parliament retains the ultimate ability to repeal
the 1972 European Communities Act and to withdraw from the Union.
However, in an ingenious article, Ian Loveland of Brunel University
(1996) raised the possibility that any such change in Britain's relations
with the European Union, as it became after the Maastricht treaty
was ratified in 1993, could only lawfully be accomplished through the
mechanism of European law. 'The European Community treaties contain no express provisions for member state withdrawal. The only way
that result can lawfully be achieved is if the EC treaties are amended
to reconstitute the Community (now Union) with one fewer member.'
That would require an inter-governmental conference. This is fanciful
and the predominant view among British judges and politicians remains
that the Westminster Parliament could pass a law repealing the European Communities Act.

Most judicial and constitutional authorities agree that parliamentary
sovereignty remains. The classic legal analysis of Hood Phillips and
Jackson (1987) argues that the European Communities Act 1972 does
not

affect the fundamental principle of the Supremacy of the United
Kingdom Parliament. . . . So far as United Kingdom courts are

concerned, constitutional law – notably the legislative supremacy of Parliament – is supreme, and Community law can take effect in this country only by force of Act of Parliament. Although decisions and opinions of the European Court of Justice on Community law are required to be followed in UK courts by section 3 of the European Communities Act, the European Court cannot (even by community law) overrule a decision of a national court.

Nonetheless, in joining the European Community Britain accepted the supremacy of Community law. This implicitly challenged key tenets of the Dicey view of sovereignty that Parliament is the only sovereign lawmaker, that one Parliament cannot bind its successor and that the courts cannot refuse to apply legislation enacted by Parliament. But, short of withdrawal, that is precisely what membership of the EU entails. The British Parliament is bound by the supremacy of European law as interpreted both by the European Court of Justice and by British national courts. As Lord Bridge argued in the Factortame judgment by the House of Lords, quoted in Nolan (1996) and at the start of this chapter:

> If the supremacy within the European Community of Community Law over the national law of member states was not always inherent in the EEC Treaty it was certainly well established in the jurisprudence of the European Court of Justice long before the United Kingdom joined the Community. Thus, whatever limitation of its sovereignty Parliament accepted when it enacted the European Communities Act of 1972 was entirely voluntary.

Voluntary it may have been, but well understood it was not at the time of entry. This was even though the treaty of Rome, as incorporated by the 1972 Act, and especially section 2, was specific that all relevant European laws would be enforceable in British courts. As Ian Loveland pointed out in the article quoted above, distinguished judges initially underplayed the significance of the 1972 Act. However, the consequences were soon recognized, even though it involved judges in the then novel activity of interpreting the intent of European legislators to ensure that the treaty's objectives were fulfilled rather than being bound by the literal wording of an Act, as has been the traditional British practice. In 1979, Lord Denning, then Master of the Rolls, said in the case of McCarthy's Ltd v. Smith's that: 'If on close investigation it should appear that our legislation is deficient or is inconsistent with

Community law by some oversight of our draughtsmen then it is our bounden duty to give priority to Community law.' Three years later, he wrote that, 'The Treaty is like an incoming tide, it flows into the estuaries and up the rivers. It cannot be held back.' In 1983, the House of Lords ruling in Garland v. British Rail implied that domestic courts must interpret all domestic legislation in a manner respecting European obligations. Any uncertainty should have been removed by the ruling of the European Court of Justice in 1978 that, where European Community law was directly applicable, national courts should 'apply Community law directly, if necessary refusing to apply conflicting provisions of national law, even if adopted subsequently. . . . It was not necessary to request or await the prior setting aside of [national legislation] by legislative or other constitutional means.'

The primacy of European law and institutions was underlined in the Single European Act – Margaret Thatcher's most important acceptance of European integration – under which qualified majority voting was extended in several areas, in place of the national veto, and the elected European Parliament was given a more important role in making laws alongside the Council of Ministers. This involved an acceptance of the law-making principles that the Community had developed over the previous generation. Moreover, the European Court of Justice has steadily broadened its remit over the years to cover a wide range of Community decisions as well as formal regulations, which are binding in their entirety, and directives, where individual member states can choose the form and method of achieving the result. British sceptics are worried that the European Court has taken on an overtly political role in furthering closer integration rather than the more passive one of interpreting existing law. But the Court is necessary to police cross-Community policies like the single market and, paradoxically, one of the British complaints has been that its procedures are too slow and its sanctions weak and ineffective. Also, over the 1993–6 period, the British government was taken to court for breaches of its treaty obligations 39 times, compared with 305 in Italy, 141 in France and 95 in Germany. The European Court has frequently ruled in favour of British interests, notably over the single market and the central issue of mutual recognition of standards before goods may be sold in any member country.

The wide implications for British courts were underlined by the

Factortame case decided in 1990, although Lord Bridge's comments were made in 1991. This arose out of a dispute over the registration as British of foreign-owned vessels. To reduce the advantages exploited by the Spanish, and to safeguard the quotas for the domestic fishing fleet, the Government brought in what became the Merchant Shipping Act 1988, which altered the registration rules to require a far higher level of British involvement in the owners or managers of a ship. Factortame, an affected company, claimed that the 1988 Act was incompatible with European law. In June 1990, the House of Lords ruled in the company's favour and granted an injunction ignoring or 'disapplying' the 1988 Act, even though it had been passed by the British Parliament. The ruling caused a sensation, leading Margaret Thatcher to claim that the decision 'was a novel and dangerous invasion by a Community institution of the sovereignty of the UK Parliament'. However, Lord Bridge argued later, as we have seen (p. 37), that there had been nothing novel in the judgment, since the 1972 Act had required domestic courts to respect the supremacy of European law, but since it had been voluntary it had not ended the sovereignty of Parliament.

Yet, as Lord Nolan suggested in his first Radcliffe lecture (1996):

> The practical result of the case, namely that the House of Lords granted an injunction to forbid a minister from obeying an Act of Parliament, was seen by many as a revolutionary development. It brought home the fact that the incoming tide of Community law was not merely lapping on to the Westminster terraces but submerging part of our statute law. It reinforced the anxieties of those who fear that the continuing development of the European Union could reduce Parliament to the status of an offshore regional assembly.

Lord Nolan, like Lord Bridge, did not accept this view since Britain could, in theory, withdraw from the European Union following repeal of the 1972 Act.

For the Westminster Parliament, the central point is that European institutions – the Commission, the Council of Ministers and, on some issues, the Strasbourg Parliament – have an exclusive right to make law in certain areas, whatever the wishes of British MPs. The House of Commons and the House of Lords have no role in it whatever, either formally or informally. The constraints were recognized in a report of the House of Commons Procedure Committee in 1989 (p. ix) which noted that European legislation was initiated almost exclusively by the Commission,

> with which the UK Parliament has no formal relationship and over which it has no direct control. More importantly, the UK has, as a condition of its community membership, bound itself to accept the collective authority of a legislative body [the Council of Ministers] only one of whose twelve [now fifteen] members is accountable to the House of Commons. These facts may be unwelcome in some quarters, but they spring unavoidably from the UK's treaty obligations.

Admittedly, the Westminster Parliament is at times required to incorporate Community legislation into domestic law, but this is an entirely secondary, delegated role. Of course the competence of European institutions is limited, but it has been steadily widened, particularly by the Single European Act of 1986 and the treaty on European Union of 1992 (the Maastricht treaty, finally ratified in 1993). At the time of British entry, the main areas of Community competence were external trade and agriculture, but these have since been extended to include the single internal market, industrial policy and state aids or subsidies, financial services, environmental and consumer protection, health and safety at work (a contentious area which has itself been broadened to cover many aspects of employment rights) and some aspects of asylum and immigration policy. However, Britain has retained control over fiscal policy (apart from some aspects of VAT rates), public spending, health, education, defence and foreign policy (despite increased intergovernmental co-operation), criminal law, industrial relations, social security and local government. At the same time, the Strasbourg Parliament has gained steadily in influence and authority following the introduction in 1979 of direct elections, held simultaneously every five years in all countries – previously members were nominated from domestic legislatures. That has created tension, and often rivalry, between national parliaments and the European Parliament.

The key issues are the extent of the competence of European institutions and the scope for the Westminster parliament to influence decision-making. Short of withdrawal, there is no scope to redefine what regulations and directives Britain chooses or does not choose to implement. The suggestion made by the British sceptics – for instance, in Lansley and Wilson (1997) – that the European Communities Act should be amended so that the British Parliament can pass legislation that is not subordinate to European law would be incompatible with Britain's continued membership of the European Union. It would provoke a constitutional confrontation – perhaps as some sceptics intend – and trigger a debate about withdrawal. Talk of repatriating powers from the European Court is a nonsense both because it is legally incompatible with British membership and because a court with Europe-wide competence is vital to police the single market. Otherwise, the main argument is about what further powers should be transferred to European institutions, notably, of course, if a single European currency is created and through the extension of qualified majority voting. All this is obviously a matter for intense political debate, depending on your view of Britain's relations with the European Union. Certainly, a full-blown federal structure would have profound implications both for the role of the Westminster parliament and potentially also for the doctrine of sovereignty. But despite the constant warnings of the Euro-sceptics such a federal superstate is not on the cards and would certainly be opposed by any likely government in Britain. In the immediate future, monetary union would affect both the accountability of British ministers for key economic decisions and where democratic control is exercised. This is because the European central bank is supposed to be independent of direct political influences. However, as I discuss in Chapter Four, the newly elected Labour government partially fulfilled one of the pre-conditions by making the Bank of England operationally responsible for setting interest rates within an inflation target set by the Government. For the purposes of this book I will concentrate on the scope for influence by Westminster on decisions by European institutions within the existing constitutional framework.

It is wrong to depict this issue as merely Westminster versus Brussels since decisions and laws are made by representatives of Britain, both by elected members of the European Parliament and, above all, by national ministers on the various councils. The interaction between ministers, the Commission and the Parliament is complicated, depending on the nature of the issue. The two most important developments of the past decade have been the extension of qualified majority voting in some areas such as the single market (thus denying any single country a veto) and the increase in the role and powers of the European

Parliament (until the 1980s still generally called the Assembly). These have weakened direct ministerial accountability to Parliament since no single nation state can block a proposal where qualified majority voting applies, while on some issues the Council of Ministers makes law jointly in a lengthy process of consultation with the European Parliament known as co-decision. There is a full British input into European decisions, but it is not from the two Houses of Parliament. There is and could be no constitutional provision for their involvement, given the nature of the European Union. Indeed, in so far as there is a villain in the story of European scrutiny, it is successive governments, which have not been eager to expand the role of the Westminster Parliament in examining their activities.

There has been much discussion about a democratic deficit within the European Union. Westminster politicians of all parties frequently question the legitimacy and authority of the European Parliament, not least because the turn-out in elections has often been half or less that in elections for the House of Commons. Whatever one's views on the desirability of closer integration, few would dispute that members of the European Parliament are much less well known, and more remote, than members of the House of Commons. Not surprisingly, Commons committees have been keen to emphasize the superior democratic legitimacy of the Westminster Parliament – a view echoed by the Major government in its approach to the Inter-governmental Conference. In practice, national parliaments and the European Parliament have different roles: the former in influencing decisions indirectly via ministers and the latter directly via its formal role in the process of co-decision.

Ever since British entry to the Community in 1973, the main emphasis at Westminster has been on examining Commission proposals before the relevant Council of Ministers reaches a decision. The exact procedure varies between the Houses, the Commons attempting breadth in monitoring the flow of documents from Brussels and the Lords seeking depth in detailed inquiries. This compares well with other systems in the EU: Denmark and now the other Scandinavian countries are the only others to approach Britain's degree of thoroughness of scrutiny. The basic principle of the Commons system – as set up in October 1973 by the Foster committee – is that a permanent scrutiny committee sifts through a mass of documents about new European proposals, together with explanatory memoranda from Whitehall departments, and alerts the House to those of political and legal importance. Then the Select Committee on European Legislation recommends those that should be debated further. Until 1990, that was usually through the form of ninety-minute late-night debates on the floor of the Commons after the main business of the day. These debates were usually ill-attended and were commonly regarded as unsatisfactory. But the procedures ensured that, except in trivial cases or where there are special reasons, a British minister cannot agree to a new European proposal until the matter has been considered and, if necessary, debated by one of these standing committees. Under a resolution of the House adopted in 1980, ministers should not give agreement in the Council of Ministers on any proposal for European Union legislation if the matter is still subject to scrutiny by the select committee, or if it is one of the proposals highlighted by the select committee as awaiting consideration and the passage of a resolution by one of the standing committees. What is known as a 'scrutiny reserve' is intended to ensure that Parliament at least has its say before ministers decide. This procedure is sometimes breached when, for various reasons, ministers reach agreement before the debate recommended by the select committee has taken place, though the number of occasions is quite small. The Select Committee on European Legislation believes (Twenty-seventh Report, 1995–6, p. xxxix) that: 'In general, the scrutiny reserve system operates well and fulfils its purpose.' However, the expansion of co-decision-making involving the European Parliament has meant that proposals are frequently revised, often in quite important ways, in the complicated process of discussion between the Commission, the Council of Ministers and the Parliament, and also that the Commons – and the select committee – are not fully involved in scrutinizing later versions of proposals before they are agreed by ministers.

In 1989 the Commons Procedure Committee recommended a series of improvements, notably that a series of standing committees should be set up to consider the matters the select committee judged worthy of full debate. The suggested five committees were, in the end, reduced to two, standing committees. While the memberships of the committees are nominated at the start of each session, any MP can attend the meetings but may not vote. A minister may be questioned by any MP for up to an hour of the two-and-a-half-hour session with the rest of the time taken up by normal debate on the merits of the measure.

The scrutiny procedures in the House of Lords are more extensive than in the Commons, partly because it has few permanent select committees. In the Commons, the seventeen departmental and other select committees involve a large number of backbenchers, meaning that fewer are available for European scrutiny work. The Lords structure involves more members than does the Commons system. In the Lords, the Select Committee on the European Communities is chaired by a senior peer who is Principal Deputy Chairman of Committees of the House. The committee has five permanent sub-committees (A, on economic and financial affairs, trade and external relations; B, on energy, industry, transport and the working environment; C, on environment, public health and education; D, on agriculture, fisheries and consumer protection; E, on law and institutions; with a special sub-committee considering the Inter-governmental Conference). These sub-committees, whose memberships rotate every few years, include several distinguished former civil servants, diplomats and industrialists as well as lawyers, including a law lord who always chairs the sub-committee on law and institutions. These sub-committees often undertake longer inquiries on fewer subjects (roughly twenty a year), taking much oral and written evidence, while the Commons committee reports quickly on a larger number of documents (as many as four hundred a year). The Lords committee also often pronounces on the merits of a proposal, while the Commons committee concentrates on whether issues of political and legal importance are raised and should be highlighted. More reports are debated on the floor of the Lords than are debated on the floor of the Commons. The two procedures are in many ways complementary, but there are aspects of the Lords' deeper and more thorough inquiries that could usefully be copied in the Commons.

These procedures suffer from several disadvantages. Some are inherent because of the constitutional limitations of the European Union on the role of national parliaments. Others are more to do with Westminster and the limited remit of the Select Committee on European Legislation, which past governments have resisted extending: the flow of reports is largely ignored by fellow MPs and the media; there is no formal connection with what happens in European institutions; the increase in inter-governmental co-operation on foreign and home affairs is not scrutinized satisfactorily by national parliaments; there is no attempt to link in with the work of British members of the European Parliament; and there is scarcely any follow-up. There is a sense of worthy work not only being unrecognized but also having no impact. As Philip Norton has written (1993):

> Debates on the floor or in European standing committees attract relatively little interest and what interest it [scrutiny] does attract is usually from members with a particular view on the wider issue of European Union. There is little if any evidence of the Commons exerting significant influence on government, or the institution of the Community, in the deliberative stage of law making.

The reports of the Lords committee are weightier and widely commended for their thoroughness: they form part of the wider policy debate on some issues, but there is little evidence that they have resulted in any change in approach by the Government in the Council of Ministers. This is like many Lords debates: they are praised, notably by peers themselves, for their rational tone, especially when compared with the more adversarial Commons, but then make little impact. No wonder MPs involved drew attention to the shortcomings of the present system in two reports of the Select Committee on European Legislation in summer 1996 and of the Procedure Committee in 1997.

It would be wrong to be too pessimistic. The British system of scrutiny has many strengths, even if they are largely unsung and unappreciated. Also, there are signs that the volume of new European legislation is declining, partly because much of the single market has been completed, and there is a trend towards a more carefully planned legislative programme and greater consultation by the Commission and Council of Ministers. The flaws are both procedural and political. Few of the various procedural improvements that I discuss in the following paragraphs will make much difference unless there is a willingness on the part of MPs and the media to take European scrutiny seriously.

There are various ways forward. First, national parliaments could be more formally involved in European decision-making, in addition to the regular consultations that occur between presiding officers or Speakers (hampered by their differing roles in various legislatures) and, more usefully, between representatives of the committees of national parliaments dealing with European affairs (known as COSAC). But these are essentially means of discussing best practice in monitoring community institutions rather than formally strengthening accountability. There has been discussion of establishing a formal second chamber from members of national parliaments. In his wilderness years as a strong pro-European, Michael Heseltine (1989, p. 35) urged the creation of 'an Upper House of the European Parliament from within the membership of our national parliaments'. Sir Leon Brittan, his old adversary in the battle over Westland before he went to Brussels to become a Commissioner, argued (1994, p. 226) that, 'If voters felt their local MPs were lending a hand to the process of Euro-legislation, it would greatly strengthen the EU's democracy and enhance its credibility.' This idea has been dismissed out of hand by the European Parliament since it would be a threat to their own exclusive legislative role by creating a second chamber in which it was not represented. An experiment in linking national parliaments and the European Parliament did occur in Rome in November 1990, with the so-called Assizes (Conference of Parliaments). This was a singularly unsuccessful and rambling affair when British MPs at least were rather distracted by the drama back home of the downfall of Margaret Thatcher. In Rome, members of the European Parliament made clear their strong opposition to proposals from French and British politicians for the creation of a congress consisting of members of national parliaments and the European Parliament. This idea got nowhere and the European Parliament later passed a resolution regretting such proposals. The Conference of Parliaments has not happened again. The European Parliament is content to keep national parliaments out of the picture in defending its role as the main legislative body. The possibility of giving national parliaments a collective influence on European decisions through a second chamber seems very remote for some time.

Second, there could be more informal co-operation between national parliaments and the European Parliament. When this idea is raised, members of the House of Commons are cautious about granting any real facilities, beyond formal access, to Members of the European Parliament (MEPs) at Westminster. In some countries, members of the European Parliament have a right to attend meetings of the main European committee. The Committee on European Union in the

German Bundestag, for example, consists of thirty-three members of the Bundestag and eleven MEPs in an advisory capacity. There is support in Britain for the idea of mutual rapporteurs between the key committees of the European Parliament and the relevant select committees of the Commons. Closer exchanges would, at least, address the problem of a lack of timely information about new developments. But, as the Commons Procedure Committee warned (Third Report, 1996–7, p. xxvi): 'Any proposals which rely on closer personal links between MPs and MEPs have however to be realistic about the practical difficulties of bringing together people whose principal places of work are widely separated. It would in our view be fruitless at this stage to think of formal structures for such contacts.' Even in countries that have more formal mechanisms for co-operation between MPs and MEPs and which are more committed to closer European integration, there is often mutual suspicion, and institutional rivalry, between members of the national and European parliaments.

Third, and most important, national parliaments could do more to try to influence their own governments before decisions are taken in the Council of Ministers. After all, the decisions of national parliaments raise the taxes that pay for European Union programmes. This is complementary to the role of the European Parliament in supervising the Commission and Community expenditure. National parliaments are in a better position to fulfil the universal aspiration to bring the European Union closer to its citizens, but there is also ample scope for improving scrutiny procedures. This involves both the willingness of European institutions to be more open in their decision-making and changes the way Westminster handles European issues. The Select Committee on European Legislation has made a number of suggestions (for instance, in its Twenty-eighth Report, 1995–6) about improving procedures – notably a requirement for a binding period of at least four weeks' notice between the provision of the official text of proposals and decisions being taken in the Council of Ministers. This is to tackle the problem that in all too many cases official texts have not been available for scrutiny by member parliaments before decisions are taken by ministers. Some of the problems occur in Brussels over the release of official texts, others in London where Whitehall departments have been slow to provide the necessary documents and information. The select committee's suggestions were taken up by the British government and in the discussions of the Inter-governmental Conference. The Amsterdam summit in June 1997 agreed that the new treaty should contain provisions to strengthen national parliaments' ability to scrutinize European legislation properly, by laying down a minimum six-week period for documents to be available. If properly implemented, they may be a help in allowing both national parliaments and affected interest groups enough time to see proposals in draft and make their views known. The Select Committee on European Legislation (in its Thirteenth Report, 1996–7) welcomed the progress made but was still concerned at the potential loopholes over timing of provision of documents and wanted a formal protocol that would allow a legal challenge in the European Court of Justice if the correct procedures were not followed. This has been complicated by the increased involvement of the European Parliament in law-making since this means that proposals are changed frequently, and in important ways, during the complicated co-decision process, which does not allow time for national parliaments and others to comment. Common foreign and security policy, and justice and home affairs, which are decided by co-operation between governments, also needs to be brought formally within the scrutiny system. Until now, the Government has been reluctant to give the same amount of detailed information in these areas that is provided on the main proposals for European legislation, but new proposals here are as important as those produced by the Commission. Another new development is the production of pre-legislative documents for consultation and, as the Select Committee on European Legislation has suggested (Twenty-seventh Report, 1995–6, p. xlv), 'there must clearly be a Parliamentary input (and scrutiny) before agreement by the council [of ministers]' on any programme or plan for European legislation.

The House of Commons also needs to improve its own procedures. Since the 1990 changes, most debates have been in the two special standing committees. But even in the minority of cases (roughly 15 per cent) where the select committee recommends a debate on the floor of the House, their suggestion can be, and is often, ignored by ministers – even, in some cases, on important issues such as enlargement, European social policy and border controls. This is a serious gap since the whole purpose of the scrutiny process is to alert MPs generally, and indirectly the public, to new developments of importance for Britain. The select committee has proposed that where it recommends debate on the floor of the House, the onus should be on the Government to move a motion to refer the issue to a standing committee. This would bring the issue out into the open. When debates upon these matters are held on the floor of the House, ministers could be questioned for part of the time, as in the standing committees.

At present, follow-up on decisions is poor. This is an inherent problem of Parliament, and the media. Interest tends to be at a maximum when an idea is being discussed or proposed. Attention then declines as detailed legislation goes through, and there is then virtually no discussion of implementation. The Procedure Committee said (Third Report, 1996–7, p. xxix) that it did not regard as satisfactory 'the absence of scrutiny of the outcome of councils [of ministers]; nor the lack of continuity between the scrutiny of draft European legislation and its implementation'. Consequently, procedures also need to be improved to ensure that ministers report back in detail on what they have done at Councils of Ministers, particularly on those matters which have been debated in one of the European standing committees or on the floor of the Commons.

But these proposals are essentially marginal unless European scrutiny becomes less of a ghetto activity for enthusiasts (on both the pro- and -sceptic side) and from the selflessly assiduous. There is also still a lingering tendency for all the old battles over Britain's membership of the European Union to be refought endlessly, especially when matters are brought to the floor of the House. At present, European issues are only occasionally examined by the main departmental select committees, apart from the six-monthly sessions of the Foreign Affairs Committee before meetings of European heads of government or the inquiries by the Treasury Committee into major issues such as monetary union. Graham Leicester has argued (1997) that national parliaments need to take a much closer look at the Community Budget and its medium-term priorities – for instance, via a new sub-committee of the Treasury Select Committee. Robert Jackson, a former minister with a close interest in parliamentary reform, has suggested (in the Commons debate on procedural reform of 22 May 1997) that the departmental select committees should be reconstituted as broader specialist committees, combining the role of the existing select, standing and European scrutiny committees. They should take on the role of both investigation and legislation, covering European as well as domestic issues and legislation in their areas. But that might risk overloading the committees and MPs with work and could narrow the number of MPs looking at important European issues. Some overlap of scrutiny by committees has advantages. An alternative is to go back to the original 1989 proposals of the Procedure Committee and expand the number of European standing committees so that they would develop more expertise.

The problem in both cases – and in several other examples to be discussed later in the book – is loading too much on to select committees. Backbenchers have many calls on their time, and with vast government and opposition front benches there is a limited pool of available and willing backbenchers. That is another argument for changes to career patterns in the House of Commons, and to the balance between frontbench and backbench service (which I discuss in Chapter Ten). But short of that radical surgery, the answer is probably a balance of expanding the existing European standing committees to, say, three or four and establishing them for the whole of a parliament, rather than just for a session, to allow time for more specialization. As the Procedure Committee noted (Third Report, 1996–7, p. xvi): 'Attending 15 meetings a year on an indigestible range of unconnected subjects is a rather less stimulating prospect than half a dozen meetings on a more limited range of issues.' This could be coupled with giving more time for debates on the floor of the House and involving the departmental select committees more in commenting on new European developments before the scrutiny process is completed. One of the difficulties now is not just over the detailed scrutiny of European legislation but the failure of some departmental select committees to recognize that Europe today enters into a wide range of policies: there is now a much shorter list of policy areas in which Europe does not matter than those in which it does.

In the end, however, it is not really a matter of procedure but of political will. Are enough MPs willing to take European scrutiny seriously? And is the media willing to devote resources to covering in detail European activities which they are eager to denounce in general? The two are related since ambitious young high-flyers in the Commons, as well as experienced former ministers, will only become involved if they think their efforts are going to make an impact and gain public attention. Westminster politicians have got to stop being so prickly and defensive about European institutions and adjust to British membership in the same way as businessmen, trade unionists and local politicians have done.

CHAPTER THREE

The Judiciary

'In recent months we have seen an entirely new development. This is an attack by politicians on the judiciary as a whole. This is without precedent in my professional lifetime and raises very serious constitutional issues.'

Lord Donaldson, Master of the Rolls, 1982–92,
Guardian, 1 December 1995

'The elective dictatorship of the majority means that, by and large, the government of the day can get its way, even if its majority is small. If its programme or its practice involves some derogation from human rights Parliament cannot be relied upon to correct this. Nor can the judges. If the derogation springs from a statute, they must faithfully apply the statute. If it is a result of administrative practice, there may well be no basis upon which they can interfere.'

Lord Bingham, Lord Chief Justice, Denning
Lecture (in Gordon and Wilmot-Smith, *Human
Rights in the United Kingdom*, 1996)

In recent years the balance between Parliament, ministers and the judges over who makes the law has faced far-reaching challenges. The first half of the 1990s was marked by a series of disputes between senior judges, including the Lord Chief Justice and the Master of the Rolls, and senior ministers, which generated public confusion over their respective roles. The various incidents that I describe in the following few pages all occurred under the last Conservative government. But it is necessary to distinguish between the possibly exceptional tensions of politicians and judges at the end of a long period of one-party rule and underlying, longer-lasting changes in the relationship between the judiciary, the executive and the legislature that might continue under the succeeding Labour government. The particular problems of the late Thatcher and Major governments may disappear, but the uncertainties over the more prominent role of judges in political debate could remain in view of the expansion in judicial review over the past two decades and the greater outspokenness of leading members of the judiciary. This has been given a further twist by the commitment of the Labour government elected in May 1997 to the incorporation of the European Convention of Human Rights into British law – which would further extend the role of judges in interpreting the actions of politicians and laws passed by the Westminster Parliament.

To the increasing alarm of many politicians, judges have steadily expanded their role, and their ambitions. There has been much confusion, misunderstanding and exaggeration about these issues, but there is at least a kernel of truth in the claim by Professor Simon Lee of Queen's University, Belfast, that: 'Law and lawyers have continued to overtake politics as a means of challenging government during John Major's premiership. It is lawyers more than opposition MPs or the media who call government to account, the brief as much as the ballot box which constrains government policy' (in Kavanagh and Seldon, 1994). This case is, as I argue in this book, an over-simplification and ignores other important shifts. Nonetheless, Professor Lee is right that, during the later years of the Thatcher and Major governments, senior ministers received their most serious reverses in the High Court rather than the House of Commons – and occasionally at the hands of the same judges when they opposed government proposals in the House of Lords. In his illuminating book on these issues, Joshua Rozenberg has given the example (1997, pp. ix to xi) of an occasion in January 1997 when five law lords, sitting in the morning as the Appellate Committee, heard an appeal over the decision by Michael Howard, the then Home Secretary, on the length of time that the two boys who murdered James Bulger should spend in custody. In the afternoon, the same law lords had moved downstairs from their room on the long committee corridor to the floor of the Lords to consider, and vote against, proposals from that same Home Secretary on mandatory and minimum sentences for some serious repeat offenders. In the same month, the law lords adjourned their hearing on the Bulger case early so that one of their number, Lord Browne-Wilkinson, could support an opposition amendment to the Home Secretary's other main measure that session, the Police Bill.

The differences of 1995–7 between Howard (aided by eager Conservative backbenchers and the more partisan newspapers) and senior judges culminated in the arguments over sentencing policy. This was dramatically highlighted in October 1995 during the Conservative party conference in Blackpool when Howard's proposal for minimum sentences for certain repeat offenders and offences provoked a statement of criticism within two hours from the late Lord Taylor of Gosforth, the then Lord Chief Justice. The following day's papers were full of the clash. The headline across the top of the *Independent* was typical: 'Chief Justice launches bitter attack on Howard's "get tough" crime plan'. Lord Taylor concluded: 'Minimum sentences are inconsistent with doing justice according to the circumstances of each case. Instead of limited judicial discretion by introducing unnecessary constraints on sentencing, the police should be provided with the resources they need to bring criminals before the courts in the first place.' Howard, a prominent and highly successful planning barrister before becoming a minister, tartly replied, 'It is Parliament's job to decide the law, not the judges'.' Lord Taylor did not disagree that it was for the legislature to decide. Rather, he regarded it as his duty to warn of the implications of a mistaken policy as Lord Bingham, his successor, did when the resulting bill was debated in the House of Lords in February 1997 – and successfully amended to give the judges more discretion.

This dispute over policy was reinforced by a series of High Court rulings against the Government, and particularly the Home Secretary, which led Howard to comment in autumn 1995 that: 'It is becoming quite difficult to predict with any accuracy how the judges are going to react.' At the same time, some senior judges were making speeches outside their courts defending and asserting their role in relation to the Government and Parliament. Ann Widdecombe, then Minister of State at the Home Office, was even more direct than Howard: 'I am worried about the pronouncements of some of the judges who appear to think there is a policy role to be adopted by some of the judiciary.' John Patten, a former cabinet minister and Home Office Minister of State, complained in July 1996 about 'our increasingly uncontrollable judges', while Lord Irvine of Lairg, then the shadow rather than actual Lord Chancellor, as he became in May 1997, had warned of the danger of 'judicial supremacism'.

To more detached observers, it was ironic that right-wing, and not left-wing, politicians were generally leading the criticism of the judiciary. Traditionally, the left has been most wary of judges for being conservative in their opinions and socially unrepresentative in view of the public school and Oxbridge backgrounds of many of them. When the revival of judicial activism first became apparent in the mid-to-late 1970s, it was through a series of rulings against the then Labour government – over Freddie Laker's Skytrain and the Tameside grammar schools – and in support of individual workers against trade unions. This was reinforced by concern, particularly among civil-liberties' activists, over the courts' failure more quickly to correct what were shown to be miscarriages of justice over the Birmingham Six, the Guildford Four and a few similar cases. Later, the courts ruled several times against the miners' union during the strike of 1984–5. But by the mid-1990s, the fire was from the opposite flank. The populist right in the Tory party and the press also accused the judiciary of being élitist and out of touch, because they were allegedly too fashionably liberal rather than too conservative. Tory MPs were also annoyed by the role of senior judges, Lord Nolan and Sir Richard Scott, in heading inquiries, into, respectively, standards in public life and allegations over the supply of arms and related equipment to Iraq. Their reports proved embarrassing for the Major government and, in the case of Nolan, led to new controls over the outside interests of MPs. The judiciary, in short, were becoming too prominent and too powerful in the eyes of Conservative politicians.

The tensions between the judiciary and, mainly Conservative, politicians reflected a mixture of short- and long-term factors: the particular attitudes of some ministers and the unprecedented longevity of one party in office, together with changes in the scope of judicial rulings. As Lord Donaldson wrote in the *Guardian* on 1 December 1995, in relation to the increasing number of judicial review decisions adverse to the Government over the previous few years:

> Whether this is due to the fact that one political party has been in power for an exceptionally long period and has become unusually convinced of its own rectitude, or to an increasingly careful scrutiny of government actions by the judiciary, or to an increasing awareness on the part of the public that they can look to the courts for protection is not for me to say. Probably all three factors have made a contribution.

This is the same Lord Donaldson who was reviled by Labour in the 1970s for his role as the presiding judge in the industrial-relations court when he made a number of rulings against the trade unions.

However, from the 1920s until the 1960s, there was a long period of judicial restraint, indeed passivity, in relation to the executive. The marked reluctance to interfere in official decisions culminated in the decisions by senior judges during the Second World War not to challenge the most draconian wartime regulations and suppression of information on grounds of Crown privilege. There was a general acceptance at the time that the expansion of the role of the state was beneficial and that the courts should not interfere. In the two decades after the war, this attitude was reflected in the regular overruling of Lord Denning's judgments by the House of Lords. In the late 1940s and early 1950s, Lord Denning expressed worries about the growing powers of the executive and argued that judges should assert themselves as protectors of freedom.

During the 1960s judicial deference to the executive disappeared. As Professor Jeffrey Jowell has argued (1997), 'in the space of a mere five years, a large number of technical barriers to judicial intervention and a purposive approach to the interpretation of statutes broke through the barrier of the literal. "The minister may" could mean "the minister must"; power granted in the form of broad discretion was no longer read as a conferral of unconstrained fiat.' There was a variety of causes for this shift: increases in the quantity of legislation, often hastily drafted and ill-phrased; the exposure of gaps in legislation which judges have filled; a much less guarded attitude by judges in delivering their rulings; and increasing concern on both left and right (at varying times) about the need for formal limits on the power of the executive. This is linked to the growth of the 'human rights' lobby, partly reflecting American views on citizen participation and rights.

The main change has been the rapid growth in what is known as judicial review, that is the ability of citizens to challenge decisions by public officials on the grounds that they have improperly exercised their powers. Contrary to the frequent headlines, this does not represent a challenge by the judiciary to Parliament. Rather it is the reverse; the courts are asked to rule whether statutes passed by Parliament are being legally and fairly implemented, not to challenge their merits on policy grounds. It is not, however, quite as simple as that since the scope of judicial review has been steadily broadened over the past twenty or so years.

The right to challenge administrative decisions may always have been there, but for the first half of this century the courts tended to take the side of ministers unless there had been some clear example of a public body claiming excess jurisdiction or making an obvious legal error. But in many cases the issue is not just whether a power has been exercised legally, but whether it has been exercised reasonably. The principles of judicial review were laid down in 1948 by Lord Greene, the then Master of the Rolls, in a ruling involving Wednesbury local authority. He argued that 'although the local authority have kept within the four corners of matters which they ought to consider, they have nevertheless come to a conclusion so unreasonable that no reasonable authority could ever have come of it'. Lord Greene was careful to add that: 'The power of the court to interfere in each case is not as an appellate authority to override a decision of the local authority, but as a judicial authority which is concerned, and concerned only, to see whether the local authority have contravened the law by acting in excess of powers which Parliament has confided in them.' The term 'unreasonableness' was redefined in 1984 by Lord Diplock as 'irrationality'. It was not really until the late 1970s that judicial review developed to cover a much wider range of grounds, ranging from the exercise of power for improper purposes, acting beyond legal powers, neglect of relevant factors, irrationality, unfairness, proportionality and over-zealous application of rules. But this creates a fine line between the legality of an action and its merits on policy grounds, which is the province of Parliament.

A Law Commission report in 1976 led to a simplification of the rules of the courts in handling judicial review and this was endorsed by Parliament in the Supreme Court Act of 1981 and reserved to judges of the High Court by the Court and Legal Services Act. There has been a seven-fold growth in the number of applications for judicial review since 1980, of which only about two-fifths are granted and lead to full hearings. Moreover, less than a tenth of all applications for judicial review against central government result in a substantive finding against the department or minister concerned, though in the instance of immigration cases, half of those where there was a full hearing went against the authorities in 1995, as did a third in 1996. Nonetheless, concern within Whitehall about the implications led to the production in 1987 of the pamphlet, 'The Judge Over Your Shoulder' by the Treasury Solicitor's Department and the Cabinet Office, which warned civil servants to be careful about, and aware of, the possibility of challenge in the courts.

During the 1980s and 1990s, the courts have rolled back the previous areas of executive immunity, accepting that the prerogative power of the Crown/executive can be challenged in the courts. It is as yet unclear how far this reflected a reaction to a record eighteen-year period of one-party rule when Parliament was seen – and not just by judges – as failing to hold the executive properly to account. Lord Bingham, when Master of the Rolls, had said in 1993 that 'the courts have reacted to the increase in the powers claimed by the Government by being more active themselves', adding the controversial comment that this had become all the more important at a time of one-party government. However, both Lord Bingham and Lord Woolf believed that the shift in judicial attitudes would continue under a Labour government. Between 1974 and 1979, the courts 'took a very forceful line whenever Labour ministers tried to exceed their powers' (see Rozenberg, p. 113).

As important has been the greater outspokenness of judges over who makes the law. For a long time, judges were banned from speaking to the media under the Kilmuir Rules of 1955 (named after the then Lord Chancellor), which stated that 'so long as a judge keeps silent his reputation for wisdom and impartiality remains unassailable'. On becoming Lord Chancellor in 1987, Lord Mackay of Clashfern made plain that individual judges should be trusted to deal sensibly with the media. This relaxation was reinforced in October 1989 by a formal letter sent to all judges by Lord Mackay, though with a warning on the need for caution about anything that might be politically controversial. In the event, problems have arisen not because of relations with the media but over carefully prepared lectures by senior judges and in their warnings about aspects of administration of justice, such as legal aid, and sentencing policy, as discussed earlier.

The difficulty of defining the right boundaries between judges and politicians emerged in a controversy over personal privacy. Successive governments have shied away from introducing a privacy law despite repeated excesses and breaches of the informal, self-regulatory code by some tabloid papers. Governments have wanted to avoid a confrontation with the press, since proprietors and editors of almost all news-papers have fiercely resisted such a law. In a lecture in May 1996, shortly before he became Lord Chief Justice, Lord Bingham reviewed the current legal position. He concluded: 'To a very large extent the law already does protect personal privacy; but to the extent that it does not, it should. The right must be narrowly drawn, to give full effect to the right of free speech and the public's right to know. It should strike only at significant infringements, such as would cause substantial distress to an ordinarily phlegmatic person.' He said his preference was for legislation, 'which could mean that the rules which the courts applied would carry the imprimatur of democratic approval. But if, for whatever reason, legislation is not forthcoming, I think it almost inevitable that cases will arise in the courts in which the need to give relief is obvious and pressing; and when such cases do arise, I do not think the courts will be found wanting.' What he had in mind was not the introduction of some general law of privacy, but enlarging the existing rights to take legal action. The next day, Lord Hoffman, a law lord, argued that: 'If the English judges were to decide that the lack of a right to privacy represented a gap in the law, there are ample materials to hand to enable such a right to be constructed. I do not think that one can expect such a right to be created by a majority decision in Parliament. But that makes it all the more important that it should be recognised at common law.' These comments were seen by Lord Irvine as 'uncomfortably like a judicial threat to legislate'. He argued that only Parliament should decide whether to replace self-regulation; and that only if there were 'a clear community consensus' over a right to privacy, should the judges create such a right. He believed there was no such consensus over privacy, and the judges risked being seen to take sides in the controversy. But what Lords Bingham and Hoffman had highlighted was the dilemma created by the failure of Parliament to act, rather than any judicial attempt to defy Parliament. This vacuum created the need for the courts to respond in particular cases, building on existing common law and the existing law of trespass, breach of confidence and the European Convention on Human Rights.

However, some judges have sought to qualify the doctrine of absolute parliamentary sovereignty on the grounds of the increasing power either formally delegated to ministers or, in practice, exercised by them because of inadequacies of parliamentary scrutiny. So the challenge of the judiciary is less to the legislature than to the only partially checked power of the executive. As Mr Justice Sedley has argued (1997):

> It is precisely because ministerial government enjoys a high degree of autonomy, enabling it in large part to control the Parliament to which it is theoretically subordinate, that it is crucial to stress the constitutional fact that the executive does not possess anything which can accurately be called sovereignty. It is in Parliament and the courts, each exercising a discrete though interdependent function of the state, the legislative and the judicial, that the sovereignties of the state reside.

From a different angle, Lord Woolf has argued that there are limits on the supremacy of Parliament in that, while Parliament is supreme in its legislative capacity, the courts are the final arbiters of the interpretation and application of the law. Both Parliament and the courts derive their authority from the rule of law and cannot act in a manner that involves its repudiation. This argument was taken further by Mr Justice Laws who in 1994 argued that there was 'a higher-order law: a law which cannot be abrogated as other laws can, by the passage of a statute promoted by a government with the necessary majority in Parliament'. On this view, the power of a democratically elected government or parliament could not be absolute and could not, for example, override the institution of free and regular elections. Mr Justice Laws drew a distinction between political and constitutional sovereignty.

The combination of the well-publicized disputes over sentencing policy and these claims by some judges prompted a special House of Lords debate on 5 June 1996, just a fortnight after Lord Bingham's lecture on privacy. The debate was appropriately entitled 'The Judiciary: Public Controversy', and initiated by Lord Irvine. He specifically warned that judges 'should never give grounds for the public to believe that they intend to reverse government policies which they dislike. That is why I regard as unwise observations off the Bench by eminent judges that the courts have reacted to the increase in the powers claimed by government by being more active themselves, and adding for good measure that this has become all the more important at a time of one-party government. It suggests to ordinary people a judicial invasion of the legislature's turf.' Lord Irvine went on to describe as 'equally unwise' statements by 'distinguished' judges that in exceptional cases the courts may be entitled to hold invalid individual statutes duly passed by Parliament. This, he said, caused ordinary people to believe not only that judges may have got over and above themselves but were also exercising a political function in judicial review cases rather than simply upholding the law. Lord Woolf, the new Master of the Rolls, defended the role of judges in being inevitably involved in public debate and in identifying areas of the law which are not at present serving the public in the way they should and which need re-examination on a case-by-case basis in accordance with the common law. The difficulty in defining the boundary of the proper development of the law was highlighted by Lord Mackay of Clashfern, who defended Lord Bingham's lecture on the law on privacy.

These problems of defining the proper role of judges will be increased by the incorporation of the European Convention of Human Rights into British law. This was proposed by Labour in the Queen's Speech of May 1997, with the support of the Liberal Democrats and a number of leading Conservative lawyers, as well as many prominent judges, including Lord Bingham and Lord Woolf. The convention has its origins in the burst of post-war idealism about European reconciliation. The UK was among ten countries that founded the Council of Europe in 1949, which decided at its launch to draw up an international agreement on human rights. British lawyers played a major part in drafting this even though the then Labour government was opposed to giving individuals the automatic right to petition or raise complaints with the European Commission on Human Rights, the initial investigatory body. Lord Jowitt, the then Lord Chancellor, was highly critical of what he described as 'some half-baked scheme to be administered by some unknown court'. This was typical of the attitude of British ministers at the time towards European integration – closer co-operation, even formal links, was all right for countries on the Continent but not for Britain. However, the UK became the first country to ratify the convention in March 1951. The convention lays down various general rights, such as right to life, no torture, no slavery, personal liberty and security, fair and public trial, no retrospective crimes, respect for private and family life, freedom of thought, conscience and religion, freedom of expression (except in the interests of national security, territorial integrity or public safety), freedom of peaceful assembly, the right to marry, effective remedies before a national authority, and no discrimination. In 1952, some additional protocols were added covering the right to peaceful enjoyment of possessions, the right to education in conformity with one's parents' religious and philosophical convictions, and the right to free elections. There is, however, a loophole to cover times of war and emergencies 'threatening the life of the nation'.

Even though the British Parliament has not formally incorporated the convention into British law, it has still had an impact on Britain – especially following the decision of the Wilson government in 1965 to accept the right of individuals to petition the Human Rights Commission. Up to the end of 1996, the European Court of Human Rights had ruled on seventy-one cases involving Britain and, in forty-four, had found at least one breach of the convention. This is worse than any other European country except Italy. However, this record is not quite as bad as it looks if account is also taken of the relative size of the UK and the fact that the right of individual petition has been allowed here for longer than in several other countries and that human-rights groups, like Liberty, are more active than in other countries. However, as the authors of the Democratic Audit study reported (Klug, Starmer and Weir, 1996, p. 47), twenty-four of the thirty-seven British violations of the convention determined by the European Court between 1975 and 1995 were the result of laws passed by Parliament. The other main reason for these figures is that, because the convention has not been incorporated into British law, complaints have to go to the European Court in Strasbourg rather than being resolved in domestic courts.

Even leaving aside the cases decided in Strasbourg, the convention has still had an impact on British domestic law, as Lord Bingham, a long-term supporter of incorporation, has pointed out (in the House of Lords on 3 July 1996, and in Gordon and Wilmot-Smith). The convention is taken into account when, for example, a statute is ambiguous, the common law is uncertain or unclear, or when the courts have to exercise discretion. In these cases the courts will rule in a manner which conforms with the convention rather than conflicts with it. Moreover, where the courts have to rule on what public policy demands, they may take into account international obligations, as in the convention and other international treaties, as a source of guidance. There is also a European twist since EU laws already formally take the convention and legislation derived from it into account, while such European laws are binding in British courts and superior to UK law. In those areas covered by European Community law, the convention is in effect indirectly incorporated into our domestic law, even though this has had little practical result so far.

Lord Nolan has argued that we 'are effectively governed' by the convention and are bound to obey the rulings of the European Court of Human Rights. But, as he argued in his Radcliffe lectures (1996), since the convention is not part of our law, 'we have too little knowledge of convention law and play no part in its development. All too often this has led us into embarrassing consequences and in my view must continue to do so unless and until it becomes part of the law administered by our judges as well as by the European Court.' However, as Lord Bingham pointed out in the Lords debate, 'the convention is not part of our domestic law. The courts have no powers to enforce convention rights directly. If domestic legislation plainly conflicts with the enforcement of the convention, then the courts apply the domestic legislation.' The advocates of incorporation argue that it is wrong that British citizens should have to go to Europe on human-rights issues rather than have their cases heard, almost certainly more speedily and cheaply, in British courts. That would also permit, as Lord Nolan has argued, a specifically British influence on the development of European human-rights thinking and jurisprudence, both in Britain and in the European Court of Human Rights in Strasbourg. Constitutional reform and human-rights groups have argued (for example, Klug, Starmer and Weir) that Parliament has been inadequate in protecting human rights. 'The United Kingdom offers far less formal protection of fundamental political rights and freedoms than international standards require and ordinary citizens are entitled to expect.' In an indirect reference to the comments of Mr Justice Laws quoted above, the lengthy audit concluded (p. 314) that 'Each of the three pillars of the "British system" for protecting rights – Parliament, public opinion and the courts – requires the additional support of a consistent set of positive rights which act as a "higher law", to which all legislation and policy must conform.'

There are four main counter-arguments. First, put forward by the Major government (despite some reservations by Conservative lawyers),

British rights and freedoms are already inherent in the legal system and are fully protected by Parliament unless removed or restricted by statute. This is essentially the view that Parliament is looking after our rights perfectly well at present and we do not need to give the judges more power to interfere. Second, as deployed by Lord Donaldson of Lymington in the February 1997 debate on the Lester bill, both the European Commission on Human Rights and the Court go beyond merely interpreting and enforcing the convention and make policy. (The same point is made about the European Court of Justice in its rulings on the law of the European Communities.) Third, and linked to the second, judicial rulings on a bill of rights would be inherently political, so that the judiciary, whether they liked it or not, would be trespassing into the territory of elected politicians. This point has been put forcefully from the left by Professor John Griffith, who has argued (1997) that a bill of rights is 'by its nature anti-democratic and authoritarian'. On his view, 'law is politics carried on by other means and does not recognize the existence of extra-legal, so-called fundamental, inalienable or natural rights'. So judges should not be called on to determine what is politically necessary. We may wish that Parliament did a better job, but 'that does not remotely justify transferring their responsibilities to the judges'. Fourth, some of the provisions would have unwelcome and unexpected effects on British law in, for example, changing the balance of justification for killing in self-defence and in the incompatibility of community-service orders with the ban on forced labour.

The most contentious issue is how far such a convention should be entrenched – in other words whether it should override the Diceyan principle that one parliament cannot bind its successor. As I discussed in Chapter Two, that has been partly qualified by Britain's acceptance of the superiority of European Community law as a result of our accession. But in most countries with bills of rights, including those with Westminster-style parliamentary systems, there is some means of entrenchment whereby the courts can strike down legislation that they consider does not comply with their rights statute. For instance, judicial entrenchment could be made subject to a parliamentary override. In Canada, for example, legislation can be tested in the courts to assess compliance with the Charter of Rights and Freedoms of 1982. However, there is a 'notwithstanding' clause so that the federal parliament in

Ottawa or any provincial legislature can declare, for five-year renewable periods, that legislation should be given effect by the courts even though it infringes these rights. This was intended to ensure that 'legislatures rather than judges would have the final say on matters of policy'. An alternative approach would involve distinguishing between different types of legislation, as in Hong Kong which differentiates between laws passed before and after the bill of rights took effect.

The more relevant example for Britain may be the New Zealand Bill of Rights of 1990. This is like any other legislation and operates as a tool of interpretation for the courts. As the Constitution Unit reports on Human Rights Legislation pointed out (1996, p. 32): 'Judges cannot overrule any other law to provide for compliance; individuals cannot take cases simply to challenge legislation for non-conformity with the rights granted in the instrument; the courts are simply entitled to refer to the bill of rights in cases that would otherwise come before them.' The New Zealand judiciary are required to interpret statutes consistently with its provisions, although the courts are not given any power to render any enactment invalid or ineffective or to decline to apply any provision. This would not undermine parliamentary sovereignty.

The various British attempts at incorporation have moved steadily in this direction. Private members' bills, introduced in 1985 by Lord Scarman and in 1994 by Lord Lester, a Liberal Democrat peer and leading human-rights barrister, originally envisaged that the courts should be able to set aside legislation inconsistent with the convention. These were modelled more on the Canadian Charter of Rights and the European Communities Act of 1972. Lord Lester argued that this was consistent with parliamentary supremacy since a future parliament could have repealed the Human Rights Act legislation just as it could repeal the European Communities Act. However, following arguments by the law lords, the Lester bill was amended, both at committee stage and, later, at report stage, to become more like the New Zealand version in being presented as an aid to the interpretation of legislation and taken into account in equity and common law. The judges were cautious, reluctant to appear to be overriding Parliament or to be drawn into political controversy. Their worries were recognized in the later version put forward by Lord Lester, which had its second reading in the Lords on 5 February 1997. This was explicitly modelled on the New Zealand experience. As Lord Lester said, 'Unlike the previous version, the present bill does not require or empower the courts to strike down provisions of Acts of Parliament which are plainly in conflict with the human rights and fundamental freedoms guaranteed by the convention.' Instead, the bill provided that, whenever a law can be given a meaning that is consistent with convention rights, that meaning shall be preferred to any other meaning. Also as in New Zealand, ministers, when proposing bills, would have to explain 'why a provision is, or appears to be, inconsistent with convention rights. This will enable Parliament to be properly informed so that it can act effectively as a constitutional watchdog in enacting and scrutinizing primary legislation.' It will also mean that, in the absence of a ministerial explanation, the courts will be able to assume that Parliament did not intend to repeal or amend convention rights by implication. Such a law would force the government of the day to be explicit if it intends to override the provisions of the convention – in a sense, requiring Parliament to think again. Critics argue that this would make the European Convention weaker in UK law than European legislation, but both the judiciary and Parliament at present seem most comfortable with an approach which would leave the ultimate power with the legislature.

The Labour Party has moved along the same road as Lord Lester. Originally, the party talked about a Human Rights Act on Canadian lines, which would have overridden all existing legislation, although Parliament would still have been able to pass inconsistent legislation, provided it made this explicit. But Lord Irvine made plain during 1996 that he was moving towards the New Zealand model so as to preserve parliamentary sovereignty. He noted that under this approach, 'the courts are required so far as possible to interpret statutes and apply the common law so as to conform, but may not strike down a statute which Parliament plainly intended should not conform'. In an interview with the *New Statesman* on 6 December 1996, he discussed the possibility of setting up a Standing Commission on Human Rights, like the Equal Opportunities Commission, to monitor protection of rights under the convention. He also stressed that the convention was a floor that would not prevent the British Parliament from strengthening rights through, for instance, a freedom of information bill. Indeed, many human-rights groups, such as Liberty, see incorporation merely as a first step towards the creation of a British bill of rights, not least because the fifty-year-old convention by definition takes no account of changes in thinking on the subject since then. There is not only no reference to the right to obtain information, but nothing is said about discrimination on grounds of disability or sexual orientation, or about protecting children.

One of the main objections to incorporation is that it would give unelected judges the power to take essentially political decisions that are the province of Parliament. However, the broadly interpretative New Zealand model of a bill of rights should minimize such a conflict, while the judges are already involved in sensitive political decisions without incorporation. And, as the development of judicial review has shown over the past two decades, the judges have generally, though not always, exercised restraint. The New Zealand model has a strong appeal to both elected politicians and judges in Britain who want to avoid a confrontation – and this model was favoured by several ministers in the discussions following the May 1997 election. After becoming Lord Chancellor, Lord Irvine argued (notably in a lecture to a bill of rights conference in July 1997) that it was essential that incorporation of the convention is achieved in a way that does nothing to disturb the balance in the separation of powers. 'It is for Parliament to pass laws, not the judges. It is for the judges to interpret these laws and to develop the common law, not for Parliament or the executive.' Incorporation 'must not disturb the supremacy of Parliament. It should not put the judges in a position where they are seen as at odds with Parliament. That would be a recipe for conflict and mutual recrimination. It is vital that the courts should not become involved in a process of policy evaluation which goes far beyond its allotted constitutional role.'

Incorporation should lead to an increase in the role of the elected legislature in scrutinizing the enforcement of rights, alongside the courts. The Constitution Unit suggested in its report on the issue (pp. 69–75) that a new or existing committee should be given responsibility for ensuring compliance with human-rights standards, both the European Convention and other international obligations in this area. This might be the responsibility of the House of Lords Delegated Powers Scrutiny Committee or a new joint committee of both Houses. Bills should be referred to the committee at an early stage in their passage (perhaps just before or after their second readings), while the committee could also monitor the activities of government departments in relation to human-rights standards.

But incorporation will inevitably provoke an intensified debate about the appointment of judges. At present, the senior judges (law lords, heads of division like the Lord Chief Justice and Master of the Rolls and Appeal Court judges) are appointed by the Queen on the recommendation of the Prime Minister, who receives advice from the Lord Chancellor. High Court and circuit judges are appointed by the Queen on the recommendation of the Lord Chancellor. This has not prevented the promotion of judges whose decisions have caused trouble and embarrassment to the Government. For instance, Brian Smedley, who presided over the abortive Matrix Churchill trial and required the disclosure of documents for which public-interest immunity had been claimed, later became one of the rare promotions from the circuit bench to the High Court. But there has been growing concern that the process is not open, that the opinions of the senior judiciary are sometimes not taken into account even in top appointments. Sir Thomas Bingham became Lord Chief Justice in 1996 on the recommendation of the Lord Chancellor, contrary to the opinion of the clear majority of criminal appeal judges, including the outgoing Lord Chief Justice, who favoured Lord Justice Rose. David Pannick, a leading barrister and writer about the law, has argued (1987) in favour of greater openness about the working of the judicial system and greater objectivity in the appraisal of the performance of judges.

> We need judges who are not appointed by the unassisted efforts of the Lord Chancellor and solely from the ranks of middle-aged barristers. We need judges who are trained for the job, whose conduct can be freely criticized and is subject to investigation by a Judicial Performance Commission; judges who abandon wigs, gowns, and unnecessary linguistic legalism; judges who welcome rather than shun publicity for their activities.'

Lord Mackay of Clashfern sought to open up the procedures to a wider field of potential candidates by introducing in 1994 the advertising of vacancies for circuit and district judges, assistant recorders, stipendiary magistrates and tribunal chairmen. Selected applicants are invited to attend an interview with a three-member panel, including a relevant judicial office-holder, a lay interviewer and a senior official of the Lord Chancellor's Judicial Appointments Group.

The Home Affairs Committee of the Commons conducted a lengthy inquiry into appointments procedures in the 1995–6 session and made some detailed suggestions for improvements, but the Conservative majority ensured that the general conclusion was that (p. lxxv) 'we have not found there is a need for large-scale change in the procedures for the appointment of professional judges and of lay magistrates'. Amendments were proposed by the then Labour minority, arguing that a disproportionate number of judges are not only upper-middle-class males and come from a narrow educational background but that a 'glass ceiling' exists to prevent those from other backgrounds progressing from the middle to the higher judiciary. There is little evidence that a relatively narrow social background makes any difference to judges' attitudes. The old left-wing myths about right-wing judges have been contradicted by the experience of recent years. As Diana Woodhouse has pointed out (1996, p. 425), 'if there was in the past a convergence between judicial and Conservative philosophy, this is no longer the case. The senior judges of the 1990s would seem to have little in common with the New Right Conservative Party and they have been prepared to air their differences.'

The most important reform proposal is for the creation of a Judicial Appointments Commission which would transfer, either fully or partly, responsibility for the appointment of judges from ministers to an independent body. This might broaden the range both of advice going to ministers on judicial appointments and of lawyers being appointed, though there are considerable variations in how such a commission might operate: whether it would be primarily advisory or have the power to appoint judges itself. The broad proposal has been favoured by the Law Society, JUSTICE, the Howard League for Penal Reform and by the Labour Party, though it has been opposed by Lord Mackay of Clashfern and the Judges' Council. The senior judges were worried that the process would become more, not less, political. The majority on the Home Affairs Committee believed that the quality of appointees would not necessarily improve if a Judicial Appointments Commission was established and that it was better to retain the present system based on consultations throughout the legal profession. However, following the May 1997 election, Lord Irvine announced consultations on the merits of establishing a Judicial Appointments Commission.

Recent controversies – and the proposals on incorporation of the European Convention – underline the case for greater transparency, at least in advice, on judicial appointments. Joshua Rozenberg (1997) makes a strong case for going further in formally separating the multiple roles of the Lord Chancellor as a leading member of the executive (in the cabinet), the legislature and the judiciary; of the law lords as active members of the legislature as well as the judiciary: and of the law officers as members of the executive who exercise quasi-judicial powers. He gives ample examples of potential conflicts of interest. I believe there is an argument for separating the judicial and the legislative roles, so that the Lord Chancellor, for example, no longer sits as a member of the Appellate Committee of the Lords (at any rate, not in any case involving the Government). The parliamentary role of the law lords is two-edged. The law lords, both serving and those retired from active service, add much to debates on legal and constitutional issues. But a greater public prominence for judges as a result of incorporation may make it impossible for them to carry on their legislative role in the House of Lords for as long as they serve on its Appellate Committee. The law officers could remain the Government's main legal advisers and be ministerially accountable to Parliament for the Crown Prosecution Service, though themselves no longer taking decisions on prosecutions or contempt-of-court proceedings. It is also questionable whether the law officers should any longer appear as advocates, not least because of the difficulty of finding suitably qualified members of the Commons. The last Scottish law officer to sit in the Commons did so in 1987, while the Blair government could not find a Solicitor General from among its record number of MPs.

The growth in judicial activism of the past twenty years and the particular tensions of the first half of the 1990s reflected a breakdown in mutual respect between some senior judges and some senior politicians. Both need to show restraint, judges over their public pronouncements and legislative role and politicians in making better law. The increasing prominence of the judiciary is not just because of a new generation of judges or a changing intellectual climate. It also reflects a failure by government in drafting laws and by Parliament in considering and debating them. From a conservative viewpoint, Andrew Lansley and Richard Wilson have argued (1997, p. 111) that Parliament should codify the grounds for judicial review; that the courts should have regard in interpreting statutes to the explanatory memoranda and notes on clauses supplied during debates on a bill; and that legislation should set out its purposes in general terms, as well as specific provisions, to allow courts to adopt a less literal and more purposive approach to the interpretation of statute. In short, if Parliament did its job better, there would be less need for judges to exercise their discretion and become involved in political controversy. But, as in so many other areas of public life, we are rapidly moving from an era of informal understandings to more formal codes and rights – and the beginnings, if not more, of a written constitution. That will inevitably mean a further change in the role of the judiciary, in judging the actions of the executive and the laws passed by the legislature.

CHAPTER FOUR

Accountability

Under our constitutional practice, executive powers are conferred by Parliament on Ministers of the Crown. Both in regard to these powers and others which derive from the prerogative and not from statute, it has long been the established constitutional practice that the appropriate Minister of the Crown is responsible to Parliament for every action in pursuance of them.

> Sir Edward Bridges, Permanent Secretary to the
> Treasury, in a memorandum, 1954, at the time of
> the Crichel Down affair

Paragraph 27 of 'Questions of Procedure for Ministers' identifies as one of the facets of Ministerial accountability to Parliament 'the duty to give Parliament, including its Select Committees, and the public as full information as possible about the policies, decisions and actions of the Government, and not to deceive or mislead Parliament and the public'. In the course of the Inquiry example after example has come to light of an apparent failure by Ministers to discharge that obligation.

> The Scott Report, February 1996

M inisterial responsibility and accountability to Parliament are the crucial links between the executive and the legislature. This has been a commonplace of constitutional discussion since well before Palmerston declared in 1838 that 'the ministers who are at the head of the several departments of the state, are liable any day and every day to defend themselves in Parliament'. Ministers are accountable both collectively as members of a government and individually for what they do in the departments in which they serve. This doctrine has been repeated, refined and clarified over the intervening years and, more recently, in the discussion generated by the Crichel Down affair, West-land, the Scott Report, and the sacking of Derek Lewis as the head of the Prison Service. But the simple-sounding concept is, both in theory and practice, elusive. It has never been absolute and has always depended on the political mood and pressures of the time. Moreover, changes in the structure of government – notably the creation of the Next Steps executive agencies and other semi-independent public bodies – has challenged traditional ideas of accountability, and Parliament has so far failed adequately to adjust. Constitutional theory, and parliamentary procedure, have not kept up with changes in management and organization. In this chapter I will discuss how the familiar doctrine has become strained and what might be done to strengthen the accountability of the executive and its various agencies to Parliament.

The Public Service Committee of the Commons noted in its comprehensive report on the issue (1995–6, p. ix) that 'there have always been elements of ambiguity and confusion in the convention of individual ministerial responsibility'. First, there is no comprehensive or authoritative statement of the convention which anyway has no binding or statutory force, so the way it is used in practice tends to be variable and inconsistent. 'It has often been as useful politically to obscure the convention as to clarify it.' Second, that inconsistency means that it has never been clear what a minister has to do to discharge his responsibility through Parliament. Third, it has never been entirely clear, either, 'how far a minister's formal responsibility for the actions of officials subordinate to him extends'. Or has it, in practice, turned into a doctrine of ministerial irresponsibility, of endlessly passing the buck? As Lord Nolan pointed out, in his second Radcliffe lecture in November 1996: 'There is no independent source of authority which can determine whether the convention has been observed in a given circumstance.'

The lengthy discussion among civil servants, serving and retired, politicians, and constitutional commentators seems too often to get nowhere. The doctrine has been reinterpreted to the point of losing much practical meaning, with subtle, though often slippery, distinctions between responsibility and accountability, between policy and operations. A large part of the problem is that the theoretical debate has tried to introduce precision into an area where precision is impossible. The questions of responsibility, accountability and, in the ultimate, ministerial resignation are relative, not absolute. They are dependent on the political mood and attitudes of the time rather than upon fixed constitutional rules. At one extreme, no one would seriously expect a minister to take the blame or to resign over an act of maladministration by a civil servant in which the minister has never been personally involved; at the other, everyone would expect a minister to resign if it was proved that he or she had deliberately lied to Parliament – as John Profumo did in 1963, and for which he duly paid the price. But the trickiest politics lies between these extremes, not in the largely pointless tabloid and opposition game of resignation chasing but in the practical exercise of determining who should be held to account and how mistakes can be put right by government.

The civil service is itself partly to blame for the fuzziness of the debate. It has suited civil servants to portray themselves as merely obedient executors of the will of elected politicians who are responsible to Parliament. The quotation from Sir Edward Bridges at the start of this chapter was, for long, the classic textbook expression of the view that ministers take full responsibility for everything undertaken in their name in their departments, and that ministers can be forced to resign by Parliament if something goes seriously wrong. One result, explicitly stated by Bridges, was that 'a civil servant, having no power conferred on him by Parliament, has no direct responsibility to Parliament and cannot be called to account by Parliament. His acts, indeed, are not his own. All that he does is done on behalf of the minister, with the minister's authority express or implied.'

This has fostered the myth – particularly cherished by letter-writers to the press from the Home Counties – that there was once a golden age when ministers did the honourable thing and resigned. Like most golden ages, it never existed. There is no evidence of any direct link between ministerial failure, even in the specific sense of being directly responsible for serious incompetence, and resignation. An exhaustive list drawn up by Professor S. E. Finer in 1956 (and reprinted in Marshall, 1989) analysed ministerial resignations over the previous century and concluded that few ministers had resigned because of the doctrine of the individual responsibility of ministers. Most were forced out of office by pressures from the Commons. In the vast majority of cases: 'Whether a minister is forced to resign depends on three factors, on himself, his Prime Minister and his party . . . For a resignation to occur all three factors have to be just so: the minister compliant, the Prime Minister firm, the party clamorous.' If the party is out for blood, it does not matter how serious or trivial the reason is. Professor Finer argued that perhaps sixteen or so cases of forced resignations over a century hardly added up to a convention since it generalizes from the exceptions and neglects the common run. Similarly, Professor Rodney Brazier has argued (1997, p. 262) that: 'It is impossible to lay down rigid constitutional rules about ministerial responsibility, at least in a way which gives practical guidance about behaviour to those holding ministerial office.' For him, the principles which have developed are 'at best elastic'.

In practice, ministers only resign when they lose the confidence of their prime minister and their parliamentary colleagues. This was true in the most famous historical case of a minister allegedly taking responsibility for the actions of his officials: the resignation in 1954 of Sir Thomas Dugdale as Minister of Agriculture. The widely held belief is that Sir Thomas was some kind of constitutional saint – the last honourable politician – because he allegedly took 'personal responsibility' for the maladministration of officials of which he knew nothing. This view is almost wholly inaccurate. Sir Thomas was not only fully aware of the decision taken by officials in the particular case of the Crichel Down land but he also accepted the policy upon which it was based concerning the rights of former owners of land that had been compulsorily purchased during the war. The reason he resigned was that he had lost the confidence of his own parliamentary colleagues. Sir Thomas, like most other ministers, resigned not on a matter of principle but because of political pressures.

The long-held myths about the Crichel Down affair were, in fact, undermined at the time when Sir David Maxwell-Fyfe, the then Home Secretary, sought to limit the circumstances when ministers would be expected to take the blame. He said, in the Commons debate on the affair in July 1954, that 'In the case where there is an explicit order by a minister, the minister must protect the civil servant who has carried out his order; and when the civil servant acts properly in accordance with the policy laid down by the minister, the minister must protect and defend him.' And, 'when an official makes a mistake or causes some delay, but not on an important issue of policy and not where a claim to individual rights is seriously involved, the minister acknowledges the mistake and he accepts the responsibility, although he is not personally involved. He states that he will take corrective action and would not, in those circumstances, expose the official to public criticism.' But in the Crichel Down case, Sir Thomas should have protected the civil servants rather than set up a public inquiry, which identified the responsible officials whose careers subsequently suffered. Maxwell-Fyfe, however, added the crucial further point that 'where action has been taken by a civil servant of which the minister disapproves and has no prior knowledge, and the conduct of the official is reprehensible, then there is no obligation on the part of the minister to endorse what he believes to be wrong, or to defend what were clearly shown to be errors of his officers. The minister is not bound to defend action of which he did not know, or of which he disapproves. But, of course, he remains constitutionally responsible to Parliament for the fact that something has gone wrong, and he alone can tell Parliament what has occurred and render an account of his stewardship.' This caveat did not, as I have argued, apply in the Crichel Down case but it was nearer to reality than the pure Bridges doctrine of civil-service invincibility. But, as the Public Service Committee noted (1995–6, p. xii), the statement is 'confusing and ambiguous, particularly so on the extent to which a minister's responsibility for the conduct of his officials extends to the general oversight of the work of the department'.

Successive governments have developed the distinction between responsibility and accountability, at the same time as admitting that the words have often been used interchangeably, and indeed are often taken to mean the same thing. These redefinitions have usually been made in response to crises. For instance, in 1986, Sir Robert Armstrong, the then Cabinet Secretary and Head of the Home Civil Service, issued what became known as the Armstrong memorandum after the Westland affair had raised questions about the proper role of civil servants. The memorandum (in Defence Committee, 1985–6) was still unclear about the distinction between accountability and responsibility. Further glosses were produced a few years later by Sir Robin Butler, Cabinet Secretary and Head of the Home Civil Service from 1988 to 1997. These statements came after the creation of the Next Steps executive agencies, in response to a report in 1994 by the Treasury and Civil Service Committee on the civil service and at the time of the Scott inquiry. The first report of the Nolan Committee on Standards in

Public Life, in May 1995, urged clarification of the rules on ministerial behaviour and accountability in 'Questions of Procedure for Ministers'. The 1990s version was that a minister is accountable to Parliament for everything that goes on within his or her department, in the sense that the minister has to stand up in the Commons, or give evidence before a select committee, explaining what has happened and what should be done to put it right. The minister is responsible to Parliament for the policies of a department. But it is unreasonable to hold a minister responsible for everything that goes on in the department of which he may not be directly aware. As the Public Service Committee pointed out in its 1995–6 report (p. xv), the substance of the difference between accountability and responsibility is 'a distinction between those matters on which ministers have merely to provide an explanation to the House, and those matters on which failures may be regarded as their own fault and which may justifiably lead to the minister's resignation'. Or, to put it more crudely, is it ever possible to define precisely situations, such as essentially administrative failures, where a minister does not have to resign if something goes wrong? The perennial attempt by the press and the opposition to attach blame and demand resignations may be less important than having a means of finding out what has gone wrong and putting it right.

These arguments were highlighted by the Scott report. This lengthy inquiry was, in many ways, a flawed and muddled exercise. Its investigatory methods did not always seem fair and Sir Richard Scott at times seemed to get lost in the morass of detail, and lost perspective about the way decisions are taken in Whitehall. He could fairly be accused of confusing legal and political procedures. However, the report did establish that ministers and civil servants had, at the very least, given partial, if not outright, misleading answers to questions about the supply of arms-related equipment to Iraq. The protagonists have argued that the policy did not change, only its interpretation. But even that was not clear, and the report gave several examples to back up the charge in the quotation at the beginning of this chapter (taken from p. 1799 of the report) that ministers had apparently failed to discharge their responsibilities to provide Parliament with as 'full information as possible about the policies, decisions and actions of the Government'. The report identified several loopholes in the definitions of accountability in 'Questions of Procedure for Ministers', notably let-out clauses relating to a vaguely defined public interest and 'established Parliamentary conventions'.

As important in the debate over accountability were the strains exposed by the removal of Derek Lewis as Director General of the Prison Service in October 1995. The controversy over the relationship between Michael Howard, Home Secretary from May 1993, and Lewis, and the circumstances of his removal, led to a legal case and even became a sub-plot in the Conservative leadership contest of May–June 1997. The underlying point at issue was the balance between policy and operations – the distinction Howard sought to maintain over the respective roles of the Home Secretary and the Director General of the Prison Service. This implied an almost arm's length relationship, which was impossible to maintain in such a sensitive area as prisons. For instance, over the four months from October 1994 until January 1995, Prison Service headquarters submitted to the Home Office just over a thousand documents, including 137 full submissions containing substantive advice about policy or operational matters. Lewis told the Public Service Committee during its inquiry into ministerial accountability (p. xlvi), that 'In the most complex and sensitive agencies, such as the Prison Service, there is difficulty in defining precisely who takes what decisions or when the Secretary of State should be involved – in popular terms, what is "policy" and what is "operational".' He gave the example of the Home Secretary's decision, as a matter of policy, that it was unacceptable for prisoners to have televisions in their cells, but the question of how much and what television prisoners should be allowed to watch in communal areas remains an operational decision. There are frequently issues – notably high-profile escapes – in which the Home Secretary will want to be informed since he will have to answer questions from the media and MPs. The line between being informed and regular interference is a ragged, and subjective, one as Derek Lewis's own account (1997) demonstrates. He argued (pp. 233–4) that the Prison Service should enjoy statutory separation from the Home Office as the police and the probation services do. 'It could be established by statute as a so-called non-departmental public body, with a formally appointed board which would have real teeth and the power to appoint and remove the Director General, rather than being merely advisory . . . It would also ensure that the Director General did not hold or lose his job at the whim of a single minister. The distinction between policy and operations could be resolved definitively.' Ministers already have powers in secondary legislation, the Prison Rules, to affect what happens in prison and Parliament could debate any changes. Also, 'the Director General should be authorized to speak in public and to parliamentary select committees on the operational implications – positive and negative – of policies set by the government. This would happen automatically with a change in the constitutional status of the service.' The question is whether ministers, and the House of Commons, would accept such a change in the legal status of the Prison Service.

The experience of Derek Lewis is an, admittedly extreme, example of the problems produced by the changes in the structure of government over the past decade. Senior civil servants and ministers have sought to claim that the traditional lines of accountability from civil servant, or chief executive of an agency, to minister and then to Parliament still exist when they are contradicted by the changes in the ways that the public sector is run. The creation from the 1980s onwards of executive agencies to administer larger areas of government work has revolutionized the management of Whitehall. More than two-thirds of the half-million plus civil servants work in agencies or closely related bodies. They cover everything from passports and the building of major roads to the main tax-collecting bodies and the payment of social-security benefits. The intention has been that the chief executives of these agencies should have considerable managerial freedom within framework agreements with the sponsoring department. These provide performance indicators, while ministers continue to decide what resources are available. The newly appointed chief executives, many recruited by a competitive process from outside the mainstream civil service, are made directly and personally responsible for the operations of their agencies. The official orthodoxy has been that chief executives are like any other civil servants and are responsible to Parliament through the ministers at the head of their parent department. At the time of the sacking of Derek Lewis, Sir Robin Butler argued that agencies had not been 'hived off', their chief executives were still civil servants and the relevant ministers remained accountable to Parliament for everything they did. Sir Robin said that while MPs could take up complaints with local managers, they must have the right of ultimate recourse to ministers. But this is not really the point. No one disputes the 'ultimate recourse' to ministers. The question is whether agency heads should have their own right to explain their position separate from that of a minister, as Derek Lewis has argued. As Lord Nolan has suggested, the Butler doctrine was 'a brave but doomed attempt to preserve the status quo'.

Previously, the civil-service heads of the relevant departments were anonymous, even if occasionally during the 1980s they gave evidence to a Commons select committee. But, in their new managerial role, the heads of the main executive agencies are public figures in their own right. They are as likely as a minister to appear on the BBC *Today* programme if a problem develops, when it would have been inconceivable for a traditional civil servant to give a broadcast interview. Of course, it suits ministers for agency chief executives to appear in public if controversies develop – as happened, for instance, with the early problems over the Child Support Agency that eventually led to the resignation of its first head – while the relevant social-security minister was less visible. Similarly, both the Home Secretary and the Director General of the Prison Service appeared almost interchangeable in interviews when a problem appeared over a prison break-out or riot. This change alone has destroyed the pretence that agency chief executives are like any other civil servant. But they are formally constrained when giving such interviews, or appearing in front of select committees, by the need to behave like civil servants in sticking strictly to the minister's line. As some have admitted privately, this has forced them to be less than wholly frank and open in their remarks. Indeed, much to the annoyance of many MPs, the replies to parliamentary questions to ministers concerning the operations of agencies are no longer given by ministers but by the chief executives whose letters are then printed in Hansard in the section devoted to written answers. But Jack Straw, Home Secretary from May 1997, changed this practice so that his ministers gave the replies to questions about the Prison Service.

A vast range of public-sector activities exist where accountability is blurred. These are usually bracketed together under the catch-all term of quango, for quasi-autonomous non-governmental organization. But this is both inaccurate and imprecise since, while it is true that these bodies are non-departmental, they are very much part of government in the broader sense. Even quasi-autonomous does not describe the multitude of tribunals that exercise judicial functions. The Whitehall lexicon prefers the term non-departmental public body for organizations that operate at arm's length from ministers. There is considerable controversy over how many such bodies there are. The official estimate in *Public Bodies*, the Wisden of bureaucracy, is that the total number declined from 2,167 to 1,389 between 1979 and 1983. There are three main categories – executive, advisory and tribunals, of which the former is the most important for this book. The quango watchers argue that these figures are deceptive since they exclude both the Next Steps executive agencies and, more important numerically, the multitude of bodies that provide services at a local level, such as training and enterprise councils, NHS trusts, grant-maintained schools and housing associations. Stuart Weir and Wendy Hall have estimated (1994) that there are 5,521 extra-governmental organizations (the evocative acronym is EGOs), which act as agencies for central government, including 629 NHS bodies and more than a thousand grant-maintained schools, over 700 further and higher education corporations and 2,700 registered housing associations. By any standard, these bodies are responsible for huge amounts of public money – nearly a third of central-government spending on the wider definition – and vitally important services such as schools, further education, hospitals, social housing and training for employment. Whatever their differences, their common feature is that they are dependent on central government, or its agencies such as the Housing Corporation or the Funding Agency for Schools, for their money.

In many cases, these bodies have taken over functions previously exercised or controlled by elected local authorities, as in the case of grant-maintained schools and the urban-development corporations. Some local authorities were both under the influence of trade unions and other producer interests and were distant from local residents. Also they often had little managerial expertise, and the changes have resulted in improved management in many areas. Ministers in the Thatcher and Major governments argued that accountability directly to consumers had been improved. This was best summed up by William Waldegrave, when he was responsible for public services: 'The key point is not whether those who run our public services are elected, but whether they are producer-responsive or consumer-responsive. Services are not necessarily made to respond to the public by giving our citizens a democratic voice, and a distant and diffuse one at that, in their make-up. They can be made responsive by giving the public choices, or by instituting mechanisms which build in publicly approved standards and redress when they are not attained.'

The counter view is that this is a one-sided analysis: that it is possible to improve services to consumers of public services and make them more directly accountable. At present, the chain of accountability is long, from a local agency, via a funding body, a sponsoring department, a minister and then to Parliament. The only direct public involvement is by parents who elect some representatives to the governing bodies of grant-maintained schools. These changes have vastly increased the power of patronage exercised by ministers and Whitehall officials in appointing members of the governing boards and councils of these bodies, creating what has evocatively been described as a new magistracy. Nominal, though in practice weak, accountability is exercised in the traditional way at a national level, while local accountability is primarily through the Citizen's Charter and other consumer-oriented mechanisms such as performance indicators and targets rather than through direct election. But managerial responsibility is not enough and Parliament cannot remotely claim to be able to monitor these myriad public bodies delivering local services, except in the most general way, or in rare wide-ranging inquiries by the departmental select committees. When something goes seriously wrong, the Public Accounts Committee holds an investigation, which can be thorough and have a wider impact through the public sector. But little more than half the executive bodies have to publish annual reports and accounts or are subject to full audit by the National Audit Office or the Audit Commission. These concerns led the committee to issue a well-publicized report in January 1994, entitled 'The Proper Conduct of Public Business', which argued that 'in recent years we have seen and reported on a number of serious failures in administrative and financial systems and controls within departments and other public bodies. These failings represent a departure from the standards of public conduct which have mainly been established during the past 140 years.' In fact, most of the examples quoted in the report were in central-government departments rather than in the new decentralized bodies or agencies.

The quango state became a popular, if imprecise, target for Labour politicians in opposition. The real issue is not the existence of such bodies to administer and deliver services, but how they are appointed and to whom they are responsible. Stuart Weir, a prominent advocate of constitutional reform, has argued (1995) that elected government is being replaced by appointive government, which 'lacks the essential democratic underpinnings of scrutiny, openness and accountability'. Any answers must involve a combination of safeguards over the power of ministerial patronage, increased parliamentary scrutiny and increased local democratic influence. The Nolan report tackled the first point, (vol. 1, p. 72) in accepting that 'the ultimate responsibility for appointments should remain with ministers', but put forward a number of suggestions for ensuring that all appointments to executive and NHS bodies were on merit and after advice from a panel or committee including an independent element. The Government broadly agreed with these suggestions, particularly the appointment of a Commissioner for Public Appointments to monitor, regulate and approve departmental appointments' procedures. This is both right and seems to be working well, with a code of practice to govern 8,300 appointments to non-departmental public and NHS bodies. There is always scope for introducing more checks and balances, both in vetting and in local nominations, but the real issue is whether the central direction and control of these bodies can be reduced. The second Nolan report, in May 1996, on publicly financed local spending bodies argued that 'if the benefit flowing from the autonomy of these bodies is to be fully realized it is no use replacing detailed local control with detailed central control'. There is a case for relaxing central-government controls on these bodies within clear policy guidelines set by accountable politicians and provided there are proper audit procedures. Managerialism needs to be balanced by accountability. However, I am sceptical about returning services, like grant-maintained schools, to local-authority control, which would risk narrowing parental choice. There are gains from the public-sector revolution of the past decade and a half which should not be lightly jeopardized. I am also dubious of making NHS trusts directly accountable to local authorities. The answer may be to build on the purchaser/provider split that has developed in the NHS and other public services. Local authorities or hybrid elected and appointed bodies could control the purchasing side, leaving the provision under more independent management control. In many ways it is as important as their structure of appointment and control that these bodies should be more open and transparent in their decision-making, with proper oversight by the National Audit Office and the Public Accounts Committee, or by the Audit Commission.

A completely new area of largely unaccountable power has appeared over the past decade with the creation by statute of regulators to oversee those industries which have been privatized. This has resulted in a plethora of acronyms – from Oftel (telecommunications), to Ofgas (gas), Offer (electricity), Ofwat (water), Ofrail (railways) and Oflot (the National Lottery). These regulators are responsible for vast swathes of British industry and have wide discretionary powers on crucial matters like prices, rates of profitability and investment. Stephen Littlechild, the Director General of Electricity Supply, may have been more responsible for reshaping British industry than either Lord Weinstock or Lord Hanson: his concentration on promoting competition in the electricity industry contributed both to the rundown in the coal industry in the early 1990s and to the associated 'dash for gas' in the substitution of gas for coal-powered stations.

The regulators are formally accountable by statute through ministers to Parliament – for instance, via the publication of annual reports and occasional appearances before select committees. But the relationship is indirect, in part deliberately so. The whole point of privatization was to remove these industries from day-to-day interference by ministers – for instance, in the holding down of prices as part of an incomes policy or ahead of a general election. But since many of the industries have remained, in whole or part, monopolies, continuing regulation has been necessary to encourage competition and to protect consumers. However, to reassure financial markets that these industries are truly in the private sector, the regulators themselves have been put at arm's length from ministers. In that sense, they have been proxies for the former sponsoring ministers in protecting the public interest. But it is a fluid situation and the scope of regulation is changing as the privatized sectors become more competitive – as telecommunications already is, in many respects, and electricity and gas are rapidly becoming. But there remain monopoly elements, notably in basic networks, which require continuing regulation.

The regulators have been remote from Parliament. The Commission set up by the Hansard Society and the European Policy Forum on the Regulation of Privatized Utilities and chaired by John Flemming (of which I was a member) noted (1997, p. 30) that:

Parliament has very few specific powers directly over the operation
of the regulatory system, particularly over the industry regulators.
Its two main specific powers are to vote appropriations to pay for
the industry regulatory bodies and to overturn ministerial decisions
which are in the form of orders (for instance, the designation of
public telecommunications operators) by passing a resolution of the
House of Commons. In addition, it can use its general scrutiny
powers, notably via the National Audit Office and select committees.

But once the original statutes privatizing the industries and setting
up the regulators had been enacted, the role of Parliament has been
peripheral. Indeed, 'There are almost no special statutory provisions
concerning the accountability of ministers for their decisions concerning the utilities.' However, appearances by regulators in front of select
committees have been irregular and usually related to some *cause célèbre*,
particularly during the inquiry by the Trade and Industry Committee
into the future of the coal industry in 1992–3 and less so during the
sensationalist and demeaning inquiry by the Employment Committee
into 'fat cat' salaries in the utilities in 1994–5. There was a flurry of
interest late in the 1992–7 Parliament with reports on aspects of regulation from the Public Accounts Committee (on the work of the main
utility regulators) and from the Trade and Industry Committee (on the
regulation of energy and telecommunications). Their main focus was
on the nature of the regulatory regime, the form of price controls
and the development of competition rather than on the constitutional
position of regulators as such. There has been a debate about how
far individual regulators should be replaced by panels or multi-person
commissions to make the process less personal.

Accountability to consumers and regulated companies could be
further strengthened, as the Commission on the Regulation of Privatized Utilities urged, by greater transparency on the disclosure of information and regulatory principles and the clarification of duties. But
there is general agreement that the regulators need to retain their
independent status. The Commission argued (p. 63) that 'one of the
central pillars of a regulatory regime for the privatized utilities should
be protection of suppliers from constant ministerial intervention. Regulators should be impartial and enjoy considerable autonomy from
elected politicians.' Ministers, the report said, have a proper role in
setting social policy objectives, but 'in their spheres of action, the Direc-

tor Generals should not be subject to control by Government ministers'. But it suggested that select committees should have the resources
to 'investigate often complex regulatory issues'. In its report on 'Energy
Regulation' the Trade and Industry Committee considered and rejected
(pp. liv to lv) the idea of creating a special Select Committee on Regulated Industries to allow Parliament to develop expertise and a consistent approach in this area. The Commission took the same view because
of the risk of increased political intervention. The Trade and Industry
Committee pointed to the difficulties of establishing the remit of such
a committee, while the existence of a single committee would not of
itself improve accountability. It would, anyway, undermine the departmental links of the present select-committee system: the Transport
Committee could hardly operate without scrutinizing the work of the
rail regulator. The real issue is the assiduity and consistency of select
committees in monitoring the work of regulators.

A further significant shift in accountability occurred within four days
of the Blair government taking office when, on 6 May, Gordon Brown
announced that the Bank of England would be made operationally
responsible for setting interest rates. This is a significant constitutional
shift and one of the main Conservative objections – made by John
Major, the outgoing Conservative leader, as well as by Kenneth Clarke,
the former Chancellor – was that it will weaken accountability to Parliament. For the previous three years, Clarke had operated a half-way
house, whereby he held monthly meetings with Eddie George, the
Governor of the Bank of England, whose minutes were later published.
The Bank was also allowed total freedom to publish its own assessment
of the prospects for inflation and whether the stance of monetary policy
should be changed. Indeed, there were public differences in the 'Ken
and Eddie' show over interest-rate changes, both for much of 1995
and in the months before the election. But Clarke had the final
say and was willing to defend his view against the Bank's in the House
of Commons. The effect of the change is to shift responsibility to the
Bank for the operation of monetary policy. Brown has sought to
enhance accountability partly through the creation of a monetary-policy
committee at the Bank, rather than through the previous sole decision
by the Governor. He has also suggested that the Bank should make
regular reports and give public evidence to the Treasury Committee
of the Commons on what he called an 'enhanced basis'. Until now, the

Governor has usually given evidence twice a year after major economic statements, but, according to Brown, the Bank would in future 'appear four times a year before the committee to give evidence and answer questions on its Inflation Report, so that the Bank's performance will be able to be judged by Parliament'. The Bank's annual report would also be debated on the floor of the House. This proposal involves a much more formal role for the Commons in ensuring parliamentary accountability on monetary policy and is similar to the regular reports on monetary outlook that Alan Greenspan, chairman of the US Reserve Board, makes to various congressional committees. But these congressional committees are far more powerful than the Treasury Committee has been since it was set up in the 1979 reforms, in part because of their constitutionally separate position in the USA. This poses questions (which I discuss in Chapter 10) about the quality of people who serve on such select committees and their role within Parliament. In the past the record of the committee in such examinations has been patchy. The Treasury has also suggested that the revamped Securities and Investments Board – responsible for prudential supervision and regulation of both financial services and banks (the latter being transferred from the Bank of England) – should also make reports to the Treasury Committee.

Chris Smith, Secretary for Culture, Media and Sport, has proposed a similar idea for the BBC, a public corporation, albeit of a different type, but with a compulsory levy in the television licence fee. According to a report of his discussions in May 1997 with the BBC governors and its board of management, he suggested that the corporation might become accountable to the relevant Select Committee of the Commons. Smith said that the governors might appear before the select committee twice a year to make the corporation more accountable for its actions. This offer was taken up by Sir Christopher Bland, chairman of the governors of the BBC, who suggested that, following the formal laying before Parliament each July of the BBC's annual report and accounts, this could provide 'a useful and precise agenda' for an autumn appearance by the corporation in front of the select committee.

The growth of the semi-detached public sector/the patronage state – Next Steps agencies, quangos, utility regulators, the Bank of England, etc. – is both a challenge and an opportunity for Parliament. Ministers may be less directly answerable to the Commons for the activities of these various public bodies, whether at Question Time, in written answers or to select committees but that does not mean that they should escape adequate scrutiny by the Commons. Three basic changes are required: in the rules governing accountability; in the amount of information provided; and in the behaviour of Parliament itself. The proposals are interlinked. It is no good setting out a tighter definition of how ministers should be accountable unless more information is provided by them, and unless Parliament is serious itself about scrutinizing the activities of the executive.

First, as the Public Service Committee suggested in its 1995–6 report, a proper framework of accountability needs to be established. It is right to be sceptical about how far such codes can change behaviour but they do establish a yardstick by which ministers and officials can be judged. For instance, 'Questions of Procedure for Ministers' (QPM) moved within three years from 'merely some tips for beginners – a book of etiquette for ministers', as described by Sir Burke Trend, Cabinet Secretary from 1963 until 1973, and unearthed by Professor Peter Hennessy, to a formal series of rules for ministerial conduct and accountability to Parliament. Not only did the first Nolan report of May 1995 suggest a number of improvements, but the paragraphs on accountability in QPM were at the heart of Sir Richard Scott's most devastating criticisms in his report of February 1996. But QPM (rewritten and retitled in July 1997 as the 'Ministerial Code') lays down what the Prime Minister – and the Cabinet Secretary of the day – expects of ministers, including duties of accountability. But it is a government document, not a parliamentary one. Under the chairmanship of Giles Radice, a senior Labour backbencher responsible for many important changes in this area, the Public Service Committee suggested a code to be adopted by both Houses about what Parliament expected of ministers. After much to-ing and fro-ing, a code was passed by the Commons and Lords in the dying hours of the 1992–7 parliament, with minor variations of format in the resolutions adopted by the two Houses. The Commons version states that:

The following principles should govern the conduct of Ministers of the Crown in relation to Parliament:

(1) Ministers have a duty to Parliament to account, and be held to account, for the policies, decisions and actions of their departments and Next Steps Agencies;

(2) It is of paramount importance that Ministers give accurate and truthful information to Parliament, correcting any inadvertent error at the earliest opportunity. Ministers who knowingly mislead Parliament will be expected to offer their resignation to the Prime Minister;

(3) Ministers should be as open as possible with Parliament, refusing to provide information only when disclosure would not be in the public interest, which should be decided in accordance with relevant statute and the Government's Code of Practice on Access to Government Information;

(4) Similarly, Ministers should require civil servants who give evidence before Parliamentary Committees on their behalf and under their directions to be as helpful as possible in providing accurate, truthful and full information in accordance with the duties and responsibilities of civil servants as set out in the Civil Service Code.

This resolution is a useful step forward in making more explicit the duties of ministers but, as Lord Nolan fairly pointed out in his second Radcliffe lecture in November 1996: 'It is possible that this [a resolution on ministerial openness] might have some effect, but it would never 'solve' the difficult cases. It is like the Lilliputians trying to tie down Gulliver. We would be better off acknowledging that Ministerial accountability is interpreted in the light of prevailing political circumstances and avoid disappointing ourselves with its application.'

Within such a code, there is a need to clarify the specific accountability of the chief executives of Next Steps executive agencies and, by implication, the main utility regulators. If they are to be made managerially responsible, they need also to be given the freedom to talk without detailed ministerial approval. They remain public servants but, within the context of the overall policy set by ministers, they should be allowed to express their views on how their agency works. Professor Vernon Bogdanor has suggested (1996, p. 35) that the Osmotherly Rules governing the appearance of civil servants before select committees (more formally 'Guidance on Answering Parliamentary Questions') should be changed for the chief executives of agencies.

This would mean that chief executives would not be appearing, as permanent secretaries and other civil servants do, merely in the role of spokesmen for their ministers. On the other hand, chief executives remain, of course, civil servants, and so, unlike, for example, chairmen of nationalized industries, they could not be allowed to comment on the merits of policy, as opposed to explaining the background to it. But they would be able to answer for their own actions in their own way on operational matters.

We are back to the familiar problem of the distinction between policy and operations. Graham Mather, a Conservative MEP and president of the European Policy Forum, which has taken a close interest in these issues, argued in his evidence to the Public Service Committee (vol. III, pp. 121–5) that Britain should move to a more formal contract system, as in New Zealand, so that senior civil servants should be held directly and personally responsible for the quality of their policy work. This would require changes to the Osmotherly Rules in effect breaking the chain of accountability through ministers. Mather noted that permanent secretaries of departments already have an accountability to Parliament in their role as accounting officers, and often appear before the Public Accounts Committee to explain and defend the financial aspects of spending programmes even though these duties are carried out under policies decided by ministers. Permanent secretaries can formally minute their objections to a ministerial action, as Sir Tim Lankester, the then Permanent Secretary at the Overseas Development Administration, did over the aid for the Pergau Dam project (a view subsequently vindicated by a separate High Court action). Mather argued that: 'In exactly the same way it is no longer appropriate to base accountability to Parliament through the single channel of the minister. Such a doctrine may have been appropriate to a pre-managerial civil service: it no longer reflects the practice of government.'

This issue was taken up by the Public Service Committee, which, in its 1995–6 report, argued (p. xix) that the working definition of ministerial responsibility meant that:

> While it is through ministers that the Government is properly accountable to Parliament, the obligation to provide full information and to explain the actions of government to Parliament means that ministers should allow civil servants to give an account to Parliament through select committees when appropriate – particularly where ministers have formally delegated functions to them, for example in the case of Chief Executives of Executive Agencies.

This view was specifically rejected by ministers in their reply, published by the Public Service Committee in its First Special Report, 1996–7, p. vii:

> The Government is not, however, prepared to breach the longstanding basic principle that civil servants, including the Chief Executives of Next Steps Agencies, give an account to Parliament on behalf of the ministers whom they serve. Were civil servants to be required to go beyond this, they would inevitably be drawn into matters on which they must refer select committees to the minister. The Government's commitment to a permanent, non-political civil service means there can be no question of apportioning between the minister and his civil servants part or parallel shares in a single line of accountability to Parliament.

The Public Service Committee reluctantly went along with this view in the wording of the resolution on ministerial accountability to Parliament quoted above, partly to ensure that it was approved before Parliament was dissolved.

But the issue will not go away. It is no longer credible for ministers to defend their prerogative powers in determining the line of accountability to Parliament when they have accepted decentralization and delegation of management responsibility. But as Lord Nolan has argued in his Radcliffe lectures, this defines accountability in centralist terms: 'If accountability is only through ministers, in respect of an agency with hundreds of offices and thousands of clients, the chain is too long, the person who should be answerable – perhaps at a local level – remains shielded from public view, and true accountability is weakened.' It becomes in effect an excuse for secrecy. He went on:

> Ministerial accountability is now in danger of being used to slow down the growth in accountability of public services. . . . This is a much more complex public service than ever before, and it demands greater attention to accountability. Such accountability can only be achieved through openness, and through requiring the people who run these services on our behalf to be openly answerable. That cannot be achieved by a chain of accountability that runs upwards from literally thousands of independent or quasi-independent bodies, of varying size, structure and legal status, to a handful of ministers, laden with half a dozen or more red boxes of paperwork to take home each weekend.

The rules need to be clarified and made more specific, and should, as Lord Nolan has argued, take account of the realities of how the public sector is now organized. But, in practice, there will never be a clear-cut distinction between policy and operations, between ministers and chief executives, as long as an activity remains in the public sector. This shifts the argument to the provision of information. Indeed, Sir Richard Scott (p. 1806) broadly accepted the argument of Sir Robin Butler, which he summarized as that 'the conduct of government has become so complex and the need for ministerial delegation of responsibilities to and reliance on the advice of officials has become so inevitable as to render unreal the attaching of blame to a minister simply because something has gone wrong in the department of which he is in charge'. However, the Scott report went on to argue that this has

> an important bearing on the obligation of ministers to provide information to Parliament. If ministers are to be excused blame and personal criticism on the basis of the absence of personal knowledge or involvement, the corollary ought to be the acceptance of the obligation to be forthcoming with information about the incident in question. Otherwise Parliament (and the public) will not be in a position to judge whether the absence of personal knowledge and involvement is fairly claimed or to judge on whom responsibility for what has occurred ought to be placed.

Professor Bogdanor has argued (in *Parliamentary Affairs*, January 1997) that Sir Richard Scott has in this way contested the traditional doctrine of ministers' accountability by saying its essence 'lies not in the threat of resignation but in the obligation to inform Parliament'. Sir Richard told the Public Service Committee in May 1996 (vol. 3, p. 68) that he 'did not regard the debate between accountability, responsibility, blame, as being the key and most important feature of ministerial accountability; I regard the provision of information as being the key to the doctrine. I think the willingness on the part of ministers to inform Parliament and through Parliament the public, or perhaps sometimes the public directly, of the matters in respect of which they are accountable is critical'. This is a crucial insight and underpins the Public Service Committee's successful campaign to have a resolution approved by both Houses laying down how ministers are expected to be accountable. But it also implies more specific requirements than the vague 'public interest' guidelines over what can and cannot be disclosed, or references to not 'intentionally' misleading Parliament. This risks creating a doctrine of irresponsibility whereby ministers can always say they were not 'intentionally' being misleading, so that awkward questions can always be evaded.

Various solutions are possible. The Public Service Committee was cautious in its 1996 report because of its desire to produce an agreed document. It mainly suggested improvements to the existing system, though even some of these about civil servants, agency heads and ministers went too far for the liking of Whitehall and the Major government. But the fiction that civil servants are merely the voices of their ministerial masters needs to be abandoned, as Bogdanor and Mather have urged. The Osmotherly Rules, governing the appearance of civil servants before committees, are a Whitehall instruction, a use of prerogative powers, rather than a resolution approved by Parliament. They should be amended, though I would not, at present, go as far as Mather. Decision-making by government would be impaired if civil servants discussed in public the detailed private policy advice they have given to ministers. They would not be frank if they thought their advice would quickly become known. Internal debate would be inhibited, which might make it harder to introduce tough and necessary, though initially unpopular, policies. Nonetheless, policy options should be more openly aired. However, civil servants should be able, and required, to give information about the application and implementation of policy rather than just operate within instructions set by ministers. I have heard senior civil servants say they have had to dissemble – a polite word for lie – in front of select committees in order not to embarrass their ministers. Under the suggested change, civil servants would always be able to say that a particular question was a matter for a minister to answer.

Crucial to any change is that the availability of information needs to be reviewed. The Public Service Committee suggested tightening up the procedures under which a government department states the grounds on which information is being withheld in a parliamentary answer, and proposed that the Table Office of the Commons should each year make available a list of questions on which ministers had refused to give information. But this is minimal tinkering. In other areas of public life, it is now accepted that not only are formal codes of conduct necessary, but they must also be monitored by an independent person. This applies, for instance, to the role of the Parliamentary Commissioner for Standards in maintaining the register of members' interests and investigating complaints against them. Sir Richard Scott suggested to the Public Service Committee that it might be possible to have someone like the Comptroller and Auditor General, who is responsible to the House rather than the Government, to investigate any disputes over the way in which any public-interest reason for not supplying information has been exercised. Yet there are problems about allowing an outsider, however eminent, to have access to confidential documents and to judge on the behaviour of the Government. Moreover, these issues are inherently political and are really the responsibility of MPs and of the Commons itself. But there is a distinction between an investigation by an independent figure to find out what is being concealed, and how MPs then fulfil their duty to hold ministers to account.

The obvious person to fulfil this role would be the Ombudsman, or Parliamentary Commissioner for Administration, who, in addition to his role of investigating complaints about maladministration, already has responsibilities for monitoring the code on open government. But not only is there a conceptual distinction between looking at the impact of administrative acts on the public and ministerial accountability to Parliament, it could also add considerably to the workload of the Ombudsman. Professor Bogdanor argued in his article quoted on page 95 that, despite these reservations, 'there remains a strong case for an independent person, whether the Ombudsman, the Parliamentary Commissioner for Standards, or an entirely new officer, to monitor the extent to which ministers fulfil their constitutional obligations'.

All this leads on to the argument of how far there should be a statutory responsibility to provide information. The Conservatives fairly claimed to have taken several initiatives on open government which improved accountability: the establishment of the departmental select committees in 1979; various measures to provide a statutory access to personal records held on computer; the publication in May 1992 of 'Questions of Procedure for Ministers' and the membership of ministerial cabinet committees; the legislation in 1989 and 1994 putting first the Security Services and then the Secret Intelligence Service and Government Communications Headquarters on a statutory footing and establishing oversight of all three services by a committee of senior peers and MPs; and an opening up of previously secret past files in the Public Records Office. A Code of Practice on Access to Government Information was published in 1994 and monitored by the Ombudsman and the Select Committee on the Parliamentary Commissioner for Administration (the Ombudsman Committee). These were important changes, and more significant in shifting the onus from secrecy to disclosure than advocates of open government usually conceded.

But these actions were on the executive's own terms. There was no statutory right to such information. The sprightly Campaign for Freedom of Information had for long been a well-informed and effective pressure group in this area. Progress on the issue was reviewed in 1996 in a report by the Ombudsman Committee on the workings of open government. It found that the Code of Practice had helped to change the culture towards openness and made a number of detailed recommendations to enable more factual analysis and research to be published and to strengthen the position of the Ombudsman in reviewing complaints over disclosure. More significantly, the committee, with its then majority of Conservative MPs, recommended (p. xli) that the system should be clarified by a single Freedom of Information Act, covering all rights to government information. This would be better than the recent move towards a more fragmented structure with different access rules for different types of information, such as health and safety, and environmental. But a single act 'would preserve the Ombudsman's important role, maintain the consistency of open government judgments and ensure that the various considerations that inform any decision on access all carry similar statutory weight. It would also give Parliament the opportunity to approve in detail the contents of the Code.' A Code of Practice makes ministers, rather than the courts, the arbiter of what it is in the public interest to disclose, even though departments usually accept the findings of the Ombudsman. But the balance would shift if disclosure was made legally enforceable. The Major government rejected the call for a Freedom of Information Act in November 1996, arguing that the Code of Practice was working well and that a statutory approach might be less flexible as well as possibly involving long and expensive disputes.

During the 1992–7 parliament both main opposition parties committed themselves to a Freedom of Information Act. The report of the

Labour and Liberal Democrat Joint Consultative Committee on Constitutional Reform argued that such an act 'would give the public proper confidence in matters of current public concern such as, for example, public health and food safety. It would also give proper access to information about the workings of government and allow individuals to see information held on them by government agencies.' The parties argued that the existing code of practice did not go far enough in ensuring that people have proper rights of access to information. However, the joint report said there 'would of course be a need for exemptions in areas like national security, personal privacy and policy advice given by civil servants to ministers, but the proposed legislation would establish independent machinery and procedures to achieve these purposes and shift the balance decisively in favour of the presumption that government information should be made publicly available unless there is a justifiable reason not to do so.' Deciding on the exemptions is the heart of the matter – the test of a commitment in principle and in practice to freedom of information. The suspicions of the open-government lobby were immediately aroused when the Blair government did not include freedom of information legislation in its first Queen's Speech. However, following this criticism, the Government promised both an early White Paper and a draft bill with legislation in the 1998–9 session. David Clark, the Chancellor of the Duchy of Lancaster, responsible for this area, stressed his personal commitment. The key issues identified in the early discussions were the need for a statutory right of access to government information; an independent commissioner to examine complaints, like the Ombudsman; and an ability to challenge decisions through judicial review.

Accountability, of course, takes many different forms, from increased procedures for consultation, to statutory rights of appeal against administration decisions, to judicial review. In 1991 the Government strengthened public accountability with the introduction of the Citizen's Charter. This was intended to increase choice and secure better value for the consumer of public services through a series of charters for various parts of the public sector (such as for parents and patients), laying down specific, and well-publicized, standards and targets for performance and, in some cases, compensation for failure to perform. The Public Service Committee noted in its report on the charter (Third Report 1996–7, p. xviii) that: 'The Citizen's Charter programme has contributed over the last five years to improvements in the delivery, culture and responsiveness of many services to the public.' This is linked to the changes in the management of the public sector noted above. The various charters have helped to strengthen direct accountability to the public, in addition to the statutory annual reports made to Parliament.

For thirty years, the Ombudsman has sought to bridge the gap in accountability to the public and Parliament. He investigates complaints from people or organizations who claim they have suffered from maladministration by government departments and public bodies, which has led to hardship and injustice. The Ombudsman has built up an impressive track record in investigating such cases and in securing remedies. According to the report published in March 1997, the number of complaints referred by MPs in 1996 was 1,920, a rise of 12.5 per cent on the previous record. Almost half the new complaints concerned the Department of Social Security, and half of these referred to the Child Support Agency: consequently, a quarter of all complaints referred to an agency set up merely a few years before in what was subsequently agreed to be hastily considered legislation – a case of a parliamentary watchdog clearing up mistakes made by Parliament itself.

However, these forms of direct accountability, while valid and important, are supplementary to accountability to Parliament, not a substitute for it. Indeed, it is crucial that Parliament take the work of accountability seriously. Ann Taylor said that ministerial accountability was one of the subjects that would be considered by the Select Committee on Modernization of the Procedures of the Commons, formally set up in June 1997. That, of course, covers a wide range of issues, from Question Time to select committees. Question Time is widely derided as raucous and adversarial. Prime Minister's Questions can often be like that and, even worse, affect the public's image of the Commons since that is often the only part of the proceedings that is highlighted on evening news bulletins. However, the other three and a half hours of questions each week are generally more subdued and, while obviously partisan, they can be more reasoned. Moreover, unlike systems where the executive and legislature are separate, Question Time ensures that the Prime Minister and other ministers have to answer on the issue of the day to members of the Commons.

The shift in May 1997 from the previous twice-weekly fifteen-minute sessions of Prime Minister's Questions to a single weekly thirty-minute session had been discussed during the 1992–7 parliament, but had been specifically rejected by the Procedure Committee in its report on the subject in July 1995. It is too early to say how this change will work out, although it does permit longer questioning on a specific issue. Longer could be allowed for questions to other ministers on some important subjects, as occurs in the House of Lords where only four oral questions are asked each day, and an average of seven supplementaries. This permits questioning to last at least five minutes and often up to ten minutes on a topical issue. An occasional alternative would be for the Speaker to allow more Private Notice Questions, after the normal hour's Question Time, on topics of urgent importance. This would be another way of allowing longer questioning on one topic, as in the Lords, but without reducing the number of questions, and topics raised, during the normal question period.

The most important change would be in the attitude of the select committees. At present, their attitude to ministerial accountability and scrutiny is patchy and spasmodic. Some committees, like the Foreign Affairs and Treasury Select Committees, are assiduous in questioning the relevant ministers before or after big events like European Councils or Budgets. Other committees are often less interested, preferring to pursue longer-term inquiries and neglecting the agencies within their remit. During the 1992–7 parliament, the Environment Committee published just two reports related to their agencies (on the Housing Corporation and on water conservation and supply), though the Trade and Industry Committee was more diligent (with its wide-ranging report in the 1992–3 session on British energy policy and the market for coal, its study of the future of the Post Office in March 1994, its report on nuclear privatization in February 1996, and its reports just before the 1997 election on energy and telecommunications regulation). But there was no requirement for annual sessions with regulators or agencies. The freedom of committees to choose their own topics of inquiry is jealously guarded and any suggestion that they should have a duty to report on this or that topic is fiercely resisted. During the discussions on the Commission for the Regulation of Privatized Utilities, my proposal that Select Committees should have a formal responsibility to report annually on the activities of regulators, as well as having a role in their appointment, was criticized primarily by the parliamentarians on the Commission. But the suggestions made by Gordon Brown over the role of the Treasury Committee in monitoring the Bank of England would increase duties for the committee in ensuring accountability. This is in contrast to the current practice where each committee can do what it wants. The same point applies in relation to spending estimates, where select committees have varied enormously in their attitudes. The Treasury Committee has regarded scrutiny of the Government's overall spending plans as a central part of its responsibilities. The Defence, Environment, Foreign Affairs and Social Security Committees have also looked closely, and regularly, at their departments' spending estimates. The record of others is patchier.

A final twist in the story of accountability is the wide range of prerogative powers, on appointments, ratification of treaties and the like, still exercised by the Prime Minister on behalf of the Crown. Many remain despite the steady process by which Parliament has by statute limited these prerogative powers and the immunities and exemptions of the Crown. The remaining prerogative powers are outside direct parliamentary control. When any major public appointment is made, the press release says that Joe Bloggs – more commonly Sir John Bloggs – has been appointed Director of the XYZ Commission, or indeed to the Court of the Bank of England, by the Queen on the advice of the Prime Minister. There is no opportunity for Parliament to vet the person's suitability, let alone to object. But if the accountability of the executive to Parliament is to have substance, it must apply to major appointments. In her main speech in opposition on reform of Parliament, to a Charter 88 seminar in May 1996, Ann Taylor suggested that 'Some senior public appointments would have to be ratified by the appropriate select committee.' After she became Leader of the Commons, she again raised this possibility in an interview in June 1997 during the BBC's *On the Record* programme, noting that there had been discussion about whether 'they should have a ratification role on some of the senior appointments'. Mrs Taylor had earlier given the example of the Higher Education Funding Councils. I would add directors of the Bank of England and members of its new monetary-policy committee, the chairman and governors of the BBC and the main statutory regulators of utilities, the heads of various quangos, possibly also of executive agencies and even the chiefs of the main services. It would be relatively straightforward to draw up such a list. As now, these appointees would be nominated by the relevant sponsoring ministers. But before the appointment was confirmed, a select committee would have limited time to question the nominee and to recommend whether the House should consider the nomination further. It might be possible to have two categories: one subject to a negative resolution procedure (that is, the nomination would automatically go through unless the select committee tabled a motion to cancel the appointment); and another whose nominations would have to be approved by an affirmative resolution (that is, positively endorsed). That might apply to a limited group of chairmen of major public bodies. Executive-minded politicians will object to the potential loss of the exclusive right of appointment, while parliamentary business managers will be worried about the time involved (not great if the number covered is restricted and the procedure is handled sensibly). However, even a committed parliamentary reformer like Labour MP Tony Wright has been sceptical (1995), arguing that: 'The House of Commons is simply not equipped to perform this role, certainly in its present form. Its partisan character will always triumph over its collegiate character.'

As serious will be fears that Britain may go down the American road with intrusive inquiries into candidates' private lives which will deter many successful businessmen and the like from taking on jobs which are, anyway, less well paid than in the private sector. But this need not mean the irrelevant and headline-grabbing partisan inquiries or the kind of bigoted obstructionism which Senator Jesse Helms has practised as chairman of the Senate Foreign Relations Committee in holding up the appointment of many American ambassadors. However, it would be possible to define strictly what was relevant in the ratification process and also to impose a formal time limit to prevent damaging delays. But such scrutiny is the necessary – and justified – price to be paid if important managerial and operational decisions are to be delegated and the lines of accountability are to be stretched. If, for example, the monetary policy committee of the Bank of England is now responsible for setting interest rates, then there is a public, and parliamentary, interest in who serves on that committee. It is not sufficient for the Chancellor of the Exchequer merely to announce the names in a parliamentary written answer, as he did. The Treasury Select Committee should have the chance to question them about their experience and suitability for such an important role.

This chapter has shown how the traditional doctrine of ministerial accountability to Parliament has become strained to breaking point by changes in the organization of central government and the growth of powerful semi-independent public-sector bodies. The official attempts to defend the line of accountability from civil servant to minister to Parliament have appeared increasingly unconvincing. Both the doctrine and the procedures need to change. New codes are being introduced with independent commissioners monitoring them. Parliament needs to recognize the reality of where decisions are taken and to be more assiduous in monitoring and supervising these bodies, which, at present, it only occasionally and inadequately holds accountable.

CHAPTER FIVE

Constitutional Reform

We gathered as the Scottish Constitutional Convention do hereby acknowledge the sovereign right of the Scottish people to determine the form of Government best suited to their needs, and do hereby declare and pledge that in all our deliberations their interests shall be paramount.

> Claim of Right, adopted at inaugural meeting of Scottish Constitutional Convention (signed by, among others, Labour and Liberal Democrat leaders in Scotland), 30 March 1989

'Sovereignty rests with Westminster because we are proposing devolution – local services to be run here by the people of Scotland. It's not separation.'

> Tony Blair, interview with the *Scotsman*, 4 April 1997

The Lords will be allowed to become a serious revising chamber only after the Commons has itself become one. Contrary to the conventional wisdom, reform of the Lords can arise only out of reform of the Commons.

> Ferdinand Mount, *The British Constitution Now*, 1992

The central role of Parliament in the British political system is under challenge from the far-reaching constitutional reform programme put forward by Labour at the 1997 general election. These proposals would not only go a long way towards creating a written constitution that would be a check on parliamentary supremacy but would establish alternative centres of power in Scotland, Wales and possibly, in time, the English regions, which would have their own democratic legitimacy and authority. Long-standing notions of parliamentary supremacy would be undermined by the proposed widespread use of referendums to approve major constitutional changes. The traditional adversarial basis of the Commons would be threatened by any change to the electoral system. Its dominant position, established in the battles of 1909–11, would be challenged by any reform of the Lords. Many of these proposals tend to be viewed in isolation, with little attempt to relate them to their implications for the position of Parliament – and, in particular, of the Commons – but, in practice, many would have a much wider impact.

My emphasis is conditional not because I doubt that several of these proposals will be enacted during the parliament that opened in May 1997: Labour's huge Commons majority should ensure that – even though there are doubts about the pace of movement towards regional assemblies and a wide-open debate over electoral reform for the House of Commons. My uncertainty is more because of ambiguities in the attitudes of Tony Blair and his senior advisers. There is an unresolved debate within the Labour Party about whether reforms should be incremental within the existing structure of the unitary state and parliamentary supremacy or whether they should be part of a comprehensive new constitutional settlement, as advocated by constitutional reform advocates like Charter 88. The Liberal Democrats have, for example, questioned existing constitutional conventions in their formal policy documents: 'The mechanical reassertion of the sovereignty of Parliament remains the stock-in-trade of most politicians. Yet this concept is ever more outdated and irrelevant. Similarly, the rule of law as set out by Dicey is primarily concerned with the supremacy of the legal order. Few question the need for such supremacy within a democracy. Yet after generations of increasing executive power, it is the nature of that order that ought to be at the forefront of the debate on constitutional government.' Unlike Labour, the Liberal Democrats have advocated a full written constitution and a formal federal structure for the United Kingdom.

The main Labour commitments on constitutional reform were made before Blair became party leader in July 1994 and, while he fully endorsed them, his attitude was different from that of the late John Smith. For Blair, constitutional reform, which he tended to describe in less dramatic terms as decentralization and giving power to the people, was only one part of Labour's programme. For instance, constitutional reform was not one of the party's well-publicized five pre-election pledges, though it was added to the versions issued in Scotland and Wales. And Blair never highlighted, or even referred much to, constitutional reform during the 1997 election campaign except, controversially, during a visit to Scotland. This was not just a matter of electoral tactics – recognition of what interested English voters in target seats. It reflected a difference of perspective, a rejection of both the enthusiasms and priorities of the committed reformers with their belief that constitutional change is central to a wider economic and social improvement. For Blair, change in Britain's constitutional arrangements is highly desirable, indeed much needed to correct an 'over-centralized government and an undeveloped citizenship', but constitutional reform should neither completely dominate the Government's legislative agenda nor put at risk its hard-won political position.

There was also a sense, shared by some of Blair's allies like Jack Straw, that the reform programme, and particularly the devolution proposals, had been devised by Scots for Scots without regard to the interests of others. The devolution plan had, for example, been drawn up in the Scottish Constitutional Convention by Scottish Labour politicians in consultation with Scottish Liberal Democrats and non-partisan representatives from business, the churches and local government, but without any real input from the rest of the Labour Party. Blair sought to provide this wider perspective, notably through his controversial proposal in July 1996 for a twin-question referendum in Scotland, and a simpler one in Wales, on the principle of devolution before legislation. During the 1997 campaign, Blair also revealed a profoundly different attitude towards sovereignty from that of many Scottish Labour MPs and the Scottish Constitutional Convention, as is clear from the contrasting quotations at the beginning of this chapter. It was not just that he stressed that sovereignty remained at Westminster and in decisions taken by English, as well as Scottish, MPs. In an interview with the *Scotsman*, he said dismissively that the powers of a Scottish parliament would be 'like those of any local authority. Powers that are constitutionally there can be used but the Scottish Labour Party is not planning to raise income tax, and once the power is given it is like any parish council, it's got the right to exercise it.' This comparison did not go down well in Scotland and seemed to many Scots all too typical of the Westminster-centred attitudes of English

MPs, who regard devolution as a concession and not a right. This is the central dilemma of the devolution debate.

Blair's comments reflect the contradictions inherent in several of Labour's proposals. Is the party really only interested in piecemeal changes to respond to particular demands and complaints? Or is it committed to the construction of a new constitutional arrangement? Is, for example, the maintenance of the Union, and parliamentary sovereignty, compatible with the view of devolution held by many in Scotland? If the referendum becomes a regular part of British practice, how far will it override the primacy of Parliament? Does sovereignty really lie with the people or with Parliament? And will referendums be held only on major constitutional decisions or will they be used also on tricky economic and social issues? However these constitutional questions are resolved, the creation of a Scottish Parliament, a Welsh Assembly, a strategic authority in London, possible eventual assemblies in the English regions, reform of the House of Lords, incorporation of the European Convention of Human Rights into British law (see Chapter Three) and changes in the prerogative powers of the Crown (as exercised by the Prime Minister and other ministers, and discussed in Chapter Four) would profoundly affect Britain's constitution. In that respect, John Major was right to talk in the 1997 election campaign about the possibly momentous implications of what was proposed, even if his warnings seemed out of tune with the public mood.

At present, the Westminster Parliament is supreme and central in theory if not always in practice. The people themselves play no formal part, except every four or five years in electing MPs. Under the dominant Dicey doctrine, outlined in Chapter One, a Parliament can do whatever it wants in relation to other political institutions in Britain. It can set up, reorganize and abolish elected local authorities as long as it has a majority in the House of Commons and regardless of the views of local people. And successive Conservative governments have done just that. In the early 1960s the Conservatives reorganized the government of London, merging several smaller boroughs into larger boroughs and replacing the London County Council with the larger Greater London Council as a strategic planning authority, which absorbed not only the old county of Middlesex but also a number of suburban county boroughs like Croydon. A decade later, the Heath government redrew the local-authority map of the rest of England, creating a two-tier structure of counties and districts, with new metropolitan counties in the West Midlands, industrial South and West Yorkshire, Merseyside, Greater Manchester and Tyne and Wear. A decade further on, the Thatcher government abolished all these counties and the Greater London Council in 1986, in part because their Labour-run councils were proving a thorn in the side of central government. The Major government went on to reorganize some of the shire county authorities, setting up new unitary authorities in some areas combining county and district responsibilities. In some cases, these reverted in effect to the self-contained county boroughs they had been a quarter of a century earlier. Not only has much of this reorganization been a waste of time, energy and, usually, a lot of money, but it has been carried out by politicians in Whitehall often at odds with those elected in the areas concerned.

This exercise of parliamentary sovereignty – or, rather, of the powers of a government that can command an overall Commons majority – casts doubt on whether Britain is genuinely a pluralist society. The weaknesses and limits of local government are reflected in the low turn-out in council elections. These changes have been linked to a centralization of financial control as the amount of money local authorities raise locally from their own tax-payers has fallen to well under a fifth of their total income. In the 1980s the Treasury's attempts to control local-government spending led to a series of new centrally imposed curbs and restrictions. As Simon Jenkins has noted (1995, p. 49):

> In September 1983, Patrick Jenkin [the then Environment Secretary] had declared that the old consensus by which local and central government had respected each other's wishes had broken down. 'The government has a duty to heed the increasingly bitter complaints of domestic and commercial ratepayers. There can be no room in our unitary state for unilateral declarations of independence by individual local authorities relying on claims of a local mandate.'

The man in Whitehall apparently knows best. The tensions between central and local were highlighted by the dismal saga of the poll tax, or community charge – a rare, if not unique, example of a major tax being introduced and repealed all in the course of one parliament.

Because the United Kingdom is regarded as a unitary state, Conservative governments in London have been able to rule Scotland and Wales, even though they have had a declining number of MPs from these nations. These tensions grew after the 1987 election when the number of Conservative MPs from Scotland dropped from 20 to 10 out of 72. In 1955, the Tories had half the MPs from north of the border. This decline fuelled demands for more direct democratic control over Scotland's affairs and led to the formation in 1989 of the Scottish Constitutional Convention by Labour, the Liberal Democrats and various non-partisan church, business, union and local-government bodies. The Conservatives declined to join, and the Scottish Nationalists took part only in the initial preparations. Crucial to the arguments of the Convention, as stated in the Claim of Right at the start of this chapter, is that sovereignty lies with the Scottish people. This is in flat contradiction to the sovereignty of the Westminster Parliament, which can decide what powers to grant and, by implication, to pull back from any Scottish Parliament. The Blair Government's White Paper on *Scotland's Parliament*, published by the Scottish Office in July 1997, stated explicitly (p. x) that: 'The UK Parliament is and will remain sovereign.' The report in 1994 of the Scottish Constitutional Commission, established by the Convention, accepted that 'entrenchment could not be achieved within the concept of supreme parliamentary sovereignty'. It sought to reconcile the contradictions by stating that 'there should be a clear commitment by the Westminster Parliament made through a declaration that the Act founding the Parliament should not be repealed or amended in such a way as to threaten the existence of the Parliament without the consent of the Scottish Parliament and people directly consulted through a general election or referendum'. This appeal to the people, rather than to Parliament, as a constitutional check should, in practice, be a powerful weapon of entrenchment.

The devolution and decentralization plans of Labour and the Liberal Democrats, based closely on Scotland in this report, involve the creation of free-standing elected authorities with tax-varying powers in Scotland, though not in Wales. But the proposals do not resolve this contradiction between the theory of the unitary state and parliamentary sovereignty on the one hand and the assertion of sovereign rights by the Scottish people on the other. The plans so far produced are aimed mainly at the demands expressed in Scotland and Wales and are the weakest on relations with the central government and the Westminster Parliament, where a series of fundamental constitutional and practice problems remains unresolved.

Financial independence has usually been crucial to political independence. But under the devolution plans financial control will remain with central government, which will decide, subject to the approval of the Westminster Parliament, how much public money is spent in Scotland and Wales. The existing formulae for allocating funds – which ensure higher public spending per head in Scotland and Wales than in England – will be called into question. The proposed Welsh Assembly will have no taxation powers and will, in effect, be ensuring a minimum of democratic control over a centrally determined and allocated block of expenditure which has been administered on a devolved basis by the Welsh Office. The proposed Scottish Parliament would have legislative competence over matters that have been the responsibility of the Scottish Office, such as health, education, local government and law and order. It would also have the tax-varying powers, of up to 3p either way on the basic rate of income tax, but this is, in practice, tiny compared with the taxation powers of a US state or large city, which largely raises its own finance. While the Conservative slogan about the 'Tartan Tax' was widely deployed by Michael Forsyth, the Scottish Secretary from 1995 to 1997, and was catchy enough to grab the headlines, the scale of tax-varying powers was a secondary issue.

But this lack of independence opens the possibility, even likelihood, of disputes between Edinburgh and London. This will happen, however clearly worded the devolution legislation is about the allocation of legislative competences (as was the case with the Government of Ireland Act 1920, which set up the Northern Ireland Parliament or Stormont). The Constitution Unit in its report on a Scottish Parliament (1996) suggested a number of mechanisms for resolving disputes, both over finances and issues of jurisdiction and competence of the Scottish Parliament. They all involve acceptance of the ultimate jurisdiction of the Westminster Parliament, or the Judicial Committee of the Privy Council (in effect the law lords) as a final court of appeal (as Labour has proposed).

The most widely discussed dilemma posed by devolution is the West Lothian question, named as such by Enoch Powell after the then constituency of Tam Dalyell, the Labour MP who argued against the 1970s proposals. This is about the anomaly created if a wide range of social and home affairs issues are devolved to a Scottish Parliament, but remain with the Westminster Parliament in England. Consequently, Scottish MPs could vote in the Commons on such issues affecting England but not when it affects their own constituents north of the border. As Dalyell has argued, this is as much a matter for English as for Scottish MPs and could be dubbed the West Bromwich or Bury North question. (There is also the mirror image question concerning the rights of Scottish MPs to raise matters affecting their constituents which are the responsibility of the Scottish Parliament.) One answer to the West Lothian question is the 'in and out' solution whereby Scottish MPs would not vote on matters dealing with the United Kingdom except Scotland. A convoluted scheme to tackle this problem was inserted, against the Callaghan government's wishes, in the 1978 devolution legislation. This provided for a further Commons vote after fourteen days where a bill which 'does not relate to or concern Scotland' is carried on a vote that makes the number of Scottish MPs decisive in the count. This could be hideously complicated, with disputes over which bills fell within the required category, and would also lead to two different types of MP. As Enoch Powell pointed out, with typical elegance, at the time, MPs were 'in the best sense of the words, peers in every respect and sit on a basis of equality of responsibility and rights'. Moreover, attempting to rule on the basis of two different majorities in the Commons – or a minority in some cases – would make coherent and consistent government impossible.

A related argument concerns the over-representation of Scotland – and also Wales – in the House of Commons compared with England. The average number of voters in a Scottish constituency is 55,000; in Wales it is 58,500; in England it is 69,500. If all the constituencies in the United Kingdom had an equal number of voters, the number of Scottish MPs would fall from 72 to 58, and the number of Welsh would drop from 40 to 33. The Kilbrandon Commission (the Royal Commission on the Constitution of 1973) argued in favour of reducing representation of Scotland in the House of Commons as an answer to the West Lothian question, after having rejected the 'in and out' solution as impractical. This would follow the precedent of Northern Ireland when, during the fifty years that Stormont was in existence, it had many fewer MPs per voter than the rest of the United Kingdom. After the imposition of direct rule, and following some haggling with the Callaghan government, Northern Ireland moved back into line with the rest of the United Kingdom from 1983.

Reducing Scottish representation at Westminster in no way answers the West Lothian question – for which the only logical answer is home rule all round or a similar devolved structure in the whole of the United Kingdom. (It could, however, be an important political response to the imbalance as Labour has implicitly recognized.) But there is no evidence of any real demand for either an English Parliament or for elected regional assemblies (as opposed to revived local government) throughout England. However, as the Constitution Unit report admits: 'Whether or not it "answers" the West Lothian question a political response in the form of some reduction in representation at Westminster may be demanded by the Opposition parties as part of the price Scotland pays for gaining its Parliament.'

Almost all these issues were raised a century ago in Gladstone's various Home Rule Bills. In 1886, Gladstone's first Government of Ireland Bill originally proposed the exclusion of Irish members from Westminster, a suggestion that was widely condemned since the Irish people would still pay taxes to the London government for imperial and defence matters excluded from Home Rule but would have no representation. As Roy Jenkins (1995, p. 548) pointed out, 'the ghost of the Boston tea party would have been raised by reserving such indirect taxes to London without Irish members in the Imperial Parliament'. The 1893 bill had a version of the 'in and out' principle, listing five areas from which Irish MPs would be excluded, notably matters 'confined to Great Britain or some part thereof'. The bill also proposed a reduction in the number of Irish MPs from 105 to 80. Critics argued that this would make cabinet government impossible, while it would, in practice, be hard to define those areas where Irish MPs could, and could not, vote. Gladstone offered to withdraw this idea, giving Irish representatives unrestricted rights of participation in all business at Westminster, though he persisted with the case for a reduced number of Irish MPs.

Alongside devolution, the biggest challenge to conventional ideas of parliamentary sovereignty would come from the increased use of referendums. Indeed, one of the most striking features of the two years before the 1997 election was how all the main parties – and not just Labour or the Liberal Democrats – proposed referendums. This was only partly because of the pressures caused by the divisions in the Conservative Party and among the public over Britain's relations with the European Union. The Euro-sceptics, and their press allies, claimed that the political élite, in the leadership of all main parties, was ignoring the strength of public feeling on Europe and hence it was necessary for people to express their views directly in a referendum – in effect, overriding Parliament. Opinions differed as to when and how such a referendum should be held. Following the rejection by the Major government – and the House of Commons in 1993 – of a referendum on the Maastricht treaty, the sceptics wanted one on any major shift of powers to European institutions. This led to the formation by Sir James Goldsmith of the Referendum Party to campaign in the 1997 election on the pledge that it would form a government for the sole purpose of holding a referendum on Britain's relations with the European Union before dissolving itself. This bizarre platform appealed to less than 3 per cent of the electorate but the underlying demand for a direct popular say over further European integration did influence the main parties. In April 1996, John Major attempted to placate demands by his sceptics for an outright commitment against joining any European single currency with the assurance that the Conservative manifesto would promise that if a future government 'decided to join a single European currency during the course of the next parliament, that decision would be subject to confirmation in a referendum'. Britain would not participate in a single currency until such a referendum had been held with a simple majority of those voting being enough to confirm Parliament's decision. The Labour position at the time was ambiguous: the party promised to obtain the consent of the people either in a referendum or at a general election. Later in 1996 that commitment was hardened to virtually the same terms as proposed by the then Conservative government, to cover the following parliament. The Liberal Democrats, which were the only main party to urge a referendum on the Maastricht treaty, proposed a referendum if the Inter-governmental Conference 'agrees to a new constitutional settlement within the European Union states'.

But the most significant development has been the proposal by both Labour and the Liberal Democrats that major constitutional change should be accompanied by a referendum. At the 1997 election, Labour proposed the most extensive series of referendums ever put forward by any party. The first, in September 1997, was a two-part one in Scotland asking voters whether they wanted a Scottish Parliament and whether it should have tax-varying powers; followed by a single one in Wales about whether voters wanted an Assembly. Both referendums occurred before full-scale legislation was introduced. The second stage will be in May 1998 when, to coincide with the London borough elections, a referendum will be held on whether to establish an elected authority for the capital and also an elected mayor. Further referendums might be held in English regions on whether to establish regional assemblies as part of a longer-term, and stage-by-stage, process of decentralization. Jack Straw, Home Secretary in the Blair government, confirmed after the election that a commission on voting systems for the Westminster Parliament would be appointed to recommend the appropriate proportional alternative to the first-past-the-post system. Labour has promised that a choice between the existing system and one specific proportional alternative will be put to voters in a referendum. The Liberal Democrats have the same broad approach, differing only in detail. For instance, the Liberal Democrats have disagreed with Labour's proposal for a referendum in Scotland, particularly the second question on tax-varying powers. This was partly because of their irritation over Labour's failure to have proper consultations before the referendum proposal was announced, and their argument that the Scottish people have already shown their clear support for devolution at successive general elections. But the Liberal Democrats have backed the proposal for regional referendums before assemblies in England are established, as well for proportional representation in elections to the House of Commons. The party also favours a referendum to ratify a proposed written constitution together with the more regular use of referendums and citizens' initiatives on economic and social issues to give people a greater voice in decision-making. Significantly, after the 1997 election, the Conservatives concentrated their attack not on the principle of holding a referendum on an issue like devolution but on holding one before detailed legislation is put forward and considered by Parliament and on the failure to involve the whole of the United Kingdom, rather than just Scotland and Wales.

But as the Commission on the Conduct of Referendums argued (1996), 'This is a striking transformation. As recently as 25 years ago referendums were commonly said to be unconstitutional. The people, it was held, have no direct play in the legislative process.' As Vernon Bogdanor has pointed out (1997), the idea was regarded as alien, somehow un-British: 'When, in 1945, Winston Churchill suggested that the continuation of the wartime coalition be put to the people, Clement Attlee, the Labour leader, replied: "I could not consent to the introduction into our national life of a device so alien to all our traditions as the referendum, which has only too often been the instrument of Nazism and Fascism." ' This argument was echoed half a century later when Michael Howard, the former Conservative Home Secretary, argued in the Commons debate on 21 May 1997, on the Scottish and Welsh referendums bill (Hansard, col. 736, vol. 294, no. 10) that: 'A pre-legislative referendum is designed to pre-empt parliamentary debate. It is not a new device. The device was the hallmark of continental dictatorships between the wars. European tyrants used the plebiscite to sideline their Parliaments; they used it to suppress the rights and liberties of their citizens.' That is because the referendums were rigged, which is not an argument against balanced questions put in a fair and open ballot.

The case for a referendum was originally developed as a conservative argument against those proposing constitutional change. It was first highlighted in 1890 by Dicey as part of his battle against Irish Home Rule. Dicey regarded the referendum as a check on party-dominated single-chamber government. Ironically, the most influential propagandist of parliamentary sovereignty himself recognized the need for constraints on the power of Parliament. This was because MPs were no longer independent-minded representatives but tightly disciplined members of party caucuses. Dicey favoured a referendum because it was 'the best, if not the only possible, check upon ill-considered alterations in the fundamental institutions of the country' and 'the only check on the predominance of party which is at the same time democratic and conservative'. Joseph Chamberlain, however, took up the idea of the referendum to press his programme of tariff reform, a pledge that was repeated at different times and in different ways over the following two decades. The referendum featured prominently in the constitutional battles of 1909–11. Indeed, the Unionists (Conservatives) went into the December 1910 election formally committed to the principle that major constitutional changes, including tariff reform, should be put to the people before becoming law. While the precise proposals varied, the general idea was that referendums should be an additional safeguard for a special category of constitutional legislation, particularly when the two Houses disagreed. Asquith, then prime minister, was worried about 'the difficulty of defining constitutional questions where there was no written constitution, difficulty of selecting a tribunal to decide on disputed cases, danger of producing a deadlock over nearly the whole field of legislation by the width of our definition'. The Liberals were worried that only their legislation might be subject to referendums if the trigger was a stalemate with the Unionist-dominated House of Lords. In any event, as Professor Bogdanor noted (1981): 'The victory of the Liberals and their allies in the general election of December 1910 signified defeat for the advocates of the referendum, and the constitutional crisis was settled not by adopting the machinery of direct democracy, but by the Parliament Act of 1911 through which the supremacy of the House of Commons was given statutory recognition.' The common view among political scientists in the generation afterwards was that referendums favoured conservative rather than progressive political forces.

So parliamentary, or rather House of Commons, supremacy was confirmed, and so it was, in theory, when the referendum re-emerged as a live issue again during the 1970s. As in the first decade of the century, the referendum was a response to an issue of major constitutional importance, Britain's membership of the European Community, which raised passions and created divisions that could not be contained within the conventional party debate. The demand for a referendum was first made by opponents of membership, such as Douglas Jay, but was taken up by Tony Benn as part of his new-found desire to increase popular participation in government. The proposal was then backed by Harold Wilson and narrowly adopted by the Labour national executive – triggering the resignation of Roy Jenkins as deputy leader – primarily as a means of minimizing differences within the Labour Party, although it also reflected a demand for some form of broader public endorsement of entry. Labour fought the 1974 election on a policy of renegotiating the terms of British membership, which would then be presented to the electorate for approval either through a general election or a referendum. In the event, the renegotiation was only completed after the October election of 1974 and the referendum was held in June 1975, when there was a two-to-one majority for staying in the Community. The referendum exposed many of the difficulties of such a device in a parliamentary system since collective ministerial responsibility was suspended on this specific issue for the duration of the campaign. Ministers joined leading politicians of other parties to fight each other in the rival pro and anti campaigns. The referendum was presented as advisory and Edward Short, the then Leader of the Commons, devised the neat formula that 'The Government will be bound by its result, but Parliament, of course, cannot be bound by it.' The result was sufficiently clear-cut – in the direction that most of the party leaderships wanted – that the Government was not faced with the dilemma of trying to force through a bill on withdrawal which a majority of MPs would oppose. That predicament would be faced, for example, if a referendum was held that overwhelmingly backed the reintroduction of capital punishment, as has been shown consistently by opinion polls, despite the opposition of a large majority of MPs in regular votes since its final abolition thirty years ago. The referendum, as used in 1975, was essentially a device to confirm the verdict of political leaders rather than to change the direction of policy. Following the exposure of the deep Labour divisions – only temporarily papered over for a few years afterwards – Labour has insisted that all ministers would have to observe collective responsibility in any future referendum.

The 1975 referendum was seen by most politicians as an exceptional expedient rather than a constitutional precedent which should be followed. Immediately after the vote, Harold Wilson assured a Conservative MP that he would not repeat this constitutional experiment. However, the Labour government headed by James Callaghan, his successor, was forced to accept further referendums over devolution, mainly by Labour opponents of the proposal. After a tortuous passage, including the withdrawal of the single bill for Scotland and Wales in the 1976-7 session and the reintroduction of separate bills for the two countries in the following session, referendums became part of the final devolution legislation. In the event, devolution for Wales was rejected by a margin of four to one. In Scotland, the position was not straightforward because George Cunningham, then a Labour backbencher, succeeded in gaining approval for an amendment requiring 40 per cent of those entitled to vote to have voted 'yes' rather than just a simple majority of those turning out to vote. This was in itself controversial in view of problems with the electoral register. But the Cunningham amendment proved a fatal hurdle since, while 51.6 per cent of those voting supported devolution, this only represented 32.9 per cent of the electorate since turn-out was just 62.9 per cent. In practice, however, the closeness of the margin among those actually voting would have made it difficult to introduce devolution. The 40 per cent rule harked back to the arguments of the 1909–11 period in creating a hurdle beyond a simple majority, either of the House of Commons or the public, for constitutional change to occur. As a result all the referendums proposed in the 1997 election envisaged just a simple majority of those voting, despite Conservative attempts to revive the Cunningham amendment.

The four referendums held during the 1970s – also including one in 1973 on the future position of Northern Ireland within the United Kingdom – may at the time have been seen as exceptional, but they created precedents for the arguments of the 1990s. There were two linked lessons: one over the use of the referendum where an issue, like Europe, produced divisions crossing party lines rather than between parties and, second, where the proposal will fundamentally alter constitutional arrangements. But there is still no agreement as to when referendums should be held, unlike in many other countries where there are formal provisions about when referendums can and should be held over major constitutional changes, or specific scope for ones triggered by voters themselves on economic and social issues (discussed in more detail in Chapter Eight). The four British examples of the 1970s, like all those proposed in the 1997 election, can be fairly considered constitutional. But plenty of constitutional changes have been approved without referendums and both the Conservative and Labour leaderships opposed one in 1992–3 over ratification of the Maastricht treaty. However, a series of polls, notably a MORI one for the Joseph Rowntree Research Trust in 1995, showed that three-quarters of the public support the use of referendums on certain important issues rather than having the matters always decided by Parliament. A similar proportion also believed it would be a good idea if the British people could force the Government to hold a referendum on a particular issue by raising a petition with signatures from, say, a million people. This partly reflects an underlying decline in public confidence in politicians and a belief that they do not reflect the views of voters.

There is no agreement on whether referendums should be before or after detailed legislation is approved by the Commons. For instance, the referendums in Scotland and Wales in 1997 were held before detailed devolution legislation had been put before the Commons, rather than afterwards as in 1979. In 1997, the referendums might be considered advisory, to establish whether sufficient popular consent exists for the legislation to be brought forward. That leaves the final decision with Parliament rather than, as in 1979, effectively giving the electorate a veto on legislation approved by Parliament. This was an important precedent since previously Commons amendments proposing manda-tory referendums had been ruled out of order. Donald Dewar, the Scottish Secretary and a veteran of the battles of the 1970s, somewhat blurred the distinction when proposing the referendum bills on 21 May 1997: 'Referendums are not unprecedented; we had them in 1975 and 1979, on matters of fundamental constitutional change in both cases. We believe that there is a case, on such occasions and issues, for an inclusive process, gathering support across party political boundaries. What we seek – whether we get it is a matter for the people – is a broadly based consensus for change.' This view of the referendum as part of the legitimization of change also reflects Tony Blair's success in mobilizing the growing number of ordinary Labour Party members to endorse his proposals, first in April 1995, for rewriting Clause Four of the party constitution and, second in October 1996, for the party's policy platform for the election.

This view of referendums makes it much harder for Parliament to regard them as merely advisory, with the Commons having the right to reject their verdict. Indeed, one of the reasons that the pre-legislative referendums on Scottish and Welsh devolution were originally pro-posed in July 1996 was as a means of minimizing parliamentary oppo-sition – in both the Commons and the Lords – to the main legislation and so avoiding the time-consuming arguments of the late 1970s. The referendum was to be used as a trump card – the people's will – against Tory obstructionist tactics, though it would hardly prevent opposition. The need for such an argument was partly reduced by Labour's huge majority in the Commons and by the Conservative wipe-out in both Scotland and Wales.

The corollary is that referendums may act as a form of retrenchment against attempts to repeal constitutional changes – even though it is dangerous to assume any finality in politics. However, the sudden changes seen in France in the mid-1980s in the methods of electing the National Assembly, from the two-ballot system to proportional representation and back, would have been much harder to achieve if such major constitutional changes could only be authorized as a result of a referendum. Referendums seem best suited to such far-reaching changes in the electoral system and transfers in the powers of Parliament which, as Professor Bogdanor has argued (1997), should not be lightly made, nor, once made, lightly reversed. If, for example, the Labour government's proposals for devolution and decentralization – for London and the English regions as well as in Scotland and Wales – are approved in a series of referendums, it will be much harder for any future Conservative government to reverse such changes merely through the possession of a majority in the House of Commons, as it did in abolishing the Greater London Council and the metropolitan counties in the mid-1980s. That change would undermine the practice, though not the theory, of the classic doctrine of parliamentary sovereignty that no parliament can bind its successor. The use of a referendum may not formally bind a later parliament but it can limit its freedom of manoeuvre in seeking substantially to amend a change approved by the public as a whole. Geoffrey Marshall, the distinguished constitutional writer, has argued (1997) that therefore 'The sovereignty of Parliament means only that no substantive objective is beyond parliamentary authority, but that the manner and form by which it enacts its measures is a matter that, for particular purposes, may be changed by Parliament itself.'

The widely different experience of referendums until now makes a strong case for agreeing standard procedures – over their regulation, funding, form of the question, threshold required, and nature of the campaign. The Commission on the Conduct of Referendums set up by the Constitution Unit and the Electoral Reform Society made a number of sensible suggestions for the running of referendums, notably the case for an independent statutory commission either on an *ad hoc* or permanent basis. Even better would be to have a permanent Electoral Commission, as exists in many democracies, to take over responsibility from the Home Office and other bodies for the administration and conduct of elections and referendums, the allocation of broadcasting time and the regular reviews of boundaries. This was urged in 1991 by the Chataway Commission set up by the Hansard Society. While many of the decisions about referendums are essentially political, there is a strong case to set up a supervisory commission if they are to be accepted as legitimate and above board.

As with the 1975 referendum on Europe, the trickiest situation may arise where a government is not itself agreed. This may occur over proposals for changing the electoral system for the Westminster Parliament. The report in March 1997 of the Joint Consultative Committee of the Labour and Liberal Democrat parties on Constitutional Reform accepted the case for the use of a proportional electoral system for the proposed Scottish Parliament and Welsh Assembly and a proportional system based on regional lists for elections to the European Parliament. The report said that both parties accepted that a referendum on the system for elections to the House of Commons should be held within the first term of a new parliament and this should be on a single question offering a straight choice between first-past-the-post and one specific proportional alternative. A commission on voting systems should be appointed early in the parliament to recommend the appropriate proportional alternative and 'among the factors to be considered by the commission would be the likelihood that the system proposed would command broad consensus among proponents of proportional representation'. The commission would be asked to report within twelve months of its establishment, and legislation to hold the necessary referendum would then be proposed.

There are a number of obvious pitfalls. First, the choice of proportional alternative would be taken by people nominated by the Labour leadership, presumably after consultation with the Liberal Democrats. The public would then be offered a simple choice of the present system or the nominated alternative. In New Zealand, the public was involved throughout. A referendum held in 1992 asked two questions: first, whether the public wanted to retain first-past-the-post, and, second, which of four alternatives they backed. The Government, the main party leaders and the business establishment favoured the status quo, but the referendum, with a 55 per cent turn-out, showed 85 per cent support for change. As Professor Bogdanor has commented (1997), one political leader remarked that the outcome showed that 'PR stood for Public Revulsion against politicians'. The second question showed that 70 per cent backed the mixed-member proportional system, as in Germany where people have two votes, one for a constituency member under first-past-the-post and another for a list of additional candidates allocated according to proportions of votes. This was suggested by the Scottish Constitutional Convention for elections to the proposed Parliament in Edinburgh. A second binding referendum, held in November 1993 at the same time as the New Zealand general election, put first-past-the-post against the mixed-member proportional system. On an 83 per cent turn-out, 46 per cent voted for retention of the existing system and 54 per cent for the mixed-member proportional system. However, the first election under the new system, held in 1996, produced messy results and an uneasy coalition of two parties that had just campaigned bitterly against each other. This has not commended the change. The Labour proposal would effectively be for just the second referendum.

Second, the Labour leadership is divided over the merits of electoral reform. This raises the prospect of a referendum being held where the Prime Minister and other leading ministers either take a neutral stand or oppose change. This would discredit the use of a referendum and might lead to the public supporting a change not favoured by a majority of the cabinet of the day. The Labour divisions are not on conventional left–right lines, as Robin Cook has been one of the leading advocates of proportional representation. Moreover, some leading supporters of change favour the alternative vote, a preferential voting system where people list candidates in 1, 2, 3 order, and the votes for those candidates polling the least are reallocated until someone has an overall majority. But this is not a proportionate system and in Australia has given one party a much higher percentage of seats in the House of Representatives than its share of votes, as under first-past-the-post. Tony Blair has said he is 'not persuaded' of the merits of shifting to a proportional system, particularly because it would give small parties disproportionate power and leverage.

Any proportional system would have profound implications for the way the House of Commons works. For a start, as Blair is afraid, the direct link between an MP and a single-member constituency would be broken – though single-member constituencies have only been universal since 1950. Before that, and particularly between the Second and Third Reform Acts of 1867 and 1884, there were several multi-member constituencies, particularly in the larger towns and cities. A shift either to multi-member constituencies or to a split between constituency and members elected on a party list might force a change in the pattern of MPs' work. In Germany, this is not a difficulty since the welfare and constituency service side is performed by local councillors and members of the regional Lander.

The other main consequence would be that coalitions would be the norm, instead of the familiar British pattern of single-party governments commanding a majority in the House of Commons. Governments would be formed and business carried through as a result of negotiation between different parties with much greater consultation, for example, about legislation. Both select and standing committees would have to operate on a different basis, seeking consensus rather than relying on automatic party majorities. This is, of course, already true in many county and district local authorities where no single party has overall control; many of the new Labour and Liberal Democrat MPs elected in the May 1997 election were already familiar with the habits of coalition politics from their work as local councillors.

The position of the House of Commons would also be radically affected if the other main plank of the reform agenda – that of the House of Lords – occurred. That is precisely why reform of the composition of the Lords has not so far happened. The main objection, as over the Wilson government's proposals in 1968–9, has come from members of the Commons worried that a reformed Lords would have greater legitimacy and authority and be more willing to exercise its power in relation to the Commons. It has always been easier for governments of both the left and the right to leave the Lords alone. Nevertheless, both Labour and the Liberal Democrats (in the report of their Joint Consultative Committee on Constitutional Reform) believe 'there is an urgent need for radical reform of the Lords. Its current composition is indefensible, in particular the fact that the majority of its members are entitled to take part in the legislative process on a hereditary basis.' Their immediate proposal is for legislation to remove the right of hereditary peers to sit and vote in the House of Lords. This was not included in the Queen's Speech on 14 May 1997, though ministers said it would be introduced later in the parliament. Rather, it hangs as a threat over the House of Lords to secure good behaviour – or minimal obstruction – from the large number of Conservative peers to the rest of Labour's legislative programme.

Attempts to justify the current composition and role of the House of Lords quickly descend into High Tory romanticism or self-serving arguments of the 'if it ain't broke, don't fix it' kind. At present, there are roughly 1,000 to 1,200 eligible members of the House of Lords, depending on the number of hereditary peers who have taken the oath, and have therefore made themselves available to speak and, more important, to vote. Roughly 750 are peers who have inherited their titles, 15 are hereditary peers of first creation, 26 are archbishops and bishops, 24 are law lords, 370 to 400 are life peers. Of these, just under half take the Conservative whip, three times the combined total of Labour and Liberal Democrat peers. Among hereditary peers, the Conservatives have an eight-to-one advantage over the other two parties' hereditary peers. But they have also maintained an edge among life peers. Following the heavy creations during the Thatcher and Major years, the Conservatives have more life peers than the combined total of Labour and Liberal Democrat life peers (only partially offset by the large number of Labour creations in July 1997). So while the Conservatives do not have a majority of the whole House, they can easily outnumber the opposition parties and generally lose votes only when they are also opposed by most cross-bench peers and by a fair number of Tory rebels. Andrew Adonis (1993, p. 237) has exploded the much-trumpeted myth of independence: 'Whilst in the working Lords [those attending frequently], the Conservatives are the largest party but short of an assured majority, in the voting Lords [in divisions] they possess a clear majority and only in a narrow range of circumstances are they vulnerable to defeat.' He pointed to a narrow range of issues – the disabled, the countryside, pensioners and constitutional proprieties – in which any government is vulnerable to defeat. This is because these interests are well represented in the Lords.

The introduction of life peers after 1958 revived what was a fast dying chamber by providing a political role for former ministers and other ex-members of the Commons, as well as leading establishment figures. The House is certainly much more active than it was, with an average daily attendance two and a half times larger in the late 1980s than in the 1950s before the arrival of life peers. The House also sits for more than twice as long each parliamentary session than it did. But the change to a House with a minority of peers dependent on current or recent prime ministerial patronage rather than on inheritance has not made the Lords any more legitimate, or easier to defend. So not only is the House of Lords not democratic, but its composition bears no resemblance to any rough measure of the party balance.

The House of Lords has only made itself acceptable by the exercise of self-restraint. When the House lost the battles of 1909–11, its powers were formally limited by the Parliament Act so that it cannot reject money bills (as certified by the Speaker of the Commons) and can only delay other bills (initially for two years, reduced, in effect, to just over one year by the 1949 Parliament Act), though it retains a veto over bills to extend the life of a parliament. The Lords can still amend bills, and often does, but within these constraints it has avoided serious confrontations with the Commons since 1911. But this produced a dilemma when there was a big contrast in the party balances between the two Houses, as, for example, after the 1945 general election when Labour had a very large majority in the Commons (though not as large as in 1997), but the Conservatives still had a big majority in the Lords. The Marquess of Salisbury, the then Conservative leader, produced what became known as the 'Salisbury convention', confirmed by his grandson, the then Conservative leader in the Lords, after the 1997 election. This was that the Lords would not oppose on second reading any bills that were in the Labour manifesto at the previous general election, though they reserved the right to amend in committee. This is a crucial caveat. There is a fine line between accepting the principle of a bill and undermining its impact by detailed amendment. Indeed, with their bias towards the Tories, the House of Lords has much more often defeated proposals from Labour governments than from Tory ones – even taking account of its greater assertiveness during the Thatcher and Major governments. During these years, the Conservative governments suffered between six and twelve defeats in the Lords every year. By contrast, the Wilson and Callaghan governments suffered an average of between 70 and 80 defeats a year between 1974 and 1979, though admittedly for much of the period Labour did not have an overall majority in the Commons and might be said to have lacked full public support.

Defenders of the Lords claim that it is more rational, more deliberative than the occasionally raucous, adversarial Commons. But there is a danger of confusing politeness and erudition with effectiveness and influence. Many of its debates are worthy, even somewhat unworldly, with a mixture of partisan argument from the front benches and the ex-MPs, and often idiosyncratic contributions from peers with fads and obsessions of their own. On issues such as the constitution, the legal system, local government and higher education, the Lords holds more impressive debates than the Commons. Law lords, vice-chancellors and the like speak with an authority often absent in the Commons. The Lords also has a high reputation for its scrutiny work, notably on Europe (as discussed in Chapter Two), though this is more praised than read. However, apart from the Lord Chancellor, the Leader of the Lords and perhaps one or two others, there are few political heavyweights on the front benches. The government side is often filled with politically inexperienced junior ministers who have to answer on behalf of whole departments or, frequently, a number. In practice, they often merely read out departmental briefs and rarely have the knowledge, authority or confidence to engage with questioners. The quality of ministers has, however, been improved in recent years by the appointment of a number of female life peers in their forties and fifties who have had careers of their own in higher education, the public sector, local government and, in a couple of cases, the Commons, before joining the Lords. Their energy and professionalism has been a striking contrast with some of the more languid younger hereditary peers, who have been Tory ministers, or the older generation of male Labour ministers.

The reputation of the Lords as a revising chamber is mainly a reflection of the shortcomings of the Commons, its haste and inadequacy in considering legislation. Most amendments are put forward by the Government to correct drafting errors found after a bill left the Commons. A detailed analysis in the most authoritative recent study (Shell and Beamish, 1993) has punctured any complacency by their lordships about their role. As Donald Shell has pointed out (p. 329), 'the vast majority of amendments made to bills were the result of second (third, fourth, and fifth?) thoughts by the Government itself as its legislation was squeezed through the so-called legislative sausage machine. This on the face of it implies a very high degree of control by the Government over the legislative process.' His conclusion (p. 333) is equally blunt about the impact of the House of Lords:

The usefulness of the House has been primarily, if not overwhelmingly, to the Government rather than to the Commons, to interest groups, or to the public. The House is a place where errors and omissions can be corrected, where at least some details can be put right even if others are ignored. From this point of view it is better to have the House than to be without it. If political ambition and ministerial vanity result in a 'legislate as you go' mentality then it is useful to have a second chamber like the House of Lords, reasonably diligent and generally dull, with a whiff of expertise but no real boldness, with conscience but not with much credibility, with a little public profile but no actual power. The House can act as a kind of legislative long-stop. If it did not exist more care would have to be taken with the earlier stages of bills, or indeed more stages would be necessary in the Commons.

The absence of any proper legitimacy prevents the Lords doing what a second chamber should do, providing a check on the government of the day pushing through big constitutional changes without due concern for the rights or interests of those affected. There are few occasions when the Lords has made a real difference; paradoxically, it did in its votes over blocking reform of the electoral system in 1917 and 1931. A notable, but rare, recent exception was its vote in 1984, which had the effect of preventing the Greater London Council from being replaced by a nominated body for its last year before abolition. Otherwise, Professor Bogdanor was blunt, but fair, in arguing (1997) that 'had the Lords been abolished in 1914, it is doubtful if twentieth-century British history would need to be rewritten'. That is not an argument for a one-chamber legislature, but rather for clear thought about what the second chamber should do – thought that had been lacking in much recent discussion.

The obvious weakness in the Labour plan is not the removal of the voting rights of hereditary peers but the lack of a coherent alternative. The report of the joint Labour and Liberal Democrat committee in May 1997 begged all the important questions about the long-term future of the Lords. It referred to 'a valuable continuing role for some cross-bench or non-party element in a reformed House of Lords. The two parties believe the cross-benchers should remain at their present proportion of around one fifth following the removal of the hereditary peers.' Also, 'it should be made possible for a limited number of those [hereditary peers] who play an active part in the work of the Lords to become life peers'. The committee's basic principle is that 'no one political party should seek a majority in the House of Lords'. Following the removal of hereditary peers, 'we should move, over the course of the next parliament, to a House of Lords where those peers who take a party whip more accurately reflect the proportion of votes received by each party in the previous general election'. In classic fashion, the report recommended that, following the removal of hereditary peers, there should be a review by a joint committee of both Houses to 'bring forward detailed proposals on structure and functions for the later stages of reform within a time limited period. This body should produce recommendations for a democratic and representative second chamber.' This interim stage could last a long time, given past difficulties of agreeing on the composition of a reformed House. Meanwhile, the removal of the hereditary peers would mean that the House would be entirely nominated. While Labour has promised safeguards against packing to one party's advantage, it does not start from a balanced position even among life peers. Does this mean mass Labour creations to even up the balance? And would the Conservatives continue to observe the 'Salisbury convention' in a House without hereditary peers?

House of Lords reform has always proved a quagmire. The report of the Constitution Unit in 1996 on 'Reform of the House of Lords' quoted a letter by Edwin Montagu to Asquith in 1909: 'The history of all former attempts at coming to close quarters with the House of Lords Question shows a record of disorder, dissipation of energy, of words and solemn exhortation, of individual rhetoric and impressive *ipse dixits* without any definite scheme of action, nothing more substantial than dark hints of preconceived plans.' A long list of suggestions has been made over the past century about the composition of a reformed House, ranging from a predominantly hereditary chamber in which a limited number are elected to serve for one Parliament by the whole peerage, through various combinations of hereditary, nominated and elected, an entirely nominated House of Lords, to an entirely elected chamber with voting on a regional basis by proportional representation. In some plans, corporate interests are represented, in others regional ones. The common theme is that the second chamber would be on a different basis, and its members serve for a different term, from the House of Commons. The motives for reform have varied. In the 1970s Conservatives favoured reform of the Lords to create a more legitimate body, which would provide a constitutional check and restraint on a left-wing government. In the 1990s Labour, like the Liberals in the 1900s, favours reform to prevent Conservatives from thwarting a programme of radical change.

But the general focus on the composition of a reformed House misses the point. It is a secondary question. The real issue is its powers or, rather, its place in a broader series of constitutional changes. Any reformed House of Lords would have greater legitimacy and would presumably want to exercise its powers in relation to the Commons. Do we want a second chamber as a constitutional check on the House of Commons – with, for example, a right to call referendums on consti-tutional issues, as a Conservative Party Review Committee suggested in 1978? Should the Lords be a regionally focused chamber as part of a federal structure for Britain? Would the reformed Lords have a special role in relation to the incorporation of the European Convention of Human Rights so that the Commons would not be able to override its veto under the Parliament Act? This would be similar to the current provision that the Lords can block any bill to extend the life of a parliament. Reform of the Lords is dependent on the extent and success of reform of the Commons, and on other constitutional reforms. A piecemeal change might do nothing, in practice, to strengthen the Lords.

That goes back to the basic question raised by Labour's constitutional reform programme. Is Labour trying to make the current unitary state, with Parliament at its centre, work better, and in a more decentralized form? Or is it trying to create a new structure with a written constitution that limits the power of the Westminster Parliament by formally entrenching rights for other institutions, such as a Scottish Parliament? That might create a role for a reformed House of Lords as a check and balance on constitutional matters. Most countries with written constitutions do have provisions for the approval of fundamental consti-tutional changes by a wider constituency than just a majority in the legislature of the party currently in power – whether constituent states or regions in federal states or the people as a whole in referendums. There are risks, also, in too inflexible a mechanism for constitutional change, as the cumbersome procedure for ratification of constitutional amendments in the United States shows. There is a balance between innovation and entrenchment. It is a myth to suppose that a consensus has to be constructed before constitutional change can occur. As the

Constitution Unit pointed out in its report (1996) on 'Delivering Constitutional Reform': 'almost every successful constitutional reform measure this century has been passed by Parliament in the face of some opposition'. An immediate question is how far the procedures of Parliament itself should be amended to cope with an ambitious programme of constitutional reform. The Blair government has proposed that parts of the detailed committee stages of constitutional bills be examined upstairs in smaller standing committees, rather than occupying large amounts of time in debates on the floor of the House, as has been the past practice. This was left as an open question by the Select Committee on Modernization of the House of Commons (First Report, 1997–8, p. xx), though the Government's support for change was clear. There are other big questions as well. Should the length of debates be subject to prior timetables? Would that be short-changing the rights of the Commons? These are not just matters of arcane procedure. They go to the heart of the question raised several times in this chapter of how Parliament adapts to a constitutional reform agenda that challenges its supremacy. The way these changes are debated by Parliament is directly related to the issue of whether some extra-parliamentary form of approval, and entrenchment, is required. These questions cannot be avoided for long, otherwise reform proposals will founder in their own inconsistencies, as House of Lords reform did in 1968–9.

At present, the Blair government's instincts seem to be gradualist and piecemeal, reforming the existing unitary state rather than creating a new constitution. But this chapter has shown that several of Labour's proposals – from devolution, to the increased use of referendums, to the position of the House of Lords – raise fundamental questions about the type of Parliament we want.

CHAPTER SIX

Quis Custodiet

That the freedom of speech, and debates or proceedings in
Parliament, ought not to be impeached or questioned in any
court or place out of Parliament.

Article 9, Bill of Rights, 1688–9

'The House of Commons itself contributed to loss of public
confidence by its failure to understand for itself that its rules
and procedures for maintaining standards of conduct had not
kept up with what is required of a modern institution.'

Lord Nolan, first Radcliffe lecture, Warwick
University, 7 November 1996

N owhere is the doctrine of parliamentary sovereignty more
strongly defended than over the right of the House of Commons
to regulate its own affairs, and the conduct of its members. At present,
members cannot be prosecuted or sued for what they say in the Commons, though they can be disciplined by the House. Also members
cannot be compelled to attend court as witnesses – even if the matter
has nothing to do with their role as MPs – though they can still be
arrested in criminal cases and, if necessary, sent to prison. Yet parliamentary self-regulation is now under challenge, as a result of allegations
about financial malpractice and other abuses by members. Proposals
by the Blair government to clarify and strengthen the law on corruption
in public life have far-reaching implications for parliamentary privilege
and self-regulation.

Charges about financial wrongdoing have, confusingly and lazily,
been lumped together with stories about sexual misconduct and infi-
delity under the catch-all term of 'sleaze', whether or not there is any
relevance to a politician's public duties and responsibilities. Stories

about both have undoubtedly undermined the public standing of MPs but it was the allegations over financial abuse that led in October 1994 to the appointment of the Committee on Standards in Public Life under Lord Nolan. The proposals put forward in the first report of the Nolan committee in May 1995 were largely, though in some cases reluctantly, adopted by the Commons. This was in itself a powerful acknowledgement that the House could not reform itself on its own and had to call in outsiders for advice, which it then had no choice but to accept. These proposals have substantially changed the way in which the House regulates the outside commercial interests and conduct of its members, introducing an independent element for the first time with the appointment of the Parliamentary Commissioner for Standards to investigate complaints. Both the post-Nolan changes and the existence of the Nolan committee as a standing body, rather than just a one-off inquiry, have meant that the House is no longer the sole master of its own affairs.

Self-regulation has long been seen as a basic strand of parliamentary privilege as a result of the seventeenth-century battles between the House of Commons, the Crown and the courts. The Bill of Rights was an assertion both of absolute parliamentary sovereignty and a 'keep-off' warning to other institutions. This was to ensure that members could perform their parliamentary duties without fear of arrest, intimidation or action in the courts. Official parliamentary documents are similarly protected. However, privilege has always had a double edge, an ambiguity that members themselves have been eager to preserve. As Tony Benn, that quintessentially seventeenth-century champion of the rights of Parliament, has argued (Nolan, 1995, vol. 2, p. 157), 'people think privilege is about the privilege of members. It is not, it is about the rights of members to have free access to Parliament so Parliament is not improperly influenced by pressures that should not exist.'

Throughout the past three hundred years the House has argued that not only the content of speeches but also its own decisions cannot be challenged in the courts. This has applied not just to legislation but also to the punishment of members for alleged breaches of privileges and rules. The House has always claimed the absolute right to decide its own procedures and to adjudicate over disputes. J. A. G. Griffith and Michael Ryle (1989) have argued: 'On no matter is there any appeal to the courts regarding anything that constitutes a proceeding in Parliament. The House is sovereign over its own business.'

The various editions of Erskine May, the ultimate guide to procedure for the Commons since the mid-nineteenth century, have provided a running and evolving commentary on the meaning of privilege. Over the centuries the House has imposed restrictions on what members can and cannot do. For instance, in 1666 the House passed the first of a number of resolutions forbidding MPs who are barristers – vividly described as 'such members of this House as are of the long robe' – from practising as counsel before the House or its committees, or advising as counsel to a private bill or parliamentary proceeding. The mid-nineteenth century was the heyday of private bills, measures with a special, local application sponsored by a private interest, notably then for the development of railways. So in 1858 the House again felt the need to ban professional advocacy in terms that strike a chord nearly 140 years later over the activities of members who are not barristers but public-relations consultants: 'That it is contrary to the usage and derogatory to the dignity of this House that any of its members should bring forward, promote or advocate in this House any proceeding or measure in which he may have acted or been concerned for or in consideration of any pecuniary fee or reward.' That appears to ban any idea of 'cash for questions' or, even, lobbying for money.

Case law has developed about what constitutes a contempt of the House leading to the suspension of members and, in rare cases, their expulsion. In 1694, Sir John Trevor was found guilty of a 'high crime and misdemeanour' in having, as Speaker of the House, accepted a gratuity of a thousand guineas (an enormous sum by contemporary standards) from the City of London after passing the Orphans Bills. He was duly expelled, as was a Mr Hungerford for receiving the more modest sum of twenty guineas for his part as chairman of the committee for the bill. This scandal led to the passing of a resolution in 1695 against outright corruption by acceptance of bribes: 'That the offer of money, or other advantage, to a Member of Parliament for the promoting of any matter whatsoever, depending or to be transacted in Parliament is a high crime and misdemeanour.'

It is ironic that, more than three hundred years later, the Government is seeking to tidy up the law on corruption to deal with just such an offence. The Corporation of London, however, was not deterred from trying to influence decisions in the Commons. As Doolittle records (p. 44), officers of the Corporation had difficulty in the 1840s in 'refuting the charge that the City had used improper means to orchestrate public opinion and ward off legislative interference. The Remembrancer [Tyrrell], who dealt with parliamentary business, was obliged to reveal that £2,750 [in addition to the 'usual' legal charges of £3,169] had been spent on opposing the Smithfield Market Bill.'

The House of Commons has also prohibited members from voting on private bills (as opposed to public bills applying to everyone) where they have a direct pecuniary interest. From time to time, allegations of corruption have also been brought against backbenchers, and even ministers.

However, there was never a golden age when MPs were all honourable gentlemen. The eminent historian Lord Blake put into historical perspective the furore of the mid-1990s over 'sleaze' when he gave evidence to the Nolan inquiry (1995, vol. 2, p. 13). He drew a comparison between the late 1980s and early 1990s and the period from the mid-1890s until the late 1920s, noting that there was relatively little trouble either in the years before 1895 or from the late 1920s until the mid-1960s. Lord Blake compared the 'get rich quick' mentality of the Edwardian era with a similar mood in recent years, though, in his view, the malpractices of the 1990s were nothing like as bad as those in the Edwardian and early Georgian period. There has been nothing comparable with the Marconi scandal of 1912 when Lloyd George, then Chancellor of the Exchequer, Sir Rufus Isaacs, the Attorney General, and the Master of Elibank, the government Chief Whip, speculated in shares on the basis of inside information – in the latter's case using Liberal Party funds. The first two managed to escape with just an apology because they invested in the American Marconi Company rather than the English Marconi Company. Even though the two companies were closely associated, the latter rather than the former had received a large government contract so, technically, the ministers had not bought shares in a company that directly benefited from the award of government work. They were also largely exonerated by an almost wholly partisan report of a special Commons select committee. As Lord Blake observed, if a similar situation had arisen today, no minister would 'have survived in public life for a moment, so our standards may perhaps be a bit better'.

Throughout this period, the House laid down a broad prohibition rather than specific rules on what was and what was not permitted. It relied on the 'good chaps know how to behave' view. Or not, in a few cases. In 1948, Gerry Allighan, a Labour backbencher, was found to have lied to a committee when he had wrongly accused fellow MPs of accepting money for disclosing to the press the proceedings of private party meetings. It turned out that this is precisely what he had done himself (Griffith and Ryle, 1989, p. 92). The Leader of the House recommended that he be reprimanded and suspended without pay, but an amendment for expulsion was successfully moved (by Quintin Hogg, later to be Lord Hailsham, twice). There was also concern about outside bodies, such as trade unions, attempting to instruct an MP, so the House passed a resolution restating its traditional principles:

> It is inconsistent with the dignity of the House, with the duty of a member to his constituency, and with the maintenance of the privilege of freedom of speech, for any member of the House to enter into any contractual agreement with an outside body, controlling or limiting the members' complete independence and freedom of action in Parliament or stipulating that he shall act in any way as the representative of such outside body in regard to any matters to be transacted in Parliament; the duty of a member being to his constituency and to the country as a whole, rather than to any particular section thereof.

As the Nolan report points out (1995, vol. 1, p. 26), the focus was very much on maintaining the privileges and freedom of action of members in relation to outside bodies, and was 'much less explicit as regards restricting the freedom of members to place themselves in a situation where they are liable to be improperly influenced'.

The traditional structure has only been challenged gradually. The first doubts crept in in the late 1960s when a Select Committee on Members' Interests was set up in May 1969 under the veteran Labour MP George Strauss. This followed newspaper stories that Gordon Bagier, a Labour MP, had worked for a public-relations firm which was trying to improve the image of the Greek colonels. At the time, the convention, though not rule, of the House was that MPs should, when speaking, declare financial interests relevant to the issue under consideration. The Strauss committee rejected proposals then being aired by some political academics and a few, generally maverick, backbenchers for a formal public register of members' interests on the grounds that 'it might be difficult to cater for every imaginable circumstance, and an attempt to do so might confuse rather than clarify the purpose of the code'. Instead, the committee opted for tightening up the traditional practices on oral declaration of interests when a member had a relevant financial interest and forbidding advocacy for financial gain. The proposed code of conduct built on the 1666 and 1858 resolutions discussed above. The intention was that MPs should keep their parliamentary and professional work absolutely separate. The committee's wording was clear-cut:

> That it is contrary to the usage and derogatory to the dignity of this House that a Member should bring forward by speech or question, or advocate in this House or among his fellow Members any bill, motion, matter or cause for a fee, payment, retainer or reward, direct or indirect which he has received, is receiving or expects to receive.

The Strauss report was published in December 1969 but was never debated, either before or after the June 1970 general election. This was in itself a reflection of the then low degree of interest in these issues. It would have specified twenty-five years before Nolan what was and what was not permissible. In March 1971, Willie Whitelaw, then Leader of the Commons, said, 'There is widespread support in the House for the view that it is right to rely on the general good sense of members rather than on formalised rules.'

However, the issue became urgent again after several members, including Reginald Maudling, the then Home Secretary, were named during the Poulson bankruptcy case in the early 1970s. In 1974 the incoming Labour government proposed setting up a public register of members' interests. A subsequent select committee set out what interests should be declared in broad categories such as directorships, consultancies, sizeable shareholdings, overseas visits and the like. But there was no requirement on a member to disclose the amounts of money he or she received from these interests. The onus was very much on MPs to make their own interpretation of the rules in registering their interests. The Select Committee on Members' Interests established in February 1976 on a permanent basis was given a very limited role 'to examine the arrangements made for the compilation, maintenance and accessibility of the register', but there was only a vague reference to considering 'any specific complaints made in relation to the registering or declaring of interests'. The main motive behind these changes was to offer the public reassurance after the Poulson affair that the House was not corrupt, and the basic framework of self-regulation was retained. Members were assumed to be honourable on their own word. In many respects, the creation of the register made matters worse because of fuzziness in definition of interests and because of difficulties in policing. As Alan Doig has pointed out (1994), 'no distinction was made between acceptable or unacceptable activities or interests, nor was advocacy to be curtailed, because it was thought that registration and declaration, together with the sense of honour and reputation embodied in individual members, would provide the necessary deterrence to dissuade MPs from doing anything which, if challenged, could be publicly disapproved of or condemned by the House.' Some hope.

A few MPs objected to the existence of the register as infringing their rights as members, in terms similar to those later used over the Nolan recommendations. Enoch Powell famously refused to register throughout his period as a member on the grounds that the resolution establishing the register is not 'binding upon members, in as much as it purports to impose obligations which can only lawfully and constitutionally be imposed upon members by statute'. The Select Committee on Members' Interests made a number of reports during the 1970s on Powell's refusal to declare his interests, and sought to persuade the House to take action to enforce the requirement to register. But no one had the temerity, or political will, to challenge Powell on his refusal to comply with the House's rules.

A big opportunity was lost when no action was taken on some of the key recommendations of the Salmon Commission, the Royal Commission on Standards of Conduct in Public Life (1976), another result of the Poulson affair. The commission believed that 'the sanctions against bribery introduced by the criminal law have now outstripped whatever sanction may be exerted through Parliament's own powers of investigation and punishment'. It continued, 'with the most genuine respect to the Committee of Privileges and the Select Committee on Members' Interests, we do not consider that they provide an investigative machinery comparable to that of a police investigation'. The commission recommended in 1976 that Parliament should consider bringing 'corruption, bribery and attempted bribery of an MP acting in his parliamentary capacity within the ambit of the criminal law'. (This is broadly the same as proposed by the Blair government in June 1997.) Nothing was done about this recommendation, though the commission's doubts about the investigative competence of the disciplinary committees of the Commons were fully borne out over the following two decades. How far the misconduct of MPs should be brought within the criminal law, and hence the jurisdiction of the courts, was discussed again by the Nolan report.

Moreover, the creation of the register of declarable interests appeared to legitimize some lobbying activities which had been outlawed by earlier resolutions. It focused merely on the declaration of outside interests, not on whether they should be held. The pre-Nolan register specifically stated that members must disclose the names of 'clients for whom they provide services which depend essentially upon, or arise out of, membership of the House'. The conflict with earlier resolutions was highlighted by the Nolan report (1995, p. 27):

> The position is, therefore, that the 1947 resolution prevents a Member from agreeing to act for a client in Parliament but the rules governing the Register of Members' Interests expressly contemplate that the Member may have received material benefits 'which might reasonably be thought by others to influence his or her actions, speeches or votes in Parliament' . . . The contrast between the 1947 resolution and the rules governing the Register is in our view totally unsatisfactory. It is small wonder that it has given rise to confusion in the minds of Members of Parliament themselves.

The confusion has been highlighted by a fascinating study of the ethical attitudes of MPs by Maureen Mancuso (1993 and 1995). She argued that 'The parameters of ethical conduct in the House of Commons remain hazy and blurred. MPs have almost nothing but an unwritten code on which to rely.' The House of Commons depends 'for the maintenance of probity on the congruence of individual attitudes with a single indistinct ideal. The basic premise is that those elected are by nature "honourable gentlemen" and that collegial experiences within the halls of Westminster ensure that MPs remain "honourable members".' In one of the rare pieces of research into the ethical attitudes of members, she interviewed 100 MPs between March 1986 and

March 1988, that is when the growth in parliamentary consultancies was occurring but well before it became a public issue and anyone had heard of the phrase 'cash for questions'. She posed a number of hypothetical scenarios about behaviour by MPs, and produced a four-fold classification: Puritans (28 of the 100), who were determined to allow neither their private interests nor their roles as representatives to exert undue influence upon their functioning as legislators; Servants (16), who had a low tolerance for conflict of interest but stressed their willingness to give primary consideration to the interests of their con-stituents; Muddlers (21), who condemned ethically questionable acts that would benefit only constituents yet condoned acts that would confer direct personal advantage on themselves; and Entrepreneurs (35), who were willing to condone almost any activity as long as it did not contravene a written statute or formal rule. The latter did not regard being a Member of Parliament as being a reward in itself and they generally believed that declaration legitimized any outside interest a member may be paid to represent. MPs of all types talked about an ethical deterioration, even if they did not share the 'ethical minimalism' of the Entrepreneurs. The latter's 'reliance on strict legalistic definition of corruption frees them from the responsibility of examining their personal conduct for compliance with nebulous standards'.

This study coincided with a sharp rise in the number of MPs with links with lobbyists. The Nolan report (1995, vol. 1, p. 22) noted that the 1995 Register of Members' Interests indicated that 26 members had consultancy agreements with public relations or lobbying firms and a further 142 had consultancies with other types of company or trade associations. Excluding ministers, this means that 30 per cent of eligible MPs had consultancy agreements of these types. A similar proportion had sponsorship arrangements with trade unions (which were intended to help finance their constituency parties rather than to benefit them personally), while 27 members had paid consultancies with trade unions. In addition, according to the incomplete register of research assistants, one-third of them in the late 1980s had registered a lobbying interest.

The lobbying business flourished from the early 1980s onwards, partly in response to the replacement of corporatism by privatization. During the 1960s and 1970s, governments relied heavily on their relations with corporate bodies such as the TUC, CBI and trade associ-ations. This ended after the arrival of the Thatcher government in

1979, while the development of privatization, contracting-out and the like increased the number, and importance, of commercial relations between government and the private sector. There were tens, indeed hundreds, of millions of pounds to be earned in contracts, advisory, banking and professional fees, and lobbyists became skilful in selling their services as intermediaries – often, however, exaggerating the importance of their own contacts and influences. Many introduced their business clients to MPs, whom they claimed had access and clout, even when they were often just parliamentary private secretaries with an impressive-sounding title but no real influence. Many MPs also saw an attractive and easy way to make money. There was a sense among many members that greed was all right, as is vividly related in the memoirs of Ian Greer (1997) whose lobbying firm flourished in this era. This was also partly a result of the rise of the full-time career politician, which I have discussed elsewhere (1993 and 1996). Fewer MPs have had an independent career or built up their own businesses before entering the House and so have looked to links with lobbyists and consultants as a means of supplementing their salaries. Many resumed associations with lobbyists for whom they had worked before becoming MPs.

The flaws in the register, and particularly its policing, became increasingly apparent during the 1980s. These were highlighted by the John Browne affair in 1989–90. This followed a complaint in May 1989 by David Leigh, the investigative journalist, that Browne, the Conservative MP for Winchester, had failed several times to register and, where appropriate, to declare his financial interests, notably with various Saudi Arabian organizations and with Middle Eastern business consultants. The Select Committee on Members' Interests (First Report, 1989–90) concluded that certain of these relationships 'influenced his parliamentary actions and conduct as a Member and should have been declared on the Register'. But the committee concluded merely: 'We have carried out our duty to the House to the best of our ability. The Committee has no power to take action: action can only be taken by the House. Nevertheless, your committee recommends that action should be taken and that the House should decide at an early date what action it proposes to take in the light of the serious nature of those of our findings which uphold the complaints against Mr Browne.'

When the report was debated in March 1990, Browne apologized for failing to register properly all his interests, but said that in the case of the Saudi Arabian contract it did not involve Parliament in any way, and he believed he was not alone in misunderstanding the rules. After a series of votes, rejecting an amendment that no penalty should be imposed, another calling for his resignation, and another proposing to suspend him for three months, the House finally approved, without a division, a resolution suspending him for twenty sitting days. He subsequently announced his intention to stand down at the next (1992) election, although, in the event, he stood, unsuccessfully, as an Independent Conservative.

In the resolution at the end of the Browne debate, the select committee was asked to look further into these issues. Its report on Registration and Declaration of Members' Financial Interests, published just before the 1992 general election, did not challenge the basic framework of the register, or the methods of investigation, but recommended changes designed to consolidate previous *ad hoc* rulings and to clarify the rules both on declaration in debates and for entries in the register. The changes, eventually approved by the House in June 1993, required the declaration of interests by sponsors of early-day motions and in the election of the chairmen of departmental select committees and, when relevant, in their inquiries. The intention was to make MPs more aware of the issues involved in declaration and registration, rather than to take a big leap forward with far-reaching reforms. In particular, there was no desire to introduce a formal code of unacceptable financial interests. But the report and the evidence given to it underlined the sense that the Commons was approaching a turning point in its methods of regulation after criticisms over failures to register or declare financial interests. John Biffen, a former Leader of the Commons, argued in a memorandum (p. 15):

> If the judgment is that the problem of corruption is growing and is potentially serious I do not believe the present arrangements based upon self-regulation can continue. The House would soon perceive the profound problems of interpretation, enforcement, and punishment. I believe these would lead to a requirement that the obligations of registration and the punishment for neglect should be set out much more specifically and contained in either standing orders or, probably, statute. The statute would indicate what level

of infringement was inconsistent with membership of the Commons. The Commons has properly had a distaste for deciding from its own ranks who could or could not remain members, as was evident in the cases of Francis Noel Baker and John Stonehouse. It would be more satisfactory if breach of registration of interest, like breach of election law, enabled a judicial judgment on eligibility for Commons membership.

Biffen argued that if, on the other hand, the problem of corruption was 'minuscule' it would be wise to remain with the present system of self-regulation operating upon a resolution of the House rather than by statute. The Select Committee on Members' Interests took the same view in deciding against putting the register and rules affecting members' interests on to a statutory footing, but accepted that this was not the last word (p. xi): 'The issue is one which the House will doubtless need to review occasionally in the light of changing circumstances and changing ethical perceptions, but the intervention of the criminal law, the police and the courts of law in matters so intimately related to the proceedings of the House would be a serious and in our view regrettable development, and would have profound constitutional implications.'

This was almost the last defence of the old regime. Writing in the summer of 1994, just as the full cash-for-questions affair erupted, Alan Doig delivered a devastating, but prescient, judgment on the work of the Select Committee on Members' Interests:

> Its determinedly reactive attitude on investigations and its unwillingness to develop a proactive role, its confusion over ends and means and its persistence in allowing MPs to be the judge of their own conduct while giving them the benefit of the doubt if they fail to take the requirements of registration and declaration seriously, together with its continuing faith in an assumed general understanding of what constitutes good sense, personal judgment and relevance, whether or not sharpened by making 'rules of registration clearer and more explicit', reflect a Committee unable or unwilling to read the messages from the various cases it had had to deal with in the past few years.

These doubts were fully exposed by the long-running cash-for-questions saga. The latter was two separate affairs. The simpler was the 'sting' operation by the *Sunday Times* in July 1994 to find out whether MPs would take cash in return for tabling questions. After a lengthy investigation by the Privileges Committee, this led to the temporary suspension of two Tory MPs, Graham Riddick and David Tredinnick. The Privileges Committee had recommended action on the ground that the conduct of the MPs 'fell below the standards which the House is entitled to expect of its members'. However, in a memorandum to the report, Sir Clifford Boulton, then Clerk of the Commons and later a member of the Nolan inquiry, noted: 'The House has never attempted to deal comprehensively with the potential conflicts of interest that can arise when the business and professional interests of Members touch upon their duties and responsibilities as Members. . . . the House has preferred instead to deal with particular instances of conflict pragmatically when difficulties arise.'

The other, far more complicated story concerned the activities of Ian Greer, the lobbyist, and the series of allegations by Mohammed Al-Fayed against various MPs, notably Neil Hamilton and Tim Smith, that he had rewarded them with hospitality and/or cash for pressing his case against the Department of Trade and Industry. The revelations, notably in the *Guardian* in October 1994 and two years later when the threatened libel action by Messrs Hamilton and Greer was withdrawn at the last minute, were damning about the failures of the existing regulatory regime. These exposed the inadequacies of the Members' Interests Committee as a watchdog, not least because Greer and a number of the MPs misled the committee during its inquiry into lobbying in the 1980s about the scale and nature of payments to members. Hamilton and several other MPs were subsequently shown to have ignored both the spirit and the letter of the admittedly more lax pre-Nolan regime. The saga is vividly discussed both in the account by the *Guardian* itself (Leigh and Vulliamy, 1997), despite its unbalanced and often self-regarding tone, and in Ian Greer's defensive memoirs (1997). The *Guardian*'s somewhat improbable alliance with Al-Fayed in airing the charges against Hamilton and others led to the resignations of Smith and Hamilton from the Government.

The shadow of Al-Fayed was long, and the long-drawn-out affair was immensely damaging politically to the Major government. The scandal surfaced again at the start of the 1997 election campaign when there was no time to publish a report into the allegations by Sir Gordon Downey, the Parliamentary Commissioner for Standards. The *Guardian* then disclosed details of some of the evidence, which led Smith to step down as candidate for Beaconsfield. The reverberations dominated the first ten days of the campaign and prompted the strangest contest in the whole election for Neil Hamilton's seat of Tatton in Cheshire. Labour and the Liberal Democrats withdrew in favour of Martin Bell, the veteran BBC war correspondent, who stood as an independent – the man in the white suit – and easily defeated Hamilton. Every single Conservative MP who had been touched, fairly or otherwise, by Al-Fayed's charges lost his seat in the election. The thorough and exhaustive report by Sir Gordon Downey (published in July 1997 as the first report of the Standards and Privileges Committee, 1997–8) clearly established that Mr Hamilton and several other former Conservative MPs had fallen well below the standards expected of MPs. By contrast, several Conservative MPs who had been at the centre of allegations about their sexual conduct survived with results little different from their neighbours – including Piers Merchant who, after the campaign had started, was 'exposed' in photographs with a teenage night-club hostess. This showed that British voters were less censorious and more mature about sexual, as opposed to financial, charges than tabloid editors.

The original Al-Fayed allegations against Neil Hamilton and others were the main reason for the establishment in October 1994 by the Government of the inquiry into Standards in Public Life under Lord Nolan, a law lord. He was not only a man of impeccable propriety and fastidiousness himself, but in time he showed a shrewd understanding of the ways of politics and politicians. The inquiry was initially described by John Major as an 'ethical workshop' to provide 'running repairs on standards in public life'. It turned into a running seminar on the workings of the British constitution conducted by the great-and-the-good of the old establishment, two peers, three knights, a dame, or, under a different definition, three former cabinet ministers, a law lord, an ex-ambassador and a former Clerk of the Commons. In a room at the back of Methodist Central Hall, the size of a small classroom, Lord Nolan held hearings three mornings a week between mid-January and late-February 1995. It was a fascinating exercise as Lord Nolan and his colleagues soon revealed their concern at what they were told by a wide range of witnesses about the growth of lobbying and the failure of parliamentary monitoring over the previous few years. Most members of the committee took the 'bad apples' view, regarding actual corruption as isolated but expressing concern about the perception that standards in Parliament had fallen. One important flaw was that, partly because of lack of time, the inquiry did not commission any research itself into the scale of misconduct by MPs and others, and concentrated on addressing the widespread perception that something was wrong. Lord Nolan signalled early on in the hearings that the rules on MPs' outside interests must be tightened – much to the concern of many, mainly Tory MPs. The first report of the Nolan committee noted the evident decline in public confidence in the financial probity of MPs and said (1995, vol. 1, p. 21) 'this unease undoubtedly has much to do with the growth of professional Parliamentary lobbying and the very substantial increase in the number of Members of Parliament employed as consultants and advisers to companies, trade associations and the like'. In the measured tones of establishment criticisms, the report (p. 31) was damning about the shortcomings of the Commons over a generation:

> The 1969 Strauss report was shelved without debate; the introduction of a Register of Interests was resisted until the Poulson scandal forced the hand of a new government in 1974; it has taken Members 20 years to accept the Register fully; with senior Members even in recent years feeling free to defy a Resolution of the House in respect of entries in the Register; and doubt has been expressed about whether justice has always been done to Members whose conduct has been judged by the House in recent years. While we accept that in the recent 'cash for questions' case the Privileges Committee has acted firmly, and this should be fully recognized, the long drawn-out preliminaries to the committee's hearings were not such as to promote public confidence. The overall picture is not one of an institution whose Members have been quick to recognize or respond to public concern.

The report argued (p. 40) that the procedures for the enforcement of the House's rules 'appeared to be less than satisfactory. Proceedings related to conduct of Members in general have been carried forward on an ad hoc basis.' The committee stressed that procedures had to operate as 'a matter of course rather than chance. The public needs to see that breaches of the rules by its elected legislators are investigated as fairly, and dealt with as firmly, by Parliament in such cases as would be the case with others through the legal process.'

The Nolan committee, however, decided to stick to the traditional framework of self-regulation by the House. It accepted the principle of parliamentary privilege that members should remain answerable to the House and not to the courts. 'Because Parliamentary privilege is important for reasons entirely unconnected with the standards of conduct of individual Members of Parliament, we believe it would be highly desirable for self-regulation to continue.' However, the report stressed (p. 41) that for self-regulation to continue it was essential that resolutions should be 'regarded as binding by all Members, and should be firmly, promptly and fairly enforced'. It concluded (p. 42) that the best way forward was 'combining a significant independent element with a system which remains essentially self-regulating'. In particular, the committee recommended the creation of 'a person of independent standing' as Parliamentary Commissioner for Standards to maintain the register of members' interests, advise on a code of conduct, and have responsibility for receiving complaints about and investigating the conduct of members in this area. The Commissioner should 'have independent discretion to decide whether or not a complaint merits investigation' and should report to a new streamlined Committee of Privileges, which would take over the functions of the Select Committee on Members' Interests. This structure was intended to monitor a new code of conduct and an improved register which should, for the first time, include declarations of annual earnings from contracts to provide services 'in their capacity as members' in broad financial bands. While accepting that MPs should remain free to have paid employment unrelated to their role as members, the Nolan committee recommended that members should be banned from undertaking services for organizations that provide parliamentary services to multiple clients or from maintaining any direct or active connections with such firms – mainly lobbyists. In addition, the Nolan committee returned to one of the main, unimplemented recommendations of the Salmon Commission of 1976, that bribery involving a member should be brought within the criminal law. But the report said that the law was still uncertain as to whether the courts of Parliament had jurisdiction in such cases, and that the Government should now take steps to clarify the law.

The report contained a clear warning (p. 31) that the Commons had to do much better than in the past:

The question is whether the House is prepared to clarify and to implement those rules fully and objectively. An elected representative has a unique position, but it cannot be assumed that this inevitably makes that person's judgment of the balance of public and private interest infallible. The House collectively has a responsibility to safeguard the public interest against the possible misjudgment of individual Members, and it has the ability to do so.

But a number of members of the Nolan committee were privately sceptical about the ability, and willingness, of the Commons to follow the spirit of its proposals.

These doubts were fully borne out by the shambolic, self-absorbed and complacent initial Commons debate on the report on 18 May 1995, a week after its publication. Its proposals affecting MPs were attacked by several Tory members, with vocal support from their colleagues, as a threat to the sovereignty of the House itself. Sir Edward Heath, the Father of the House, who had always taken a minimalist view of disclosure, argued that when he entered the House in 1950, 'we recognized every Member of Parliament, man or woman, as a person of integrity. That was the attitude, and it was fully accepted. We have now reached a stage at which every man and woman in the House is an object of suspicion.' This was one of the few occasions when Sir Edward was loudly cheered by his own side. Several other Conservative backbenchers made similar points, arguing that Lord Nolan was unworldly and was threatening the future of the professional middle-classes in the Commons. This reflected a widespread misreading of the report, at least on the Tory benches, since Nolan had specifically rejected the suggestion that all members should be full-time and explicitly supported the retention of suitable outside interests. The report said (vol. 1, p. 23) that 'it is important that the House of Commons should continue to contain members from a wide variety of backgrounds. We should be worried about the possibility of a narrowing in the range of able men and women who would be attracted to stand for Parliament if members were barred from having any outside paid interests.' However, many Tory MPs saw a twin threat to their pockets and to Parliament itself. Typical was the intervention of Geoffrey Clifton-Brown: 'If the judgment of Members of Parliament is so suspect that – for the first time – this place must be judged by somebody else, democracy will be irredeemably damaged.' Later, Sir Edward Heath told the Carlton Club, and wrote (1995): 'I don't believe that outsiders should run Parliament. Members know far more about what is happening in the House than any bureaucrat from outside could ever learn. A line must be drawn. If we cannot run our own affairs, how can we run other people's affairs?'

But that was precisely the public doubt. Judging by opinion polls, many voters did not believe that MPs *could* run their own affairs. A MORI poll, taken for the Joseph Rowntree Reform Trust's 'State of the Nation' survey in April–May 1995, at the time of the publication of the Nolan report, showed that three-quarters of the public favoured a ban on MPs working for lobbying firms and any paid company links, while two-thirds backed a ban on MPs speaking or voting on issues in which they had a financial interest. The public did not share MPs' belief in self-regulation as a centrepiece of parliamentary sovereignty. A mere fifth favoured the Nolan approach of tightening up existing rules enforced by MPs without involving the police, courts or an outside body. Nearly two-fifths believed that the rules should be made law, with an independent commission and civil courts overseeing MPs' conduct. One in three backed the view that the rules should be made law, making breaches a crime investigated by the police and punishable by the criminal courts. By contrast, the then status quo was supported by just 7 per cent.

Nonetheless, the party leaders recognized the strength of public feeling. After an intensive series of meetings, a special Select Committee on Standards in Public Life reported by the middle of July 1995 with a series of proposals – in some cases tidier than Nolan – to set up a Parliamentary Commissioner for Standards and a streamlined new Standards and Privileges Committee to replace the two former committees on Privileges and Members' Interests. The committee was initially deadlocked on controls relating to outside interests and disclosure. This was partly because of doubts over Nolan's loosely worded recommendations, but reflected more a division along party lines. Eventually, at the end of October 1995, the committee recommended in its second report a ban on paid advocacy in Parliament because it regarded the Nolan proposal to prohibit relationships with multi-client consultancies as unworkable. The report argued that the distinction between single and multi-client consultancies was hard to make and that the Nolan committee's attempt to regulate types of outside bodies would not work. Indeed, the select committee's own proposal to concentrate on actions by members went in some respects much further. It recommended a distinction between paid advocacy in Parliament (unacceptable) and paid advice (acceptable provided it is properly registered and declared). However, the Tory majority on the committee rejected proposals from Labour members and the one Liberal Democrat that the amounts involved in providing such advice should be disclosed, as the Nolan report had recommended. The report argued that, given the ban on paid advocacy, which had not been envisaged by Nolan, there should not be a requirement to disclose remuneration. However, a sizeable Tory minority recognized the strength of public feeling on the issue and, in the debate on 6 November 1995, John Biffen supported the disclosure of earnings from consultancies because of the public unease. He warned that MPs should not avoid 'forces outside this chamber'. In the end, twenty-three Conservative backbenchers voted for a Labour amendment requiring disclosure of earnings from consultancies related to membership of the House. This was carried by 322 votes to 271.

The net effect was that the House had to accept substantial changes in its regulatory arrangements against the wishes of a large number of the majority party. The new Parliamentary Commissioner for Standards – Sir Gordon Downey, a distinguished public servant and former Comptroller and Auditor General – was an officer of the House and responsible to the new Standards and Privileges Committee but, in effect, had an independent status and standing. It would be hard for the committee to reject his recommendations. He soon became like a French examining magistrate, deciding whether there was a case to answer. He quickly dealt with a number of minor complaints against MPs over their alleged failure to make a full declaration of outside earnings without involving a lengthy inquiry.

However, the post-Nolan process is flawed: in the operations of the register; in the resources and powers available to the Parliamentary Commissioner; and, above all, in the working of the Standards and Privileges Committee. The basic question of whether the House can adequately regulate itself remains open. First, the new rules over the disclosure of outside financial interests were interpreted in widely differing ways. In particular, some MPs, such as Sir Edward Heath, claimed that their business consultancies had nothing to do with their membership of the Commons, and therefore their earnings did not have to be declared. David Mellor, the former National Heritage Secretary, listed eleven consultancies in the January 1997 register, including a number of leading British companies such as British Aerospace and GKN. He claimed in the 1997 register (p. 99) that: 'It is not now, and never has been a contractual duty, implied or otherwise, that my services are provided in my capacity as an MP. The existence of these contracts is not dependent in any way upon my being an MP, nor does the duration of these contracts bear any relationship to any Parliamentary timetable.' Mr Mellor was never accused of abusing his position to ask questions or do anything of that kind in Parliament on behalf of his clients. The issue was more whether these consultancies arose because of his membership of the Commons, or were separate and would continue if he lost his seat. That claim will be tested since he lost his Putney seat in the whirlwind of 1 May 1997. Before being elected he had been a barrister, not a businessman, though he had converted himself into a businessman–broadcaster after losing office in September 1992. He was only the most candid of those not declaring earnings.

Sir Gordon Downey recorded in his introduction to the 1997 edition of the register that in relation to the declaration of 'fees or benefits from the provision of services in his or her capacity as a Member of Parliament', there 'continue to be apparent inconsistencies in the interpretation of this requirement. At some stage the Select Committee [on Standards and Privileges] may wish to consider whether these are sufficient to justify a review of the guidance and its interpretation.' While informal exchanges do occur between the Parliamentary Commissioner and MPs, the declaration process has proved to be reactive. Only if a formal complaint is made is an investigation triggered. First, as guardian of the register, the Commissioner should be given powers to identify those failing to follow the rules which themselves need to be tightened over the scope for consultancies to be declared. A distinction might perhaps be drawn between a business agreement existing before someone enters the Commons and one agreed later.

Second, the resources and powers available to Sir Gordon Downey have proved inadequate. While he dealt expeditiously with the series of small complaints in the summer of 1996, he was inundated by the weight of paper associated with the cash-for-questions affair. For instance, while its report of March 1997 into the groundless allegations against Michael Howard by Mohammed Al-Fayed amounted to four short paragraphs, the accompanying memorandum from Sir Gordon Downey was a dense and closely argued 118 pages. This was before he – with the help of a QC – had examined the mountain of papers linked to the complaints against Neil Hamilton, Tim Smith and other members. To some extent the Al-Fayed affair is an exception because of the bizarre nature of the allegations and the personalities involved. As Sir Gordon wrote (p. 39) of Al-Fayed and Tiny Rowland, the other main business protagonist in the affair, 'Purchasing information or suborning employees from the opposite camp (or elsewhere) are treated as commonplace. They seem anxious to outbid each other in extravagant claims. Others involved in their affairs – politicians, business associates, employees, official investigators – are all liable to be accused of dishonesty, stupidity or other personal failings.' But however unusual and weird, the saga has raised questions of whether the Commissioner's staff needs to be expanded and whether he should have the power to make his reports public even before they have been considered by the Standards and Privileges Committee. This would enhance his standing and status. The Commissioner should also have greater powers to carry out inquiries on his own initiative, without receiving a formal complaint, though reporting on the results to the committee.

Third, even the streamlined procedures of the Standards and Privileges Committee are defective. The single committee may be smaller but it suffers from the same inherent difficulties of trying to investigate alleged misconduct and then stage what amounts to a trial into the conduct of parliamentary colleagues. Many of the familiar problems remain of issues being decided on partisan grounds. This has been aggravated by the decision to hold hearings in public, which invites playing to the cameras by members of the committee and works against natural justice and proper questioning of the MP under suspicion. These flaws were all too apparent in the inquiry into the behaviour of David Willetts as a junior whip, which led to his resignation as Paymaster General in December 1996 after the Standards and Privileges Committee had criticized his conduct. In his first full week as a whip in October 1994, Mr Willetts had written a silly note about a discussion with Sir Geoffrey Johnson Smith, then chairman of the Members' Interest Committee, which could be taken as implying that he was trying to influence the committee. The obvious explanation was that he was being too eager as a new whip and, in his keenness to impress, he had exaggerated his role. But the words used indicated the attitudes of the Conservative whips at the time towards the Members' Interests Committee. When he gave evidence Mr Willetts exacerbated his position by appearing devious in his answers. His position was fatally undermined when inconsistencies in his evidence were pointed out by Quentin Davies, a fellow Conservative MP who had become increasingly independent-minded after remaining for a decade on the backbenches. The Standards and Privileges Committee concluded (First Report, 1996–7, p. xiii) that 'we cannot accept much of the memorandum submitted to the committee by Mr Willetts, nor much of his oral evidence, as being accurate. We are very concerned that any member should dissemble in his account to the committee and believe that this response by Mr Willetts has substantially aggravated the original offence.' Mr Willetts immediately resigned as a minister, though there was sympathy that he was to some extent a scapegoat rather than a sinner. He was guilty perhaps of hubris and foolishness, and not much more.

In the light of the Willetts case, there was some debate about how the process could be made less partisan and more focused, especially given that the hearings were in public. One step was the decision by Ann Taylor, the Leader of the Commons from May 1997, not to become chairman or serve on the committee herself, as her predecessors had. There is also a strong case for improvements in the methods of inquiry. Following the John Browne case, Michael Ryle, a distinguished former senior Clerk of the Commons with a close interest in parliamentary reform, argued (1990, p. 318) that it would be a mistake for the committee (then the Members' Interests Committee) to attempt to copy the procedures of the courts since its members were not necessarily lawyers and were certainly not neutral. However, following the Willetts case, the Standards and Privileges Committee agreed to take evidence on oath, more like in a court. But if the committee behaved like a court, Ryle suggested, there would be a demand for an appeals procedure, though, in a sense, that existed anyway since the full House has to vote on any punishment of a member. However, he stressed the importance of ensuring natural justice for the member, subject to inquiry, the point of complaint in the Browne case. He suggested that both the complainant and the member should be represented by counsel if they so wished. It might also be desirable to separate the prosecuting and adjudicating roles of the committee so that one member could lay down the facts of the case and lead its examination of witnesses, as the Attorney General previously did on the Committee of Privileges. This view is accepted by at least one of the members who has been publicly investigated by the Standards and Privileges Committee.

There was a lengthy debate during the Nolan inquiry as to how far an independent element should be introduced. Lord Howe of Aberavon argued (vol. 2, p. 469) that there might be a role for 'independent participants in the proceedings, both in the investigation and presentation of matters for consideration and in the pre-final adjudication'. He was backed by a number of constitutional lawyers. But Tony Newton, the then Leader of the Commons, was characteristically cautious (vol. 2, p. 171) in noting that 'there is some potential sensitivity given that we are talking about people whose responsibility is to the electorate, who are accountable to the electorate, in introducing either into committees of the House or into disciplinary procedures some person or body that is appointed rather than elected and could, in some sense therefore, be seen as superior to Parliament'. That point was partly addressed by making the Parliamentary Commissioner for Standards an officer of the House. In so far as these matters remain with the Commons, an important caveat, there are limits to the involvement of outsiders. I believe that it would be hard to introduce non-MPs on to the Standards and Privileges Committee itself. Rather, the committee should adopt a more judicial format, along the lines suggested by Ryle, and the independent element might come with the appointment of a legal assessor to advise the committee who would be allowed also to question witnesses. This would be separate from the role of the Parliamentary Commissioner in conducting the preliminary inquiry. As now, final decisions on whether and how to punish an offending member would be taken by the full House.

But the real question is how far these matters should remain exclusively with the Commons. Can Parliament any longer be left to regulate itself? In particular, should the conduct of MPs be subject to the criminal law and the jurisdiction of the courts? After the cash-for-questions affair, the Nolan report and the well-publicized problems of spring 1997 over the Downey report into the Al-Fayed allegations, it was much harder to argue that MPs should be left to regulate and discipline themselves. There was growing support for the establishment by statute of a commission outside Parliament – like the Independent Commission against Corruption in Hong Kong and similar bodies in other Commonwealth countries – to investigate complaints against the conduct of members and then to make recommendations to the Speaker of the Commons. The House would have the duty of accepting such findings unless it formally voted to overturn them. This would be similar to the work of the election courts, which were established in the nineteenth century to prevent the Commons becoming clogged up with time-consuming arguments over disputed elections, although this was in the days before the secret ballot when bribery was rife. This is an attractive, but flawed, parallel, since the election courts deal with the behaviour of people outside Parliament before they have won a seat rather than what they have allegedly done once they have become members. Any attempt to create a permanent commission to investigate alleged wrongdoing by MPs and other people in public life would be an important constitutional innovation, with wide implications for the role of Parliament. It would be an explicit challenge to parliamentary sovereignty.

Equally tricky issues are raised by the suggestion that bribery involving members should be explicitly made a criminal offence. This would not remove all regulatory matters to an outside body but it would affect parliamentary privilege and the Bill of Rights. The debate turns on both constitutional and practical questions. Defenders of continued self-regulation cloak themselves in Article 9 of the Bill of Rights, protecting freedom of speech in the House from court action and parliamentary privilege. But as Earl Russell, the eminent historian of the seventeenth century, and independent-minded Liberal Democrat peer, pointed out in his evidence to the Nolan inquiry (vol. 2, p. 493):

> It is argued sometimes that any restriction on Parliamentary privilege would infringe Parliamentary sovereignty. I think this is a misunderstanding on what sovereignty is. Sovereignty is the supreme power to make the law; it does not confer an immunity to break the law. That is a point which goes back to the due process clause of Magna Carta. It was brought to the attention of our Kings in a long, long series of conflicts – finally very reluctantly accepted. I think saying that Parliament is sovereign and saying that Parliament must keep the law are not incompatible propositions.

But the Bill of Rights has acted as a powerful constraint on laws affecting MPs. The Salmon Commission argued that neither the statute nor the common law relating to bribery applied to members. Under legislation passed in 1889, 1906 and 1916, neither the Commons nor the Lords counts as a public body, nor does membership of Parliament constitute a public office for the purposes of the common-law offence of misuse of public office. According to Salmon, this left acts of bribery involving MPs as matters of privilege for either House. That is why the commission recommended that corruption and bribery of members, acting in their parliamentary capacity, should come under criminal law. It put to one side the traditional objection, arguing that 'Article 9 is a charter for freedom of speech in House, it is not a charter for corruption.' That is both sensible and correct, but it still requires legislation to limit the application of the Bill of Rights.

However, the widespread view that MPs could not be prosecuted under existing law was challenged in a case brought in 1992 against Harry Greenway, a Tory MP. This was dropped because of flaws in the charges. But, in preliminary hearings, Mr Justice Buckley challenged the Salmon Commission's interpretation and ruled that an MP did hold public office (as quoted in Robertson, 1997). The judge maintained that it was a common-law crime for an MP to take a bribe and that Article 9 of the Bill of Rights was not a bar to prosecution. He argued:

> That a Member of Parliament against whom there is a *prima facie* case of corruption should be immune from prosecution in the courts of law is, to my mind, an unacceptable proposition at the present time. . . . The Committee of Privileges is not an appropriate or experienced body to pass sentence. Why should a Member be deprived of a jury and an experienced judge to consider his guilt or innocence and, if appropriate, sentence? Why should the public be similarly deprived?

Geoffrey Robertson, a flamboyant barrister, who had acted for the *Guardian* in the abortive Hamilton and Greer libel action, argued that this ruling was authoritative and it was 'astonishing' that the Al-Fayed allegations against Smith and Hamilton had 'never been properly investigated by the police or the Director of Public Prosecutions'. The Nolan committee was aware of this case, but apparently felt that it was not conclusive since it had never been tested in the higher courts. Its report argued (vol. 1, p. 43) that 'it is likely that members of Parliament who accepted bribes in connection with their parliamentary duties would be committing common law offences which could be tried by the courts. Doubt exists as to whether the courts or Parliament have jurisdiction in such cases.' Consequently, the committee recommended that 'the Government should now take steps to clarify the law relating to the bribery of, or the receipt of a bribe by, a Member of Parliament'.

A Home Office discussion paper in December 1996 on the law relating to bribery of MPs accepted that the existing position was ambiguous. Moreover, even if corrupt acts involving members of the Commons were likely to constitute the common law offence of misuse of public office in England and Wales (though not in Scotland), 'some evidence which might be necessary to establish the guilt or innocence of a member might not be available to the courts by virtue of Article 9 of the Bill of Rights'. That is the flaw in Robertson's case; even if a legal action can be brought against a member, it is unlikely to succeed because of the current inability to cite what an MP has done within Parliament. Unless parliamentary privilege is altered to permit the use of such evidence relating to what is said or done in the Commons or Lords, allegations about the bribery of a member are likely to fail.

The problem has been highlighted by two recent cases. The House of Lords decided in Pepper v. Hart in 1993 that the courts were entitled to refer to Hansard reports of the parliamentary passage of domestic primary legislation as an aid to interpretation, despite objections by the Attorney General that this would breach Article 9 and infringe parliamentary privilege. However, the Lords ruling was strictly limited and was just about interpreting ambiguous legislation and the use of Hansard for reference purposes. The courts cannot use evidence of reports to impugn parliamentary conduct since this would undermine the basic tenet of Article 9 that a member can speak freely without fear that what he or she has said will later be used in court. In Prebble v. TV New Zealand in 1994, the Privy Council held that it was an infringement of parliamentary privilege for anyone involved in legal proceedings to question words spoken or actions taken in Parliament by suggesting that they were untrue, misleading or instigated for improper motives. Since the defendant intended to rely upon what had been said and done in the New Zealand House of Representatives and to question such statements, this would have breached Article 9. Moreover, even while privilege can be waived, breaches of Article 9 cannot be. Consequently, if members are to be prosecuted for accepting bribes to ask questions or otherwise to affect their conduct in Parliament, the member's parliamentary conduct will become a live issue in the case and there will be a breach of Article 9 and of parliamentary privilege. This led to the conclusion in the Home Office paper that an offence of bribery involving an MP might be feasible if it were subject to the consent, or conversely objection, by the relevant House, and reports of parliamentary conduct or speech could not be used in evidence by the prosecution or defence. The offence would need to be made out without recourse to such material.

The Home Office paper discussed various options: from relying, as now, solely on parliamentary privilege to deal with accusations of bribery; subjecting members to the present corruption statutes in full; distinguishing between conduct that should be dealt with by the criminal law and that which should be left to Parliament itself; and making criminal proceedings subject to the approval of the relevant House. The first has been shown to be deeply flawed, both over methods of investigation and sanctions, while the second, though feasible, raises all the issues discussed above about the use of reports of parliamentary conduct or speech in evidence in inferring motives for the conduct of a member. However, in an ironic twist, the Bill of Rights was amended in the Defamation Act of 1995, at the direct instigation of Neil Hamilton and his supporters, to give him the option of waiving its application to themselves, at their own request, in defamation cases. However, a similar arrangement in criminal cases would not work if the decision whether or not to waive the application of the Bill of Rights was left to the member, in effect allowing the member to prevent evidence of his or her guilt being put before the court but allowing evidence in his or her favour to be considered. However, a general waiver for cases of bribery might be possible.

The suggestion that the relevant House of Parliament would itself decide whether criminal charges should be brought in a particular case of alleged corruption, or whether the issue should be dealt with by the House itself, looks unworkable. It would put an enormous onus on the House, and, as the discussion paper pointed out, 'It might be seen by the public as importing a political element into prosecution decisions. It would be particularly difficult presentationally if a decision to allow, or not to allow, a criminal prosecution were seen to have been taken on party political lines. There could be a suspicion that members of

the majority party were less likely to face prosecution than others.'
In most Continental parliaments, the legislature does decide whether
charges against members should be brought before the courts, but it
is often a political process and risks undermining respect for members
and the House. Moreover, a decision could not be taken until after there
had been a full investigation, and discussion, which might prejudice any
later criminal proceedings.

The most plausible option would be to attempt to distinguish conduct
that should be dealt with by the criminal law and that which should
be left to Parliament itself. This would involve each House determining
in precise terms – and much more precisely than now – which sorts of
conduct should be dealt with as breaches of privilege and which under
criminal law. The courts would then have to decide whether the conduct in that case was covered by the resolution of the House. There
would be bound to be some tricky initial judgments on where the
boundaries lie.

Defenders of self-regulation have a point over the difficulty of draw-
ing a line. There is a variety of practical questions. Who would lay the
charge before the court? Are current rules of conduct on outside earnings (even post-Nolan) too imprecise for court action rather than disciplinary action by your parliamentary colleagues? Indeed, many of the
payments received, or allegedly received, by members in recent controversies may have been unacceptable and against the post-Nolan rules,
but they would not be classified as bribes and thus liable to the criminal
law. Many entirely legal payments for consultancies are considered
improper if they are paid to members when related to their parliamentary activities. But they are not bribes as such. The post-Nolan distinctions are still imprecise. Not only is a better definition of permitted
and prohibited arrangements necessary, but it is questionable whether
the police and the courts should be involved in charges against members
over activities and payments banned by Parliament but which are perfectly legal if undertaken by non-MPs. If the law on corruption and
bribery is to be clarified, as it must be, MPs should be treated in the
same way in the criminal law and the courts as everyone else, whatever
disciplinary code is adopted and regulated by the Commons itself.
Non-criminal disciplinary matters should be kept out of the courts.

In any case, court action can be lengthy and costly, even though
recent inquiries in the Commons have hardly been swift. This might

anyway make the rules inflexible. There would also be problems if the charges appeared politically motivated. This would not only challenge the sovereignty and authority of Parliament, but also the independence and neutrality of the judiciary. There are objections to judges becoming involved in the day-to-day regulation of the practices and conduct of members. But this should not prevent serious allegations, such as bribery and corruption involving members, from becoming criminal offences to be judged in the courts, as applies with every other member of the public. This would leave the Commons and the Lords with the responsibility of handling other disciplinary and privilege matters, albeit with improved procedures and an independent investigatory and advisory element. The post-Nolan framework needs tightening up, but that is not a case for abandoning self-regulation totally. The courts should be involved only with crimes, not ordinary disciplinary matters. The House must decide and police its own rules, albeit with more outside help. In many respects, the Al-Fayed saga was exceptional, and a new parliament should be given the chance to show whether it can deal swiftly and, if necessary, toughly with other serious breaches of its rules on financial misconduct.

That is why it is not straightforward just to make bribery of MPs a criminal offence, or 'Government Declares War on Sleaze' as the Home Office press release baldly stated in June 1997. The Home Office published a consultative paper on 'The Prevention of Corruption', outlining a new offence of corruption covering both the public and private sectors and extending current, and often confusing, statutes to cover misuse of public office. This raises a variety of legal questions about a possible reversal of the burden of proof – for instance, (p. 5) 'where a person is expected to exercise impartial judgment, it is arguable that that person should order his or her private affairs in such a way as to avoid any impression of corrupt activity. It may be reasonable therefore to expect a person in these circumstances to justify any questionable payments made to them.' But the major questions are about parliamentary privilege; and the Government simultaneously announced the setting up of a joint committee of both Houses to review the purpose and extent of privilege, including the whole relationship between Parliament and the courts. As Ann Taylor, Leader of the Commons, said in a statement when the consultation document was issued: 'The basic protection of freedom of speech in Parliament is very important and must be retained. However, the way in which parliamentary privilege works can prevent the courts from looking at issues where there is public interest for them to be scrutinized.' Noting that in recent years the boundaries between Parliament and the courts have been redrawn in response to particular events – such as amending the Defamation Act – she said that this and other changes had 'taken place without a fundamental review of how Parliament's legal immunities operate alongside the courts'. This shows again how apparently desirable individual measures can have much wider implications for Parliament than are at first realized – and how the challenges to the position of Parliament have to be considered not in isolation but as part of a wider picture of political and constitutional change.

CHAPTER SEVEN

The Media

'It would be shocking to have debates in this House forestalled, time after time, by expressions of opinion by persons who had not the status or responsibility of MPs . . . on this new robot organization of television and BBC broadcasting.'

Sir Winston Churchill, 1955

'The decline in press coverage of Parliament must have a serious effect on the public's understanding of our democratic system.'

Jack Straw, 1993

The main arena of British political debate is now the broadcasting studio rather than the chamber of the House of Commons. For many older MPs the decreasing attention paid to debates in the chamber is one of the most significant, and regrettable, changes of the past generation. Politicians and the media have both altered and adjusted their behaviour so that the proceedings in Parliament, and particularly on the floor of the House, are now merely one, subsidiary, feature of political coverage in the media. Television has become a direct means for political leaders to communicate with the public and speaking in the House of Commons is merely one way of doing so – and by no means the most satisfactory one for politicians eager to define the terms on which they appear since their words are juxtaposed with those of their opponents.

On big days when an important story is breaking, the chamber is often deserted and even the members' lobby just outside the chamber, the Rialto for gossip between MPs and journalists, can be fairly empty, certainly of those in the know. Instead, the assiduous journalist will wander across the road to College Green, or a hundred yards away to

4 Millbank, the home of the studios of the BBC, ITN and Sky. Ministers and their shadows will be found there in a round of interviews. Jean Seaton, an academic with an acute understanding of relations between politicians and media, has talked (1997) of 'a geographical effect ... television has shifted the location of political happenings from legislatures and conference halls to where television discussions and interviews take place'. She has described 'the windswept triangle of grass' of College Green as

> a nationally recognized platform, and part of the unwritten constitution. It is a very rule-governed triangle: it is understood, for example, that it is here that parliamentarians offer instant opinions about each other under the dominant broadcasting regulation of political balance. The sense of a parliamentary environment and backcloth – outside the House, but also outside a studio – offers a necessary informal intimacy and neutrality, before MPs rush back into the House.

Similarly, when a major policy initiative is to be launched, it will invariably have been leaked/previewed in that morning's newspapers. The relevant minister will have appeared on the *Today* programme on Radio Four. It is hardly surprising therefore that, apart from the annual Budget, the Commons chamber is usually sparsely attended for the subsequent statement by the minister about the details of the new plan. Stephen Dorrell sounded faintly ludicrous in March 1997 when, during a breakfast-time interview, he said rather huffily that it was the custom for ministers to give details of a White Paper to the Commons rather than on the *Today* programme. Why then had he agreed to appear on the day that the White Paper was being published? And why then had he set out the broad outlines of his proposals? Even the fiction that ministers first report to Parliament was looking pretty tattered.

When a newly elected MP asked me, after the 1997 election, whether anything he said in the chamber would be reported, I said no. He would only attract media attention by his activities outside the chamber, writing pamphlets for think tanks and articles in the press, or participating in broadcasts. His speeches and interventions on the floor of the House were basically aimed at his parliamentary colleagues, and particularly his party whips. They were to show that he was a sound, hard-working chap, who deserved favours and promotion. A solid performance in the chamber is necessary to impress other MPs, not to achieve public prominence or to build up a reputation. But since the first steps on the ladder of promotion are usually thanks to the whips, such activity in the chamber is still necessary, even if it is largely ignored by the press and the broadcasters.

Two parallel changes have occurred: the increasing dominance of television and radio in political debates and the declining attention paid to Parliament itself. Until forty years ago, there was a formal rule banning the discussion of issues on radio and television that were due to come before either chamber over the following fortnight. The fourteen-day rule was a wartime invention, initially maintained afterwards by an informal gentlemen's agreement. In 1953 a formal request by the governors of the BBC for the ban to be lifted was rejected by the Government. The issue came to a head two years later when a group of MPs on a popular live discussion programme, *In the News*, publicly criticized the restrictions on free debate resulting from the ban. Some Liberal MPs then tabled an early-day motion in February 1955 saying that 'This House, which is the servant of a people which cherishes its right of free discussion, deplores the ban . . .' But the restriction was supported by both the main party leaders. The comments of Sir Winston Churchill quoted at the beginning of this chapter were echoed by Clement Attlee, then about to step down as Labour leader after twenty years: the authority of Parliament should be sustained as 'the main forum of discussion'. Churchill himself was never publicly interviewed on radio or television during his final premiership from 1951 until 1955.

So, when, in July 1955, the BBC said it would abandon the fourteen-day rule unless formally instructed otherwise, the Government duly obliged. The order came from, of all people, Charles Hill, who had first come to public notice in the 1940s as the mellifluous Radio Doctor. He was then Postmaster General and was later to complete a unique double as chairman of both the Independent Television Authority and the BBC. But, in July 1955, he issued a formal diktat to both the BBC and the fledgling ITA (whose stations were about to start broadcasting) that no discussion or *ex parte* statement should be broadcast during the fortnight before a political issue was debated in either House of Parliament. Moreover, when legislation was introduced in Parliament on any subject, no broadcast by an MP might be made between the introduction of the legislation and the time when it either received the Royal Assent or was withdrawn or dropped. That would have ruled out any of the current radio and television current-affairs programmes. No *Today*, *World at One*, *PM*, *World Tonight*, *Newsnight*, *Breakfast with Frost*, *On the Record*. The Dimbleby brothers and the Snow cousins would have been redundant. Coverage in the 1950s was still largely on politicians' terms, not just because of the restrictions on the broadcasters but also because, as Anthony Seldon has written (1981, p. 425) about the final Churchill administration, 'Many of the journalists themselves, compared to their successors a decade later, were comparatively docile and deferential to establishment figures.' Senior ministers were socially and personally distant from working journalists. There was little attempt to probe differences within the cabinet and there was only limited news about Churchill's declining health.

The fourteen-day rule, the symbol of that more restrictive era, did not long outlast the departure of Churchill and Attlee. As with so much else in British politics, the Suez crisis of autumn 1956 proved to be the turning point. As Michael Cockerell has written in his absorbing history of prime ministers and television *Live from Number 10* (1988, p. 51), 'With the crisis dominating parliamentary business every day for weeks on end, the television companies decided completely to ignore the rule.' As the crisis ended, the Government suspended the rule for six months and then, in July 1957, it was suspended indefinitely by Harold Macmillan, the first British prime minister to exploit television properly. Indeed, the Suez crisis, when the Government was strongly criticized by many newspapers, triggered a generally more assertive style of journalism, linked to the appearance of a better educated and less deferential generation of lobby journalists (see Seldon, 1981, p. 425).

At the same time, the caution of the BBC about reporting on politics was being challenged by the arrival of independent television. The BBC had been wary of covering election campaigns at all, apart from the results programmes pioneered by the perennially enthusiastic David Butler, who has done more than almost anyone else to explain politics by linking the academic, political and media worlds. The BBC took a cautious view of the 1949 Representation of the People Act. That interpretation was challenged by the new Granada television station and by ITN in covering the Rochdale by-election in 1958. This opened the way for full coverage of general elections from 1959 onwards and of by-elections. At the same time, broadcasters were becoming more adventurous and demanding in their interviews, led by Robin Day in his lifelong role as questioner on behalf of the viewing and listening public. Current-affairs programmes such as *Panorama* and the early-evening *Tonight* built up high viewing figures as well as respect for their professionalism. Their success was followed in the early 1960s by much greater irreverence towards politicians, epitomized in the self-conscious satire 'boom' of the late Macmillan years when *Private Eye* was founded and *That Was the Week That Was* briefly flourished on television.

However, it took the best part of two decades for the now familiar format of news and current-affairs programmes to develop. It was not until the early 1980s that breakfast television and Channel Four arrived and not until the 1990s that news became a twenty-four-hour-a-day phenomenon with the appearance of Sky. The demands of these programmes forced politicians to respond. Their own handling of television became more sophisticated, partly after observing and imitating American campaigning techniques. Terms like sound-bite, instant or rapid rebuttal, news cycle and the ludicrous 'spin doctor' (since they have neither the subtlety of spin bowlers nor the professionalism of doctors) became part of the jargon of the media and of the grandly titled communications directors of the parties, who had previously been known as press secretaries.

Politicians have adapted to the demands of the broadcasters. The snappy and catchy are preferred over the reflective and considered. Pictures are better than words, personalities than policies. Rows, scandals and crises are more likely to catch attention than analyses, differences of nuance and emphasis and changes in procedure. Politicians and their media advisers have become skilled at conveying their messages in ways appealing to the broadcasters. Inevitably, the more deliberative way that Parliament functions is less glamorous, less newsworthy. Important legislation can go through largely unnoticed unless there is a rebellion. Coverage is dominated by Prime Minister's Questions, after May 1997 just once a week, to the exclusion of almost everything else unless a minister is in trouble. PM's Questions has become the best known Commons activity since sound broadcasting was introduced from the House in 1978 and the television cameras were admitted in 1989 (after a lengthy debate which divided members in all the main parties). On the main evening news bulletins, a short clip from PM's Questions is often the only direct reference to anything that has happened in Parliament and it normally features as just one part of a report covering all aspects of an issue. In many respects, this is justified since the parliamentary exchanges are often less significant than what has happened and what is said outside Westminster on a particular issue – whether it be by the head of an executive agency, a company chairman, a trade-union leader (less during the Tory years) or a spokesman for a pressure group. In terms of the main television coverage, events in Parliament are now just one aspect of political news.

Television has reduced the role of the political party as an intermediary between leaders and voters, according to Colin Seymour-Ure (1994), a long-standing observer of the relations between politicians and the media. It has also played up the importance of leaders themselves, and, in particular, the Leader. He has argued somewhat optimistically that, 'The threat that television might bypass Parliament was more from MPs preferring the studio to the chamber than from MPs being shut out of television altogether. Even so, the televising of the Commons came not a moment too soon for the institution's reputation.' It has been a double-edged blessing, as I argue above, in emphasizing atypical aspects of the work of the House like Prime Minister's Questions, though these are the events best attended by members. The arrival of the cameras was fully justified on democratic grounds – voters should be able to see their MPs and hear what they say. Moreover, the impact on the House and on the behaviour of members has been less than was predicted beforehand by the opponents of televising the House – apart from relatively trivial and short-lived features like 'dough-nutting', when members sit deliberately behind the MP speaking and so appear in camera shot. Initially over-restrictive rules of coverage, insisting just on head-and-shoulder shots of the member speaking, were in time relaxed to allow more reaction shots and views of the chamber. The Parliament Channel on cable television provides a straight, unedited report, like C-Span in the USA, but it is only available to a minority and is for political buffs. Some of the television companies provide good weekly programmes on events in Parliament, but these are generally shown at inconvenient times – more out of a sense of duty by the broadcasters than out of a belief that they will capture a big audience. Occasionally, when someone at the centre of a current controversy is questioned by a select committee, the hearings are shown more widely on the main news bulletins. This has been one of the successes of televising Parliament, not least in that it has given a chance for lesser known backbenchers to make an impact. Televising the Commons may have increased interest in what goes on, but there is little evidence that it has reversed the decline in the standing of Parliament. The cameras may have added to the pressure for reform, as Suzanne Franks and Adam Vandermark have argued (1995), both because of the apparent incomprehensibility of some of the proceedings and the raucousness of big setpiece occasions. 'Practices and procedures which appear sensible and logical to insiders may not appear so when viewed by outsiders.' There is pressure to cut out the jargon; and Budget speeches have been shorter since the arrival of the cameras. But Westminister-based coverage on Radio Four is being cut.

Over the past twenty years, there has also been a huge change in the way Parliament is reported in the press. The most dramatic development has been the virtual disappearance of direct gallery coverage, that is full reports on what is said on the floor of the House, on dedicated parliamentary pages. In 1992, Jack Straw, then a member of Labour's shadow cabinet with a close interest in the media, organized a study of the quantity of press reporting of Parliament over a sixty-year period. This study (summarized in the *British Journalism Review*, 1993) showed that the systematic daily reporting of parliamentary debates, what was said on the floor of the Commons, in broadsheet papers had dropped very sharply. In *The Times*, the daily coverage of Parliament varied between 450 and 1,050 lines on a series of sample dates between the early 1930s and the late 1980s, and was often nearer the upper end. In the *Guardian*, the average was between 300 and 700 lines. But by 1992, the year of the study, fewer than 100 lines a day were dedicated to the proceedings of Parliament in either *The Times* or the *Guardian*, and since then the total has dropped. The same broad trend was confirmed in a more recent study by Bob Franklin (1996), using a slightly different definition of coverage.

The decline in traditional direct reporting on what is said in Parliament, gallery coverage, began during the 1980s. As political editor of the *Financial Times* between 1981 and 1988, I played a role in the change by ending the traditional distinction between the gallery coverage and lobby stories, which provide background and descriptions of activities outside the chamber. Frequently, what was said in the chamber fitted in as a few paragraphs within a broader political story also including remarks broadcast on television, a lobby (that is, non-attributable) comment by a minister or backbencher and interpretation of the implications. In this period on the *FT*'s Parliament and Politics page, there was usually a mix of such stories plus one or two more traditional gallery reports. Even in *The Times*, home for so long of the dedicated parliamentary page, the balance had begun to shift during the 1980s. I believed, and still believe, that such a mix offers the reader a fuller picture of what is going on in politics. However, even the few remaining gallery reporters had become extinct by the early 1990s. The most dramatic change came in 1990 when Simon Jenkins, the new editor of *The Times*, scrapped its full parliamentary page. As he later told the Nolan inquiry (First Report of Nolan Committee 1995, vol. 2, p. 7): 'I stopped it because I couldn't find who read it apart from MPs. We are not there to provide a public service for a particular profession, or, for that matter, for a particular legislative chamber.' Simon Jenkins overstated his case. He was right that no broadsheet paper exists to be the house journal of any interest. But the question is, rather, whether the virtual abandonment of gallery coverage has deprived readers of information about an important part of the political debate. Brian Mawhinney, who had an abrasive relationship with the media, as with everyone else, when he was Conservative Party chairman, remarked in a thoughtful lecture in February 1996 that:

'It is ironic to note that journalists operating without access to word processors or even typewriters, without computerized printing presses, without anything more sophisticated than the most primitive form of hot metal, were a century ago able to provide the voting public of their time with a dramatically better account of events in Parliament than any voter can gain today. And since commentators are wont to lament, from time to time, that no modern politician has the public impact of Gladstone or Disraeli, may not a politician occasionally note that no speech delivered in parliament today would receive even a tenth of the coverage given to the Grand Old Man and his rival?'

The sharp decline in reporting by the press of what is said by MPs on the floor of the House has led to widespread criticism of this kind, and questioning of the role of the parliamentary press gallery. The press has no legal right to report on Parliament and, indeed, newspaper coverage is still theoretically a breach of privilege (as was discussed in a still pertinent report on conditions by a Parliamentary Press Gallery Committee in 1964). Journalists based at Westminster continue to believe that they are allowed on the premises on sufferance. Unlike all other staff working in the Palace of Westminster, the press has no formal representation on any of the management committees and relies on informal contacts over space and accreditation.

The change has occurred for a variety of reasons. First, and most important, is that the focus of political debate has shifted outside the chamber to select committees, news conferences and broadcasting studios. There is, of course, an element of chicken and egg here. Politicians are more reluctant to say anything of importance in the chamber because they know they are unlikely to be reported, and papers report less because nothing of importance is said there. It is striking, for example, that two of the best contemporary Commons performers – Kenneth Clarke and Gordon Brown, the Chancellor and Shadow Chancellor for most of the 1992–7 parliament – engaged almost entirely in knockabout when they faced each other in the House a few times a year. They had fun, to amuse themselves and the two or three dozen members in the chamber. None of Mr Brown's series of major speeches changing Labour's economic policies was made in the Commons. They were all made outside Parliament, and usually trailed beforehand in the press.

Jack Straw himself suggested (1993) that the change also reflected the impact of the televising of the Commons from the autumn of 1989; the relative unimportance of events in the chamber during Lady Thatcher's heyday in the 1980s; a generational change among the political editors of broadsheets and a consequent change in the behaviour of MPs. As Straw pointed out, 'In the near absence of any coverage of chamber speeches which they make, MPs have resorted more and more to the press release in a bid to get their views publicized.' Paradoxically, the arrival of television cameras in the chamber has mattered less for what is now shown of proceedings on the floor of the House than because of the associated creation of the Millbank television and radio studios within five minutes' walk of the members' lobby. This has made it much easier for MPs to give broadcast interviews. Politicians value time in these studios more highly than when they are on their feet in the chamber because they know that what they say on television and radio is likely to have a greater impact and to reach more of their constituents. Moreover, the press can fairly say that they are only following the example of members themselves. Attendance by MPs in the chamber has dropped sharply, apart from prime-time slots like Question Time. This trend has been aggravated by the availability of a direct feed of the proceedings on the floor of the House on television sets in the office of every member, and incidentally also the press galleries. Sir Terence Higgins, one of the parliamentary stalwarts of the past thirty years, complained in his valedictory report as chairman of the Liaison Committee (First Report, 1996–7, p. 4) that the provision of sets has had 'a major impact on attendance in the chamber . . . Members have tended to remain in their rooms, from time to time watching television coverage of the floor of the House while working on constituency matters.'

Most political journalists, particularly of the younger generation, welcomed the shift in emphasis of coverage, while regretting the complete disappearance of gallery stories (as I still do). Replying to Jack Straw's paper, I argued (1993) that the reduction in coverage of exchanges on the floor of the House did not reflect any overall reduction in political coverage. The balance had changed with more coverage of select committees, behind-the-scenes manoeuvres, what is happening in Whitehall (every broadsheet has a correspondent dedicated to Whitehall) and to what is happening within the political parties. The public, I wrote, 'now knows more of what is going on as the result of assiduous work by reporters in the lobbies than would ever be gleaned by sitting in the press gallery'. I am now less sanguine.

Both the quantity and quality of coverage of politics has declined since the early 1990s. And this is not just because of the virtual disappearance of direct gallery reporting of speeches on the floor of the House. The main reason is the change in approach of all the main broadsheet papers. This reflects the impact of the price war and increased competition, both among newspapers and with television and other media outlets. It has put a premium on items that are believed to attract new, and younger, readers. Detailed political coverage is low on that list, reducing the amount of space devoted to politics in all its forms. The news and feature, though not opinion, pages of all the main broadsheets are now aimed at attracting a wider and younger market with shorter, more easily digestible stories. Select committees, if they appear, have to live alongside the Spice Girls. More serious analysis has to co-exist with snappy personality stories and pictures that appeal to casual readers. The critics argue that most papers have moved down-market with the '*Daily Mail*ization' of their news and night desks. Bob Franklin noted (1996) an increasing emphasis on scandal and miscon-duct rather than policy issues such as health, education or law and order, or, I would add, questions of procedure and structure. The 'backbench' on newspapers that decides which stories appear generally prefers scandal and personalities to analysis and policy, though the latter still appear in truncated form. The outrageous is more likely to be reported than the significant if it is less newsworthy in conventional terms. Publicity-conscious MPs now know that to attract coverage, they need to include catchy sound-bites in press releases or in broadcast interviews.

Bob Franklin highlighted other trends: a growing preoccupation with the activities of government and senior politicians to the relative neglect of backbenchers and minority parties (the Liberal Democrats have had to struggle constantly for coverage except when they win by-elections); an increasingly critical tone, 'more polarized, less measured and less willing to be neutral in its appraisals of parliamentary affairs'; and parliamentarians are given few opportunities to express their views directly through quotations.

The overall result is that political coverage is less comprehensive than before. But this is about much more than the decline in direct gallery reporting of what is said in the chamber, with which MPs are perhaps understandably concerned. The real question is whether the overall quality of reporting has declined: whether the public knows as much as they should about what is happening in politics. There are gains. Analysis of political trends and of detailed policy is better than twenty or thirty years ago, in part because of the rise of respected specialist correspondents. The debate within government on key issues, like Europe, is more fully reported. Some big parliamentary stories are still covered reasonably well in the main broadsheets and on the main current-affairs programmes, even if accounts of what is said in the House are only a minor part of reports. On a few important occasions, when there is a big vote or an important subject is being debated, *The Times* will still offer a traditional gallery story of several hundred words.

Revealingly, these reports have recently been as often from the Lords as from the Commons.

However, the coverage in most papers lacks depth and context, as well as being squeezed in size. Personality differences are exaggerated. Every dispute becomes a split. Every small shift in position becomes a humiliating climbdown. Stories about policy developments, the activities of backbench groups, the work of think tanks, new initiatives from backbenchers and even who is doing well are given a low priority. There is little consistency or follow-up. Readers may be told about a story for the few days when it is big news in conventional terms – of a row, scandal or possible ministerial resignation – but they are seldom told what happens then. For instance, the report by Sir Richard Scott on the supply of arms-related equipment to Iraq dominated the headlines for two or three weeks in February 1996. There was speculation about its contents before its publication; massive coverage on the day itself, despite the very short time to absorb and produce stories, let alone detailed analyses; and the report was at the centre of attention for more than ten days afterwards. There was pressure on Sir Nicholas Lyell and William Waldegrave to resign. This lasted until the Government won the subsequent Commons debate by one vote, and the two ministers survived. But from then onwards there was virtual silence, even though the report raised important issues about arms-sales policy, the handling of intelligence and of government information in trials and, not least, ministerial accountability to Parliament. Only a very few journalists interested in constitutional matters, or Scott report buffs, followed the subsequent investigation by the Public Services Committee of the Commons and its discussions about a formal resolution defining ministerial accountability (which I discussed in Chapter Four). This patchy treatment is typical of many matters with procedural or constitutional implications. Parliamentary reform is virtually ignored in the press.

Few would dispute that the focus of attention, of the public and many MPs themselves, has moved away from the chamber. Parliament itself has seemed less important in relation to other sources of power, such as Europe, the judges and the new public-sector bodies. In that respect, the media are following rather than setting trends. The parties have also changed their approaches. Their media strategists are less concerned with the Commons. For them what happens in the Palace of Westminster is now just one part of the permanent campaign. When Tony Blair became prime minister in May 1997 and replied to John Major in the first of the weekly thirty-minute sessions, he joked that he could hardly complain about one obvious 'sound-bite' question designed for the evening news bulletins since he had done much the same himself. A conscious part of Labour's pre-election tactics was to ensure that Blair also deployed a catchy 'sound-bite' phrase in his second or third question, and success was measured by whether it appeared in the early and main evening news bulletins.

There is a danger of exaggerating the influence of such media strategies, and the role of 'spin doctors'. A mini-industry has grown up – notably among current and former BBC correspondents – writing about media manipulation (most thoroughly in Nicholas Jones, 1995). There is a risk of the employees of Auntie sounding like archetypal maiden aunts protesting about heavy-handed molestation by lascivious party press officers. The broadcasters do face greater pressures than newspapers because of their prominence as well as the legal constraints on balance under which they operate. But this case is really just a 1990s' version of the complaints made in the 1980s about manipulation of the lobby and management of news by Sir Bernard Ingham, Margaret Thatcher's chief press secretary. Sir Bernard could, and often did, bluster, but he was essentially the Prime Minister's voice. It was up to journalists to put his 'bunkum and balderdash' into context. Complaints about manipulation in lobby briefings ignore the more open world of television-dominated politics. The critics also often fail to distinguish between the daily briefings by 10 Downing Street, which are usually about the routine details of the Prime Minister's day, and the access enjoyed by accredited lobby correspondents at Westminster – notably the conversations that take place in the members' lobby on an unattributable basis. But such conversations are really only the free exchange that exists between any group of journalists and their sources, and has always existed. Peter Hennessy and David Walker, leading scourges of the lobby system, quote (in Seaton and Pimlott, 1987) the comments of Joseph Chamberlain about a cabinet discussion in November 1880 on 'the subject of communication between Cabinet ministers and the press'. He noted that 'several of the ministers were in intimate connection with Editors of newspapers' and 'it was pointed out that without special intercourse it was impossible to secure in the press an adequate defence of the decisions and policy of the Government'. Or, alternatively, the newspapers were able to inform their readers about the debate inside the Gladstone cabinet.

The critics of the lobby system and of spin doctors assume that the media are merely passive and uncritical recipients of news; that they cannot and do not seek alternative views and interpretations. But the Lobby, the common collective term for accredited correspondents, is not an uncritical mass. It is not just, though it can be, merely a conduit for news management. One of the joys of being a political journalist is the multiplicity of sources. Not only is the opposing party eager to present its view, but any minister, even a prime minister, has rivals who want to put over their side. Admittedly, the process can become ridiculous with press officers – so much more prosaic, if less sinister, than 'spin doctors' – of the parties following each other round the corridors and crammed rooms of the press gallery. They offer instant rebuttal and preview speeches and even party-election broadcasts the day before they happen. There are risks here: a press officer can create a sense of dependency by promising a preview of a future event or initiative, but only to those who do not rock the boat. And political reporters, and news desks, are always frightened of not having covered a story, however trivial. The night logs of newspapers are generally exercises in protecting the backs of those concerned, so that one paper always 'matches' the stories in another. Competition can produce sameness rather than diversity.

Similar complaints about the decline in quantity and quality of media coverage have been made in the USA over the treatment of Congress. A collection of essays published by the American Enterprise Institute and the Brookings Institution (edited by Thomas Mann and Norman Ornstein) noted (1994, p. 4) that, while Congress has always been criticized, the tone has become much more unfavourable in recent years. 'Stories focus on scandal, rivalry, and conflict to the exclusion of policy and legislative process. They routinely portray members of Congress as self-interested, self-indulgent politicians who exploit the process for personal gain.' Moreover, the amount of political coverage on the three main networks has declined from an average of 124 stories a month between 1972 and 1978 to 42 a month between 1986 and 1992. Until the mid-1980s, the networks broadcast on their main evening bulletins about thirteen stories on policy matters for each report on ethical lapses, but since then they have shown nearly one story involving scandal for every three on issues. This partly reflects a shift in power from Washington bureaux to head offices, commercial pressures from new corporate owners, changing technologies and softer definitions of news.

But these reflect more general worries about the changing nature of political coverage. John Deardourff, a veteran American media consultant, has noted (1996) several adverse trends, which are also true in Britain: excess cynicism, bordering on outright contempt for politics and candidates; preoccupation with the horse-race dimensions of campaigns; and the narrowing of the circle of privacy around the personal lives of candidates and other public officials. In short, the press has become less interested in the substance of political debate, particularly matters of process and organization, and has concentrated more on personality and scandal. This is, in part, an unfortunate by-product of the Bob Woodward/Carl Bernstein investigative tradition, which encouraged a whole generation of journalists and television producers – in Britain as much as in the USA – to have contempt for politicians and little interest in policy and institutional arguments.

Another serious concern is the degree to which the press itself has become more partisan. Of course, newspapers have often, even usually, taken sides in the party battle: in the nineteenth century and in the early decades of this century, a few papers were subsidized by the parties. Columnists and commentators, like myself since 1991, have been employed by papers to express our views and not just to report the news. Our function is both to be opinionated and to give insight into developing debates within government and opposition (by far the best discussion of the distinctive role of political columnists is in Tunstall, 1996). There has also been a lengthy debate (in Linton, 1996, and Curtice, 1997) about the influence of the press on the results of elections. I believe the press reinforces opinions rather than creates them, and its influence is over a long period of years rather than during the few weeks of an election campaign. The line taken by newspapers in leaders also follows the views of readers more than is commonly supposed. But the nature of the partisanship has changed. Papers, and some journalists, have not been content to report and to analyse but have sought to be part of the process. This has been shown vividly by the rise of Euro-sceptics to influence within the Tory party, which was aided by a group of sympathetic journalists on the *Daily* and *Sunday Telegraph*, the *Daily Mail* and various News International titles. The latter have not, however, been monolithic and a cheerful pluralism has existed on *The Times*, allowing the expression of many views, as I well know. Nonetheless, the prominence given to the sceptic viewpoint in traditional Tory-supporting papers from the late 1980s onwards has had a significant impact on the debate within the Tory party and has reinforced the general shift of public opinion in a sceptic direction. The risk is that the political aims and hopes of editors, and in some cases of proprietors, can override and distort news reports. This was shown by the inglorious record of many newspapers in reporting the Conservative leadership election of July 1995. Not only were almost all the traditional Tory-supporting papers very – and in some cases viciously – hostile to John Major, but their front pages tended to write off his chances. There were tendentious estimates of what the 'danger' level of votes against him and abstentions might be for Major. Most of these analyses turned out to be wrong, as Philip Cowley of the Centre of Legislative Studies at the University of Hull has pointed out (1996) in what should be uncomfortable reading for many journalists.

The career paths of journalists and politicians, both elected and unelected, have become increasingly blurred. It has always been true that some people have spent time in journalism in their twenties and thirties before becoming members of the House of Commons. And there has been a distinguished trickle in the other direction, notably Bill Deedes and Matthew Parris. But, now, more journalists combine writing, and occasionally broadcasting, with being politically active. That does not matter if they are not writing about politics and policy. But some are. Of course, journalists cannot be political eunuchs. It is nonsense to argue, as some American journalists do, that political writers are compromising themselves by voting in a secret ballot. We have views, and often strong likes and dislikes. But having a partisan commitment, such as being active in a party, inevitably creates obligations and can prevent a journalist being critical when necessary. Some journalists make no secret of their party affiliations – like Alastair Campbell before he became Tony Blair's press secretary in 1994 – and are treated on that basis as having clear partisan links and loyalties. But in other cases the commitment can become more obscure and more insidious, with the journalist arguing for a particular faction or person within a party.

This is linked – both in Britain and especially in the USA – with the rise of the highly paid celebrity journalist, both the household-name anchors or correspondents and the newspaper pundits who appear on the main chat-shows. They are detached from any real reporting and the concerns of ordinary people and closer, both financially and socially, to many of the people they are, in theory, covering. This produces the risk of arrogance, of journalists thinking they are more important than the politicians they cover and, hence, of presuming to determine what is rightfully the province of elected politicians. This is, in part, because many journalists are better educated than many MPs and there is no longer the social gulf that used to exist between the press and politicians. There was a curious ambivalence in the media about the decision of Martin Bell, the acclaimed BBC war correspondent, to challenge Neil Hamilton in the 1997 campaign. Was Bell in some ways the media candidate? Was he morally superior because he was not a conventional politician?

This appears rather a bleak picture of a trivial and partisan press ignoring issues of substance. That should not be exaggerated. American journalists visiting Britain during the 1997 election commented upon the seriousness of the press conferences. Whereas in the USA, the main focus would have been on the latest poll trends, in Britain questions were being asked about substantial policy issues even at the end of the campaign. But the coverage of politics, and especially of Parliament, is skewed and inadequate. I do not believe in some idealistic version of civic journalism. That brings the risk of journalists themselves becoming advocates of particular policies, however desirable they may seem in theory. What the media needs – the broadcasters as much as the press – is a sense of detachment and perspective, of significance rather than sensationalism. Kenneth Walsh, a leading White House correspondent, has argued (1996, p. 302) that 'Journalists should stand apart from their sources and the special interests they cover, especially the rich and famous. Appearing too clubby only drives a wedge between us and the public, which is increasingly sceptical that we represent their interests against those of entrenched power.' Mann and Ornstein have urged (p. 7) in their study quoted above that professional norms of journalism need to be strengthened, 'refusing to air rumours without solid, independent confirmation; distinguishing between the private behaviour of public officials and their performance of public duties as subject for news coverage; and emphasizing coverage of substantive performance over scandal-driven allegations'. Tell that to the editor of the *Sun*. The tabloids may not be interested, but the editors of the broadsheets should at least pause to reflect on what has been lost in the recent changes in their coverage of politics and Parliament.

The media should be reporting what matters in Whitehall and Westminster. However, it is not only hopelessly unrealistic to believe that there will be a return to the days of extensive gallery coverage of what is said on the floor of the House, but nor should there be. The floor of the House is not where the real decisions are being taken, where the main political debates are occurring, or where political influence is being exercised, except on rare occasions. The media has a duty to report and analyse what is done by the country's politicians – to let readers and viewers know how they are governed. The MPs are elected, and journalists are not. But it is not a blanket obligation. The media has to interest and retain the attention of its readers and viewers in an increasingly competitive market. Parliament has to show it is worth reporting – not just that its procedures are comprehensible but that what happens in the Palace of Westminster in itself matters. MPs have to show that they are not engaged in an empty partisan ritual, but that they are holding ministers to account and scrutinizing legislation properly. They have to demonstrate that the programme of reform launched in 1997 will make Parliament more effective, a place where political influence is exercised, rather than just votes counted. They have to show they deserve more extensive coverage. Parliament needs to open itself up, to explain its activities and procedures more fully. But this is not just a one-sided process. The media should take politics seriously. They should report on whether the new procedures for considering legislation work, whether bills are really being improved. I can already hear the yawns of news editors bored by stories about procedure and process. But the press cannot have it both ways, though it often does. If the media ignores Parliament, it cannot at the same time complain about public disillusionment with politicians and Parliament. If the immediate onus is on the politicians to make Parliament more influential, and hence newsworthy, the media should respond. I am not hopeful.

CHAPTER EIGHT

Anti-politics

'The growing integration of the world economy – in which capital, and to a lesser extent labour, moves freely – means that it is not possible for Britain to sustain budget deficits or a tax regime that are wildly out of line with other major industrial countries. One of the requirements of our tax structure is to attract enterprise into the UK from overseas.'

Tony Blair, Mais Lecture, 22 May 1995

'Something for the benefit of the country as a whole. What should it be I thought? Become a blood donor or join the Young Conservatives? But as I'm not looking for a wife and can't play table tennis, here I am.'

Tony Hancock, *The Blood Donor*, 1961

Parliament is increasingly seen as irrelevant to the main challenges and decisions facing Britain. Conventional politics, and the main political parties, are regarded as out of touch with the main decisions affecting people's lives and unable to cope with economic and social pressures that cross national boundaries. That is an increasingly widely held view, among economists, social scientists and political analysts without a direct interest in Westminster. It is not just the formal institutional challenges, such as European institutions, the judiciary or constitutional reform, which I have discussed in the previous half-dozen chapters. Other, more elusive but no less important, challenges arise from a combination of globalization and technological changes, and issues, such as the environment, drugs, youth culture and feminism, that are mainly developing outside the conventional political framework. On this view, national governments, and hence parliaments, are increasingly constrained in what they can do. Not only have they surrendered much of their control over fiscal and monetary policy to international capital markets but they have no direct mechanisms for influencing, let alone controlling, such transnational phenomena as global warming and the rise in the use of hard drugs.

Also, at a national level, power is increasingly shared among a variety of formal and informal networks of pressure groups, companies and entrepreneurs, forcing governments to adapt their approaches and policies rather than to set the agenda. This adds up to an anti-politics, or rather anti-Westminster, thesis. But it is not entirely convincing. There is still a role for national governments, and parliaments, even if it is more limited and constrained than in the heyday of nationalist collectivism between the 1920s and the 1980s.

The most widely discussed constraint on the freedom of manoeuvre of national governments is seen as globalization – that is, the increasing integration of world economies through the reduction of barriers to trade and financial flows. The combination of jet air travel, improved telecommunications (including in the 1990s the Internet), twenty-four-hour trading in the main financial markets, and the marketing of the same products throughout the world have all broken down national barriers. These changes have profound economic, social and political effects. No national government can ignore such outside pressures. As the quotation from Tony Blair at the start of this chapter shows, this acceptance of globalization has been one of the central themes of his 'new' Labour approach. In a speech in Australia in July 1995 to that most transnational group Rupert Murdoch's News Corporation, Blair argued that, 'what is called globalization is changing the nature of the nation state as power becomes more diffuse and borders more porous. Technological change is reducing the power and capacity of government to control its domestic economy free from external influence. Free movement of currency means free movement of capital which seeks the highest return worldwide. New names from the Far East have become part of the western consumers' vocabulary – Sony, Toshiba, Hitachi. BT and ICI now have listings on the New York and Tokyo stock exchanges.'

But, as Blair himself accepted, this does not make national governments redundant. Just as the state did not wither away under communism, so it has not under capitalism. As a proportion of national income public spending has risen in the major industrialized economies since

1980, the supposed era of the rediscovery of free markets and deregulation. However, there have been wide variations in the levels of public spending despite common international pressures. In the USA, public spending of all types is just over 30 per cent of national income, while it has been around 50 per cent in Germany, with Britain right in the middle. Different countries have maintained very distinct attitudes towards levels of welfare provision, income redistribution through the tax and benefit system and the extent of public ownership and regulation. These remain intensely political decisions taken by national governments and parliaments responding to domestic political pressures.

National legislatures can still take important decisions, though the scope for their action is narrower. Globalization, for example, means that national politicians have less control over levels of short-term interest rates – formally recognized by the Blair government in May 1997 in its decision to make the Bank of England responsible for implementing monetary policy. Governments are also being pushed by financial markets to contain and reduce their levels of borrowing and debt, as was reflected in the somewhat naïve discovery of the power of bond markets by some of President Bill Clinton's advisers after he took office in January 1993. The same was true when the 'socialism in one country' experiment of François Mitterrand failed disastrously in the first two years of his presidency. Of course, market constraints existed in earlier years as Britain's stop-go cycle and repeated emergency budgets of the 1950s, 1960s and 1970s showed. But floating exchange rates, the freeing of controls on financial movements and the integration of capital markets means that the markets punish erring governments more quickly and severely than before. This is in itself a deterrent and a discipline on their behaviour.

In some respects, we have returned to conditions of before the First World War when the gold standard reigned supreme and there were high levels of trade and investment flows between countries. Governments then accepted the discipline of a fixed exchange rate (as would occur with European monetary union) and associated policies like a balanced budget. No one, however, doubted that both Britain itself and the Westminster Parliament were sovereign. Rather, limitations on what elected politicians could, and should, do were generally recognized. In that respect, the era of ubiquitous government from the 1940s until the 1980s may be the exception.

No one would argue, however, that all governments are the same. Even leaving aside the extremes of, say, North Korea and Singapore, it is clear that varying policies decided upon by politicians, elected in most cases, can have a big influence on the performance of their country's economy and its well-being. For instance, the Conservative governments of the 1980s and 1990s in Britain pushed through far-reaching reforms in the public sector, leading to both privatization and deregulation. But, in the same period, successive French administrations of both left and right have failed to introduce similar changes in the face of stiff resistance from trade unions. The political culture, as expressed by elected politicians, is very different. Moreover, the world, even western industrialized countries, is not just a single market where capital and labour are completely mobile. Global pressures certainly limit the ability of national governments to alter levels of tax and regulation, but only limit, not prevent. Linguistic and cultural differences, as well as immigration controls, prevent most workers, even skilled ones, from just moving to countries with low taxes. The truly internationally mobile – top executives in multinational corporations, stars of entertainment and sport – may be a relatively small number, but they can still influence the attitudes of business and government.

The International Monetary Fund (IMF) has frequently argued that globalization has accentuated the benefits of good policies and the costs of bad ones. As Martin Wolf reported in the *Financial Times* on 13 May 1997, 'contrary to fears that globalization has sidelined governments, elected bodies have an important role in implementing sensible national policies'. The IMF study he quoted, listed five determinants of successful economies: the quality of governance, macro-economic stability, openness to the world economy, the quality of investment and the skills of the workforce. In recent years, there has been increasing awareness of the first point and not just in extreme conditions of civil war. The rule of law and the absence of corruption are crucial to inward investment, while bad governance encourages the transfer of money by the well-off to safer havens, capital flight, since they have the ability and contacts to dodge controls. Other factors are environmental regulation, health standards, the provision of a social safety-net, policies to aid the transfer and development of technology and systems to help promote savings.

Similarly, the World Bank argued in its World Development Report of 1997 that 'Globalization is a threat to capriciously governed or weak states. But it opens the way for effective, disciplined states to foster development and economic well-being.' The application of predictable rules and policies is vital for attracting private investment, and the lack of them has deterred foreign investment in some countries of the Commonwealth of Independent States, the former Soviet Union. Along the same lines as the IMF study, the World Bank report highlighted five crucial functions that governments, rather than markets and private bodies, must provide: legal foundations, an effective macro-economic policy environment, investment in basic social services and infrastructure, a comprehensive safety-net for vulnerable members of society, and basic environmental protection. This institutional framework, the report maintained, underpinned the success of the East Asian economies. This is little to do with levels of public spending: indeed, those governments which spend the highest proportions of national income have been among the most corrupt and lawless, and least attractive to business. What matters is the rule of law and a framework of business and civic ethics, together with strong institutions separate from government. Those countries with weak 'state capability' on this definition, notably in Africa, have increased their income per head by only 0.5 per cent a year over the last three decades. There has been a deterioration in conditions in some central African countries. Over the same period, income per head in countries with 'strong capability', as in East Asia, expanded on average by 3 per cent a year. The World Bank report concluded: 'Good government is not a luxury – it is a vital necessity for development.'

However, elected politicians in western democracies do not always recognize either the constraints on their role imposed by global economic integration or the scope for action that remains. Some still hanker after active intervention in monetary and fiscal policy, while some go to the opposite extreme of the minimal state. A central part of Blair's 'reinvention' of the Labour Party was a redefinition of the role of government to take account of globalization. He accepted and recognized the constraints of international financial markets on levels of public borrowing and taxes, but still saw a role for active government. As he argued in his Australian speech, 'The role of government is to represent a national interest, to create a competitive base of physical infrastructure and human skills to attract the capital that will produce the wages for workers and the profits for investors.' On this view, governments should act, in partnership with the private sector, to help Britain become more competitive, notably by improving educational standards and skills, and by addressing the insecurity and social divisions associated with globalization.

So while the fashionable notion of the powerless state is a myth, there are areas where national governments – and elected politicians – have proved remarkably ineffective. The globalization of international finance markets has not only made any national controls on capital flows ineffective but it has also made it much harder to regulate and prevent fraud in such markets. National financial regulators and supervisors have repeatedly been shown to be impotent in the face of frauds covering several countries. It has not mattered where a company is registered or controlled from; the fraud can be perpetrated anywhere. That has been exposed by the collapse of the Bank of Commerce and Credit International (BCCI), by Nick Leeson's speculations in Singapore over Japanese financial contracts, which brought down the mighty London banking house of Barings; and by the massive losses experienced by Daiwa Bank in New York. National politicians, and their central banks, do co-operate more in the hope of preventing both fraud and financial instability. But they can only monitor, not control, such markets. A parallel and, in the case of BCCI, directly related problem is international crime, particularly the trade in drugs, where cross-border banking transactions are crucial to the payments links between suppliers, distributors and users, and the associated money-laundering. This trade is beyond the control of any national government and legislature, however much they may try to ban the use of certain types of drug.

Related to, and underpinning, the impact of global financial markets has been the spread of technology and telecommunications. The Internet offers a way of spreading information round the world, as well as a way of communication between voters and politicians, and between voters themselves. The spread of the satellite dish, and of international media operations like CNN, as well as the BBC, has broken down national barriers on politics. No longer can any one country's politics be regarded as entirely domestic when the latest riot, inter-ethnic atrocity and even election can be, and is, broadcast live around the world. National politicians cannot control what is shown. The bloody struggle for autonomy in Chechnya was undoubtedly helped by the presence of western television crews. The pictures that appeared on western, as well as Russian, television screens constrained Moscow in suppressing the breakaway. Television reports about atrocities were also a powerful pressure for external intervention in Bosnia. Of course, the international spread of telecommunications – the Internet as much as television – is no guarantee of freedom and democracy, as is shown by Burma and China. Censorship still exists and some international media groups are willing to kowtow to authoritarian regimes to gain access to their media markets for their satellites.

Another challenge that crosses national boundaries is the deterioration in the global environment, notably the phenomenon of global warming. This threatens far-reaching changes in the world's climate, affecting not only ocean levels but also agriculture and food supplies. It is caused by emissions of gases from power stations, chemical plants, motor vehicles and the like. The problem is that one country can be, and is, affected by emissions from another country. Therefore, unless many countries agree on action, it is in no one country's interests to introduce measures to control this form of pollution which will add to the costs of its domestic industries. That has bedevilled a succession of international conferences on the issue because of the different interests of various countries. Since national governments on their own cannot produce results, there is a disincentive on national politicians to do more than express pious hopes.

Green issues have risen up the political agenda but, in general, outside mainstream politics. This is partly because the main parties have been constrained by the producer interests that finance and back them. So it has been pressure groups like Greenpeace and Friends of the Earth that have made the running, and have operated at a transnational level via groups in many countries. At times, this has given them more influence than any individual party, or even national government, over some multinational corporations. The classic example was the success in June 1995 of Greenpeace in forcing Shell UK to abandon plans to sink the Brent Spar oil platform in the Atlantic. Greenpeace waged a Europe-wide campaign, including consumer pressure against Shell's garages and petrol stations in Germany. Local Greenpeace groups lobbied a variety of European governments and the European Commission, which urged the British government and Shell UK to change their approach. This underlined the vulnerability of even the largest international corporation to widely organized pressure. While Greenpeace has claimed at its peak to have more than three million supporters worldwide, it is in no sense a democratic organization. It may canvass the views of supporters but decisions are taken by a small group of senior management and salaried staff. In this respect, it is more like a highly disciplined cadre of the type envisaged by Lenin.

The success of environmental groups is seen by some political analysts as symbolizing a new type of politics, disillusioned with traditional power structures of party and hierarchy. This anti-politics thesis has been popularized in Britain by some former Marxists such as Martin Jacques and by the think tank Demos. The latter's founder and director Geoff Mulgan entitled his first book on the issue *Politics in an Antipolitical Age*, and a collection of edited essays from Demos publications, *Life After Politics, New Thinking for the Twenty-first Century*. His central argument (1994, chapter 1) is that traditional hierarchical politics, based on 'monopolist' nation states and government, is increasingly being bypassed by the growth of anti-politics on the margins – that is, 'movements that pioneer new social themes against the orthodoxy, of personal salvation against public stultification'. Such analyses always teeter on the brink of avant-garde pretentiousness, and sometimes fall into a radical-chic vacuousness.

Mulgan has argued (1994, p. 18) that some of the big new issues present challenges that conventional politics cannot handle. 'While the parties and parliaments went on talking, what had previously been non-political issues became the great matters of life, the real issues by which people defined their position in the world. Some of these issues, such as global warming or the spread of AIDS, are by their nature macrocosmic and worldwide in scope, and so beyond the realm of practical politics.' Others, he argued, are microcosmic, 'intensely personal, concerning identity and purpose, battles over sexuality or home life, neighbourhood and culture, and the unprecedented quantity of decisions forced on individuals and institutions without the guidance of tradition. Much the most important of these has been the empowerment of women.' In the Mulgan view, these issues are

soluble less through the passing of laws and degrees than through changes of culture and behaviour. Sovereignty, the monopoly power of violence and law, becomes impotent and even foolish in the face of such a challenge, since the softer realms of culture are beyond the reach of its rigorous and hard law. Traditional politics . . . carries on with a momentum of its own, the massive inertia of great parties and career ladders, but finds itself ever less able to resonate or to provide satisfactory sanctuaries for people's hopes and cares.

This thesis exaggerates a nugget of truth into an unwieldy structure which does not bear the weight of its claims. Social changes occur, and always have occurred, independently of government: for instance, the shift from the countryside to the new big industrial cities of the nineteenth century or the sharp rise in female participation in the workforce in the twentieth century. Social life is now more private and less collective, thanks to technological change and affluence, but that still presents problems that require a response from government. Laws and taxes are not the whole story, but they are part of it. Of course, its means of response have varied. In the nineteenth century, they were more local and voluntary. In the twentieth century, central government has gradually extended the welfare state, in part offsetting the decline in voluntary provisions and the breakdown of the social support of the extended family. The state cannot provide total solutions through 'the passing of laws and decrees', but it can help.

Similarly, governments have responded, at least in part, to both the macrocosmic and microcosmic challenges listed by Mulgan. The striking feature of the response of the British government to AIDS was not how little has been done, but how much, given that the decision-makers were almost all middle-aged, or older, heterosexual men not known for their instinctive sympathy for the gay community. But, as Sir Norman Fowler commented in his unfairly underestimated memoirs (1991, chapter 13), the Thatcher government responded with a sense of urgency. This was not by moralizing and attempting to change the moral climate of society but by a hard-hitting publicity campaign aimed at preventing more people contracting the HIV virus. The record on global threats to the environment is less satisfactory, for the reasons I discussed above, but successive British governments have moved in a green direction on tax and planning policy.

The Mulgan thesis is also wrong over what he has called the microcosmic challenges over identity and culture. Governments may have been slow to respond to the empowerment of women, but they have responded: for instance, by introducing child benefit paid to the mother (despite the opposition of male union leaders and politicians) and with equal-opportunities legislation. The manifestos of all the main parties in the 1997 election showed greater concern with the demands of working women for improved child care and the problems faced by single mothers in getting back to work. The virtual doubling in the number of women MPs, up to a sixth of the Commons, at the 1997 election is in itself a partial, and limited, response to the changing role of women. The 101 women Labour MPs were predictably dubbed 'Blair's babes' by the press. Not only was this tritely patronizing, but it also missed the more significant development: many of them were also working mothers with school-age or even younger children. They should have been called 'Blair's mums'. This change shows that traditional politics can respond to such social changes, albeit belatedly.

Nonetheless, Mulgan and his colleagues give some valuable insights into what they call the 'disconnection from politics'. As he and Charles Leadbeater have pointed out (in the essays edited by Mulgan, 1997), 'In most countries, faith and interest in politics seems to be becoming a minority attachment.' They cite low involvement, limited choice, and poor delivery of results. This is reflected particularly in the inflexibility of traditional government structures, and the long-term decline in membership of, and loyalty to, political parties. Their central argument is that government has failed to adapt in the way that modern businesses – what they call 'lean' organizations – have by focusing on core tasks and products; by always looking outwards to customers and supplies; by removing unnecessary layers of bureaucracy; and by being highly skilled. By contrast, in the Mulgan and Leadbetter view, the political system is perpetually shifting its focus and is at a distance from voters. Their solutions involve continual innovation in new forms of government – 'as a broker and energizer rather than a provider or direct regulator' (similar to some of the ideas of Rod Rhodes discussed below) – and the addition of mechanisms of direct democracy on to the representative system.

The growth of the state to a mature condition – that is, attempting to improve what it does, rather than add new roles, or increase its relative size – has added a further, generally unrecognized constraint. In the past, governments, and hence parliaments, have had more freedom of manoeuvre in decisions because the state was expanding. New policies and programmes could always be added. The era of limited government has narrowed the options for decision-makers. Richard Rose and Philip Davies (1995) have highlighted the importance of the inheritance of past programmes. They have calculated that in 1989, after ten years of the Thatcher premiership, only a third of government programmes had been introduced by her, and two-fifths dated from before 1945. The contrast is even larger when programmes are measured in money terms: three-quarters dated from before 1945 and a mere tenth from the 1980s. They concluded:

> At no point in time did an administration decide how many or what kind of programmes government ought to undertake, or make an *ex ante* decision about how much money should be spent, or how it should be allocated. The record of each successive administration is largely a record of more of the same; the great bulk of the programmes it administers and finances are inherited from the more or less distant past.

As I have argued (in my contribution to Jones *et al.*, 1997), Rose and Davies have a fair point, but they exaggerate. Significant changes can be made to long-established policies, as the Conservatives did in modifying and cutting back the scope of social security entitlements from the mid-1980s onwards. But incoming ministers face entrenched views, often a consensus, on particular policies formed by civil servants, think tanks, implementers of policies such as local authorities, pressure groups and voluntary bodies. Even strong-willed politicians with large majorities in the House of Commons, such as Margaret Thatcher, found it hard to shift long-formed Whitehall policy positions, as she often protested at the time, as well as later.

Another way of viewing these constraints on central government, and hence Parliament, is provided by political scientists, notably Professor Rod Rhodes (1997), who have challenged the Westminster model and argue that policy-making is much more fragmented and spread through a network of organizations. His thesis is that the traditional model of the hierarchical, bureaucratic state is no longer valid as the state has become hollowed out with some functions shifted upwards to the European and others downwards to agencies and quangos via privatization, contracting-out and public–private partnerships. So instead of ministers and civil servants issuing orders, they have increasingly to negotiate with the private and voluntary sectors to deliver services. In this view, no one has the information, expertise, influence or policy instruments to decide unilaterally. Central government sets the boundaries to the actions of these networks and often funds them, but it has become increasingly dependent on them. Stripped of the numbing jargon of political science, this analysis highlights how the pervasive Victorian, and Diceyan, view of ministerial accountability to Parliament is now heavily circumscribed in practice (as I discussed in Chapter Four). In many ways, it has always been circumscribed. Successive administrations' health and education policies have depended on the co-operation of doctors and teachers, whatever centrally imposed organizational changes have been introduced. Rhodes's point was once made to me succinctly and plainly by the late Sir Keith Joseph in 1981 when I asked him how he was finding his new post of Education Secretary. He said, typically, that he had not yet found the levers – and he never did. But some ministers can, and have. Governments can still make a difference, even though ministers have to contend with well-organized pressure and campaigning groups who can count on sympathetic media treatment in their calls for additional expenditure on this or that programme. Of course, policy does not just emerge from Parliament at the whim of ministers. It usually reflects lengthy discussions among a wide range of people – civil servants, think tanks, affected groups as well as ministers and their advisers. But it is ministers, dependent on a majority in Parliament, who decide which option to pursue.

Political parties, the central organizations within Parliament, still matter as important, but by no means the sole, players in determining policy within tight limits set by a wide range of domestic and international factors. The main parties can no longer be described as mass organizations. Membership of the Conservative party is authoritatively reckoned to have peaked at around 3 million in the early 1950s, though this is inevitably an estimate since the party has not had a national membership scheme and people join locally. Nevertheless, even if the precise figures are suspect, the trend is clear. While membership was declining only slowly during the 1960s and 1970s, a sharp decline began from the early 1980s onwards. From a total of 1.2 million in 1982, Tory membership dropped to little more than 600,000 by 1992 and down to between 350,000 and 400,000 in 1996, according to estimates compiled by Michael Pinto-Duschinsky, a leading authority on party organization and finance. And even this could easily be an over-estimate, since he suggested (1997) that the records of many local parties were out of date, and included people who had died, moved or were otherwise no longer members of the party. Some senior Tories reckoned that the true figure could be as low as 250,000, roughly the same as Labour in its low point in the early 1990s. While Labour's membership figures are hard to compare over time because of changes in the way in which they have been compiled, the party suffered the same trend as the Tories. Labour's membership probably peaked at more than a million in the early 1950s and declined sharply from the 1960s onwards. However, its nadir appears to have been in the early 1990s when its membership rose from about 250,000 in 1992 to well over 400,000 by the time of the 1997 election.

These trends can in part be attributed to changes in social habits and use of leisure time. When the immortal episode of *The Blood Donor* was first broadcast in 1961, the studio audience would have laughed at Hancock's reference to the Young Conservatives. By the 1990s, few would even have heard of the organization, let alone known anyone in it or considered joining themselves. These lines from *The Blood Donor* were quoted by Jeremy Richardson (1995) in an article about the market for political activism, in which he discussed the growth of interest groups as a challenge to political parties. Those interested in politics have many other outlets for activism, from non-partisan civic organiza-tions to single-issue interest groups. On this view, people distinguish between voting as an occasional civic duty and participating in politics – for a small minority by joining a party or, for an increasing number, via single-issue groups. Indeed, many of the new Labour MPs first elected in May 1997 had been active in such pressure and single-issue groups, notably those to do with the welfare state, such as lone parents, housing rights and pensioners, or with overseas aid and the environ-ment. In some cases, their involvement in such activities preceded their involvement with the Labour party, in most cases it was in parallel. Among voluntary groups, the Royal Society for the Protection of Birds had a membership in the mid-1990s almost as large as the Conservative and Labour parties combined. In the early 1990s, Greenpeace had a membership of 400,000, substantially higher than Labour at the time, though it then fell sharply, in part reflecting the high membership turnover of all such groups.

Some political scientists – notably the American Robert Putnam – have suggested there has been a broad civic disengagement from group activities. In a widely quoted article (most easily available in Britain in *Prospect*, 1996), he has contrasted the sharp decline in organized ten-pin bowling leagues in the USA and the rise in individual bowling. His 'bowling alone' thesis has been challenged by those who argue that there has not been a decline in joining, but rather a shift from old, collective workplace groups and social clubs to sports and single-issue groups. In Britain, the membership of political parties, trade unions, the British Legion and the Women's Institute has declined, while membership of environmental groups, civic bodies and health clubs has risen. In some cases, there is merely an indirect, credit-card involvement rather than an active participation. Professor Putnam has pointed out that in America, organizations such as the powerful American Association of Retired Persons and various environmentalist groups have experienced explosive growth since membership merely involves writing a cheque. By contrast, those groups in which membership involves meeting others are withering.

The sharp rise in Labour party membership since the early 1990s is in part a response to these trends and a recognition that people will not join an organization just for the pleasure of turning up on cold nights to lengthy meetings dominated by bores and obsessives. Labour has offered its new members not only a flow of information (reinforced by regular requests for money), but also a direct opportunity to participate in the party's decision-making via postal ballots on a one-member one-vote basis. These occur every year in the elections to the party's national executive committee but have also been held over the rewriting of clause four of the party constitution (on a consultative basis) and, in the autumn of 1996, in winning approval for the party's draft manifesto. This is regarded by the Labour left as a cynical exercise in plebiscitory democracy by the national leadership which merely wants, and secures, the approval of the party for its desired initiatives and does not really give individual members a chance to participate in decisions. There is something in this criticism, though one-member one-vote ballots are far better than domination by small groups of committed activists, which have, in the past, been unrepresentative of Labour supporters generally. The new Labour approach does, however, offer a clear incentive for people to become involved in parties, and therefore in the mainstream political process. The candidates in the contest for the Conservative Party leadership in May–June 1997, particularly the eventual winner William Hague, pledged to follow Labour's example in the hope of reviving the flagging Tory membership.

Parliament does have a problem of legitimacy in view of its low standing in opinion polls and the fall in turn-out in elections (to the lowest level since 1935 in the May 1997 general election). Of course, there are various ways that turn-out can be boosted, from improving the electoral register to allowing voting for a longer period, or entirely by post. But the anti-politics school argues that more radical solutions are needed. Geoff Mulgan sees part of the problem in the nature of representative democracy. He has argued (1997, pp. 204–5) that

> representation separates citizens from decisions by concentrating power amongst a relatively small group of professionals. As a model of democracy, it was fitted for an uneducated electorate, and for an era when travel and communication were difficult. Its effect through the electoral system is to bundle decisions together, usually leaving citizens only binary choices between two different parties and pro-grammes. Worse, it leaves legislatures oddly unrepresentative, skewed towards men, towards professions like the law and teaching, and towards the relatively rich. All of these features undermine the authority of representatives and make them less able to take responsible decisions.

In this view, modern government is both exclusive and élitist.

In recent years several suggestions have been made for strengthening democracy – or, rather, supplementing the conventional model of four- or five-yearly elections to the House of Commons. Some have been in response to the reduction in powers and role of local government imposed by the Thatcher and Major governments. Others have been in reaction to the managerial revolution in government, the creation of executive agencies and similar bodies. Both developments have been criticized for weakening democracy, though (as discussed in Chapter Four), Conservatives argue that the rights of the citizen as consumer, rather than as voter, have been strengthened by widening choice in public services and by providing more public measurements of perform-ance in citizens' charters and the like. One solution is to strengthen local accountability by reviving local government and freeing it from Whitehall controls.

The anti-politics school argues that more direct forms of participation are desirable, not least in the light of technological changes such as the Internet. There is, however, the real danger that the loudest and most organized will exploit these forms of communication, whether the Internet, fax machines or e-mail to make decision-making by elected representatives much harder. Those fashionable futurologists, Alvin and Heidi Toffler, who have the ear of Republican House of Representatives Speaker Newt Gingrich, have urged a 'semi-direct' democracy, giving ordinary people a say. Experiments have been held in the USA in televoting or electronic town meetings, based on the New England tradition of assembling the citizens of a town once a year to decide on its budget and other important issues affecting their communities. This worked when each town might have had just a few hundred citizens, but it is hard to copy this now, however sophisticated the use of telephones and televisions. Experiments have been tried in Columbus, Ohio, where local leaders have debated issues while viewers have periodically registered agreement or disagreement through their interactive cable systems. I would love to have read James Thurber, that great son of Columbus, on such an experience. It might have rivalled such comic classics as *The Night the Ghost Got In*.

Most experiments have involved sending a random sample of voters the necessary information and asking them to express their view. James Fishkin of the University of Texas has linked up with Channel Four to conduct what he calls 'deliberative polls'. This involves assembling a group of voters, intended to be broadly representative, for a few days, normally a weekend, to listen to experts offer a briefing on a particular issue, before they are then asked to give their opinion. Such polls, involving 230 to 300 people, have been held on crime, Europe and the monarchy. These are interesting, occasionally illuminating, and are a novel experiment in current-affairs television, but no more. They can never be truly democratic. Some local authorities have applied a parallel technique of 'citizens' juries' of a smaller number of people to consider alternative options. Deliberative polling, televoting and citizens' juries are, by definition, unrepresentative since the mass of voters are excluded, but such direct methods can be a consultative or advisory addition to the election of representatives.

Referendums could also be used more frequently and on a wider scale. All the main political parties now advocate the use of referendums on major constitutional issues (as I discussed in Chapter Five). William Hague's first policy initiative as Conservative Party leader in June 1997 was to call for a referendum on the Amsterdam treaty. One problem is defining when referendums should occur. Should they also be held on major economic and social issues, as in the USA and Switzerland? In the USA, nearly half the fifty states allow referendums, normally known as propositions, or initiatives put to the ballot by the demand of voters. This is a legacy of the progressive movement at the beginning of the century. Such initiatives, normally voted on at the time of legislative elections, can have far-reaching effects – as have those imposing term limits (on the length of time that legislators can serve) or restricting taxes. The success of Proposition 13 in California in 1978 was a turning point in the taxpayers' revolt and movement to limit the size of government in the USA. Andrew Adonis and Geoff Mulgan (in the Demos essays edited by Mulgan, 1997) have urged the use of not only voter juries to consider the pros and cons of various contested policy proposals and voter feedback via combined television and telephone networks on cable, but also voter vetoes. These would give citizens at national and local level the right to call consultative referendums on strongly disputed legislation or council decisions. At a national level, a million citizens would need to sign a petition for a referendum to take place. Some local authorities have used such referendums to guide them on setting levels of spending and the council tax, or even on issues such as refuse collection. Indeed, in 1981, Michael Heseltine floated the idea of forcing local councils to hold referendums before they could introduce what were called 'excessive' increases in local rates. The idea of consultative referendums on policy has been discussed by Paddy Ashdown, the Liberal Democrat leader, partly as a means of providing greater public support and legitimacy for decisions on taxation. But, apart from major constitutional issues, the main objection to the frequent use of referendums at a national level is that the complicated choices facing ministers every day – on, say, the balance between taxes and spending on a range of programmes – can seldom be simplified into a yes or no question on a ballot paper. That is why we have a representative system.

This chapter underlines how much of the political debate is now conducted away from Parliament. But that does not mean that Parliament, and the familiar party exchanges, are irrelevant. National governments, and therefore legislatures, are more constrained than in the past. Their room for manoeuvre on overall levels of taxation, expenditure and interest rates is narrower. And the managerial revolution in government has altered the way in which decisions are taken and implemented. But this still leaves ample room for governments to do good or ill. Moreover, apart from the occasional use of referendums on clear-cut constitutional matters, the various alternatives to a representative system are unconvincing as a means of expressing the will of the people. They can be useful as a means of communication, but no more. But the fact that their use is being urged, and discussed, highlights the problems facing Parliament in persuading the public that it is doing its job properly.

CHAPTER NINE

Parliament's Response

The balance of advantage between Parliament and government in the day-to-day working of the constitution is now weighted in favour of the government to a degree which arouses widespread anxiety and is inimical to the proper working of our Parliamentary democracy.

Select Committee on Procedure,
First Report, 1997–8

'Parliament is weak in this country. I've been in it for twenty-two years and I think it's got weaker every single year I've been in it. We just don't check the executive properly in our system. We have only got the power of publicity . . . We do have an elective dictatorship.'

John Smith, leader of the Labour party,
at Charter 88 meeting, 1 March 1993 (quoted in
Adonis, 1993)

Parliament has not stood still. The House of Commons and the House of Lords have both altered their procedures considerably over the years, as earlier chapters have shown. The Commons has barely stopped examining its own workings with a major inquiry at least every ten years, followed by at least limited changes. This chapter will examine how far these reforms have succeeded in meeting the challenges facing Parliament and discuss the state of the debate about further change.

Much of the discussion over reform has a repetitive character, with similar complaints about the power of the executive over the legislature. In part, that reflects the nature of a representative system based on strong parties (as I discussed in Chapter One). So the reformers have merely been complaining about the inherent character of a system dominated by party discipline and loyalties where the executive is bound to use its majority to seek to control the legislature to get its business through. For that very reason the reformers are always going to be disappointed – though the boundaries between the executive and the legislature can be, and have, shifted. What was regarded with horror by the immediate post-war generation of senior politicians, and with scepticism by their successors in the 1960s, was eventually accepted in the 1980s, and is now largely unquestioned. Nonetheless, the House of Commons cannot be like the American Congress unless we have a formal separation of powers, as opposed to a differentiation of functions. Parliament can never govern or control the executive. It is better, therefore, to focus on the more limited objectives of ministerial accountability and scrutiny of the executive and its proposals: what Bernard Crick (1964) has described as putting 'relevant facts and fancies before the electorate which sits in judgment upon governments'. In his view, 'Parliament is the broker of ideas and information: the Government must carry the final risks and responsibilities.' We are governed through Parliament, not by Parliament. As will already be clear, I believe the traditional debate has obscured the newer institutional challenges and the internal structural weaknesses of Parliament. The legislature has not kept pace with either the far-reaching changes in the executive of the past decade or completely external threats to its position.

The Government has had the upper hand in the control of Commons business since the reforms introduced by Gladstone in the nineteenth century. These were reinforced by the changes introduced by Balfour in 1902 and taken further by Morrison in 1945–6. The Attlee government in 1945 rapidly set up a select committee with the specific instructions to 'report as soon as possible upon any scheme for the acceleration of proceedings on Public Bills which may be submitted to them on behalf of Her Majesty's Government'. The main change was that all bills should be referred to standing committees, apart from bills of 'first-class constitutional importance' and small, non-contentious measures. Previously, the committee stages of most major bills had been on the floor of the House. This change greatly strengthened the executive's ability to get through its legislation. But Labour ministers, and their Conservative successors in the 1950s, resisted the creation of specialist select committees, though these had been used in the nineteenth century to investigate major social problems, such as the employment of children, or military disasters, like the Crimean War. But they went into decline in the first half of this century, apart from the Public Accounts Committee. The Estimates Committee, established with limited powers in 1912, was strengthened after the Second World War following the successful experiment of the National Expenditure Committee. But it was only able to examine expenditure and administration, rather than policy. The suggestion of Sir Gilbert Campion, then Clerk of the House, for establishing a new Public Expenditure Committee, combining the Public Accounts and Estimates Committees, was rejected by the Government. However, the work of committees was broadened in the 1950s by the creation of the Nationalized Industries Committee in 1956, which over the following two decades proved to be an innovator by taking evidence in public, questioning ministers as well as civil servants and appointing special advisers.

Disquiet among backbenchers surfaced in a debate in January 1958 when several MPs called for the more extensive use of committees to scrutinize the executive. A number of suggestions, such as time limiting some speeches, were made, which took nearly thirty years to implement. But ministerial opposition to change was underlined by R. A. Butler, the Leader of the Commons, who, in the Commons debate, then rejected the call for specialized committees on finance, defence, foreign affairs, etc., since they would 'create something absolutely opposite to British constitutional development, because the fact that there is a certain degree of power and authority delegated to those committees in America, and in a different way in France, is largely due to our friend Montesquieu. Their constitution is different from ours. The executive does not sit, and is not perpetually badgered and bullied, in the legislature itself. The executive is not part, as ministers are here, of the legislature itself. It is almost impossible to have a system of standing committees à l'Américain with the British constitution and the executive being present in Parliament as occurs here.' Nonetheless, a new Select Committee on Procedure was established and considered a wide variety of suggestions, including the more expeditious dispatch of business and taking matters off the floor of the House, though it turned down the idea of specialist committees or morning sittings. Even several of its very modest suggestions, in practice little more than tinkering with current procedures, made no progress in view of the conservatism of both government and opposition front benches.

However, the broader national mood of introspection in the early 1960s led to a renewed interest in parliamentary reform. The complaints then were less sweeping than in the 1930s when there had been a sense that Parliament was weak and almost impotent in face of the world depression. The criticisms in the early 1960s were more about the effectiveness of Parliament in scrutinizing the executive, over, for example, science, technological research and development, and the long-term planning of public expenditure. Typical were Andrew Hill and Anthony Whichelow, the pseudonymous members of the Clerks' department who, in *What's Wrong with Parliament?*, argued (1964, p. 94) that all the faults 'would be moderated, and some of them wholly rectified, if the House of Commons were to reform its committee system. It could do so, without any appreciable increase in expenditure.' In the same year, ten Labour MPs and two peers produced what was in effect a manifesto for reform in a supplement to the Labour right publication *Socialist Commentary*. The group was chaired by Reg Prentice, the future Labour cabinet minister and later a Conservative MP and minister, and included Horace King, a future Speaker of the Commons. They called, among other suggestions, for timetabling of legislation, for carrying over of business from one session to the next, for time limits on speeches during parts of a full-scale debate, for an extension of select committees, and for the Commons to be televised. Many of their ideas have been acted upon since then; others are still on the reform agenda in the late 1990s. Writing at the same time, Bernard Crick was an optimist about the potential for reform and urged a system of committees covering broad subject groups, based on the pattern of the thriving specialist committees which both parties then had. He preferred this to departmentally related committees, which he feared 'would carry a greater risk of interference with the routine work of departments'. Professor Crick was well ahead of his time in urging a committee on legal and judicial affairs (successfully resisted by Lord Hailsham when the departmental committees were set up in 1979) and one on the machinery of government (which was not separately formed until the Public Service Committee was created in December 1995). He favoured reducing the amount of time the House of Commons spent in considering legislation and increasing the amount of time spent both in examining and publicizing the broad outlines of future legislation and policy, and in examining the efficiency and effectiveness of the day-to-day administration of the country. However, he warned that 'the executive mind on both sides of the House has little patience with even the existing opportunities of Parliamentary participation in the process of Government'.

Under the influence of Richard Crossman as Leader of the Commons from 1966–1968, specialist committees were created on agriculture, education and science, overseas aid and development, race relations and immigration, science and technology, and Scottish affairs. As the Study of Parliament Group report of 1976 pointed out (p. 6), 'The Committee on Race Relations and Immigration resulted from an initiative by the Home Secretary, James Callaghan; Scottish Affairs seemed a small price to pay to contain some of the pressures on a Labour Government of Scottish nationalism, which were renewed in the late 1960s.' But ministers and civil servants often sought to limit their range of inquiries, and, with the exception of the Select Committee on Overseas Development, the committees based on departments did not succeed in establishing themselves and were not reappointed. In particular, the Agriculture Committee's attempt to invade sensitive territory over relations with the then Common Market led to its quick disbandment. This was similar to the fate of other experiments introduced under Crossman, like morning sittings, which were dropped after one session. The main change in the early 1970s was the replacement of the Estimates Committee in 1971 by a Select Committee on Expenditure with the specific terms of reference 'to consider public expenditure' and six sub-committees to examine more detailed aspects. These committees were usually appointed for a whole parliament rather than for just one session and their staffing and resources were increased. Nonetheless, the Study of Parliament Group took a sceptical view of the changes in 1976 (p. 31): 'The introduction of new select committees in the mid-1960s was made in the hope that they would improve the substance of debate about government policy. Yet the evidence shows that they have largely been so effectively absorbed into the system that it is now difficult to assess what changes they have effected apart from the creation of an extra burden of work.' It concluded (p. 38) that 'over the past decade there has been a steadily growing disenchantment with the concept of specialist committees. Their reports have failed to command great attention in the House; they have made little impact on the limited section of the public that takes an interest in parliamentary affairs.'

Despite these doubts, a lengthy inquiry by a diverse group of MPs on a new Procedure Committee led to the most ambitious – and at the time oversold – changes to scrutiny of the executive in 1979. In practice, both the Procedure Committee of 1976 to 1978 and the decisions of the Commons in 1979 reflected a traditional interpretation of the role of the House, despite some overblown rhetoric. The Procedure Committee declared in its report of July 1978 that the House should be able 'to exercise effective control and stewardship over ministers and the expanding bureaucracy of the modern state for which they are answerable, and to make the decisions of Parliament and Government more responsive to the wishes of the electorate'. The committee concluded that these fine-sounding aspirations were not being achieved: 'Despite the considerable growth of the select committees since 1964 and the changes which have taken place in their powers, the facilities available to them and their methods of work, the development of the system has been piecemeal and has resulted in a decidedly patchy coverage of the activities of government departments and agencies, and of the major areas of public policy and administration.' The House, it added, 'should no longer rest content with an incomplete and unsystematic scrutiny of the activities of the executive'.

Enoch Powell was, typically, one of the few dissenters in the discussion of these ideas, arguing that the balance of the Government and the Commons had seesawed over time. As often, he had a point, since influence has varied in relation to political circumstances. But he underestimated the structural changes which had, and have, weakened legislative scrutiny. The Procedure Committee proposed the creation of about a dozen select committees covering the activities of particular departments. These would replace the broad subject-oriented committees then in existence, apart from those dealing with statutory instruments, European legislation and the Public Accounts Committee. The new committees were to be given the broad brief of monitoring 'expenditure, policy and administration', but not legislation. The report talked of striking a new balance through changes 'not of a fundamental or revolutionary character, but by changes of an evolutionary kind, following naturally from the present practices'. A classic exercise in

British establishment reformism then – change under a conservative cloak.

The proposals were generally welcomed in a two-day debate that the Commons held in February 1979, just before the fall of the Callaghan government. The most notable dissenter was Michael Foot, the then Leader of the Commons, who was as wrong in most of his warnings about the implications of the proposals as he was about virtually everything else in his long political career. His fear was that the Procedure Committee's proposals threatened the supremacy of the chamber, and the access to it which 'is the supreme attribute of the House of Commons'. Foot believed that the existence of the committees would drain attention away from the chamber and would interfere with the position of members who wanted to raise issues covered by the committees, while acting as a shield for departments. Only the latter worry has been partially borne out. As Norman St John Stevas, as he then was, pointed out in his role as shadow Leader of the Commons, 'The debate is not a choice between the chamber and committees. We need both and have always had both. In the time of Elizabeth I we had a much more developed committee system than we have today.' Following the May 1979 election, the Thatcher government quickly came forward with proposals for departmental select committees, along the lines proposed by the Procedure Committee, though differing in a number of details about remit and scope. As Geoffrey Howe noted in his memoirs (p. 261), the committees were established 'very largely as a result of Norman St John Stevas' tenacity at the beginning of the 1979 Parliament. Margaret [Thatcher] had reluctantly accepted Norman's implementation of plans for the establishment of Commons Select Committees, originally prepared under Francis Pym's guidance'. (Lord Pym is the largely unacknowledged architect of the changes.) It was in the debate of 25 June 1979 that St John Stevas, by then Leader of the Commons, made his misleading comment about redressing 'the balance of power to enable the House of Commons to do more effectively the job it has been elected to do'. Doubts were expressed by, among others, Tony Benn and Gerald Kaufman. The latter was worried that the proposed system would place select committees 'in direct contention with the Government departments they are designed to shadow'. He thought that could be 'very dangerous'. Some thirteen years later, after a long period on the opposition front bench, Mr Kaufman became a highly successful, and waspishly effective, chairman of the National Heritage Committee in 1992.

The departmental select committees have been one of the most studied aspects of Parliament. The verdicts have generally been favourable. While the Commons, and its committees, could never have power as such, which remains with the Government, they have gained in influence and improved scrutiny. As Michael Ryle, a former senior Clerk, said in evidence to the Procedure Committee inquiry of 1989–90, this impact has been in various ways: more frequent and systematic examination of the policies and acts of government (by being permanent, having a wide remit and being bolder); the provision of more information about the workings of government; improving the contact between Parliament and the people; opening up the arguments of pressure groups; and increasing the influence of Parliament on government policy. Academic observers, even instinctively cautious ones like Nevil Johnson, have accepted (in Ryle and Richards, 1988, p. 167) that the post-1979 system 'has operated to strengthen the sense of accountability to Parliament on the part of the executive, and indeed has added a new dimension to the traditional procedures on the floor of the House for asserting the accountability of government'. He argued that the process was best described as the pursuit of 'explanatory dialogue' since the committees did not change policy, levels of expenditure or the way in which public services are administered. The main inquiry by the Commons itself, by the Procedure Committee in 1990, described (p. lxxix) 'the change to a system of departmentally-related Select Committees as worthwhile and as a success'. In particular, the 'holding of ministers and officials to account for their policies, actions and decisions . . .' is carried out 'by the departmentally-related committees in a far more rigorous manner than is feasible on the floor of the House, where it is all but impossible to tie down an able or reasonably well-briefed minister in a few minutes at Question Time'. Like Ryle, the committee also stressed other positive effects, such as the discovery and publication of information, the platform committees give to outside organizations and individuals to express their views, and 'the enrichment of public debate on various issues'. But the record is patchy; the evidence-taking has at times been weak and over partisan and some reports have been slight.

From my own observation, the most important impact has come

from the public hearings, questioning of ministers, civil servants and others. This has forced ministers to produce more detailed answers than are required on the floor of the House. Select committees are now part of ministers' lives and therefore part of the policy-making debate. This has applied particularly where committees have held regular sessions on important policy issues, notably after Budgets or before European Councils. This has broadened the debate. The committees have also tackled controversial matters, such as monetarism, the Pergau dam and aid to Malaysia, London's health service, the future of the BBC, the operation of the Child Support Act, and various privatization measures in ways that would never have happened before 1979. In most of these cases, the gathering of evidence was more important, and certainly more influential, than the subsequent reports.

The champions of select committees find it harder to produce cases where their reports have changed government policy. It would in some ways be odd if they did on important matters. Of course, ministers have to provide detailed replies to reports and that concentrates minds in Whitehall – as does the need to present evidence. But ministers can, and frequently do, disregard or ignore findings with which they disagree without much of a political stir. The Procedure Committee report of 1989–90 argued that the Home Affairs Committee had had an influence on the abolition of the 'Sus' laws, while the Foreign Affairs Committee report on the future of Hong Kong and the Treasury and Civil Service Committee's recommendations on the publication of annual departmental reports were also quoted as being influential. More recently, it is possible to point to the work of the Social Security Committee on the Child Support Agency and the mis-selling of pensions, and to the Trade and Industry Committee's report on pit closures. These are the exceptions rather than the rule. I would draw a distinction between major expenditure decisions or, say, privatization, where the influence of select committees has been small, and organizational questions, such as the civil service or relations with the Bank of England, where their influence has been greater. In part, this is because the former is more contentious between the parties, while the latter is less a matter of ideological division. But the Procedure Committee accepted (p. xxix) that 'Select Committees are not an alternative Government, nor Royal Commissions producing detailed blueprints for the future.' The then Treasury and Civil Service Committee broadened the debate on economic policy, but there is no evidence that it had any real impact on decisions taken by Sir Geoffrey Howe or Nigel Lawson during the heyday of the Thatcher governments.

The committees have generally not done well in conducting post-mortem investigations into policy errors and scandals, with the exception of the regular and long-established audits involving the Public Accounts Committee. The inquiries that have been carried out, such as on the sinking of the *Belgrano*, the Westland affair, the Pergau dam, arms for Iraq, BSE, and Gulf War Syndrome, have exposed some of what has gone wrong, but they have not been entirely successful. This is partly because such inquiries are usually into what has been done by the current administration and therefore are, by definition, highly contentious and partisan. The government members on the committee are pulled by their party ties into not being too critical of the ministers they support every evening in the division lobbies. There is also the danger of such investigations turning into disciplinary tribunals, questioning and criticizing named civil servants. As important are the practical problems of conducting such inquiries, not because of a lack of staff resources, but because of a shortage of members' time and the danger that such inevitably lengthy investigations will squeeze the time for regular inquiries into the expenditure, administration and policy departments. Also, few MPs are skilled in conducting, and sustaining, forensic questioning, while with a committee of nearly a dozen there is always pressure to allow every member a chance to intervene, which disrupts a sustained line of questioning. Both the Trade and Industry and the Public Service Committees have suggested setting up special parliamentary commissions to establish factual information on complex subjects which would otherwise occupy too much of a committee's time. The model might be that of the National Audit Office, which conducts investigations to establish the facts and then reports to the Public Accounts Committee which, if necessary, questions the civil servants concerned. The committee itself is not at the cutting edge of the investigation. There may also be a case not just for special committees or parliamentary commissions, but also inquiries being carried out in the first instance by non-parliamentary teams.

An important weakness of the departmental select committees has been their patchy treatment of public expenditure. Some committees have regarded this as a central part of their responsibilities, notably the

Defence Committee since arguments over spending and value for money are at the core of the Ministry of Defence's eternal battles with the Treasury. The Social Security Committee has been similarly assiduous, but the Procedure Committee noted in its 1990 inquiry (p. x) that just over half the departmental committees had claimed to have devoted some attention to the scrutiny of expenditure. Of course, it is not always possible to draw a clear distinction between expenditure, policy and administration, but the plans produced by the Government each year should be subject to regular scrutiny. However, there is a tendency for some committees merely to argue for more money for the department they are scrutinizing. They act as parliamentary lobbyists for the department and the interests it sponsors. There is a danger of committees becoming too closely identified with pressure groups. Douglas Hurd noted, however, in a lecture (1997) that: 'Parliament has the indispensable job of balancing out the general interest. It would be a disaster if Parliament simply became a collection of advocates of particular causes.' Apart from the Treasury Committee, there has been little attempt to examine spending priorities. Few committees have ever suggested possible cuts in programmes, though some have a good record in signalling the rising cost of long-term programmes, notably the Defence Committee, as well as, of course, the Public Accounts Committee in its later examination of how money has been spent.

Similar points can be made about the scrutiny of Next Steps executive agencies. As I discussed in Chapter Four, there has been a running debate about how they should be accountable and over relations between ministers and their chief executives. The Liaison Committee concluded in February 1997 (p. xv) that 'To date executive agencies have not been sufficiently accountable.' But a more serious worry is whether Parliament exercises sufficiently the powers it already has. For instance, a number of witnesses to the Public Service Committee inquiry into ministerial accountability (p. lxv) argued that committees should 'take a more serious and long-term interest in agency performance and administration'. The typically forthright Professor George Jones of the London School of Economics went much further in his evidence to the Procedure Committee inquiry of 1990. He argued (p. lxxvii) that the 1979 changes took the House 'off in the wrong direction' since the terms of reference of the new committees were too wide and they lacked a sharp focus. Professor Jones was worried that the committees pursued the hobby-horses of their chairmen or individual members. He argued that the post-1979 committees had 'ignored their proper target – administration – and had become involved in attempts to tackle policy issues by a consensual approach. This, he claimed, went "against the grain of the British constitution", since it ignored the role of the House of Commons as an arena for debate and for the clash of party opinion.' Jones was seen by the Procedure Committee as being provocative, but he had a partial point. It is not that it is wrong for the departmental select committees to examine policy, but too often this has led to a neglect of expenditure and administration, and especially of executive agencies and the multitude of other new public-sector organizations, such as the utility regulators. This is one of the least discussed, but most important, gaps in the scrutiny work of the Commons.

A related issue, discussed in more detail in the next chapter, is the involvement of departmental select committees in public appointments. Ever wary of ministerial patronage, Tony Benn had unsuccessfully argued in the Commons debate when they were set up in June 1979 that they 'should have the right to vet at least the chairmen of all the major public corporations before they are appointed ... A select committee should be able to recommend to the House that a candidate should not be confirmed.' However, since these are prerogative powers, exercised by ministers in the name of the Crown, the committees have no formal role, except where some, like the Comptroller and Auditor General, are accountable to the House. But the Liaison Committee report of February 1997 contained several examples of where committees have been informally involved. For instance, the Defence Committee has for some time taken evidence on appointments to the post of Chief of Defence Procurement where outside candidates are considered. The committee took written evidence in advance on the criteria for selection and oral evidence subsequently from the new incumbent. Michael Colvin, the committee chairman before the May 1997 election, concluded (p. 26) that 'for the time being we believe that this scrutiny should be confined to prior information on the criteria for selection and subsequent evidence from the person chosen and not any participation in the selection process. In the case of senior military appointments, we are particularly wary of introducing political considerations into a choice which is ultimately made on advice to the Crown'. Gerald

Kaufman, chairman of the National Heritage Committee, noted (p. 54) the committee's recommendation that 'when (after consultation) the Secretary of State proposes someone for a Governor's position, the committee should have the opportunity of interviewing the candidate before the nomination is confirmed'. The Major government did not agree. Paul Channon, the pre-election chairman of the Transport Committee and a former cabinet minister, discussed the idea of whether the approval of committees should be required before those nominated to senior public appointments took office. He noted (p. 89) that committees do not necessarily hear evidence in a way that would be conducive to a fair appraisal of different candidates, while 'it would seem strange for a select committee to be able to veto an appointment by a Secretary of State, who has the responsibility for the executive and would have to work with the appointee. There is also the danger that if committees were to have such formal powers, they would attract more interest from the whips, thus endangering their independence.'

A frequent criticism is that too few reports are debated on the floor of the House, though now a number of morning debates are specifically reserved for committee reports. This is a red herring. Such specially arranged debates are dominated – and sometimes almost exclusively attended – by members of the select committees congratulating themselves on the wisdom of their report, plus the minister and a shadow spokesman. The process is largely incestuous. Far more important is that the evidence and findings of select committees now form part of the broader information on which MPs draw in all kinds of debates rather than those focused specifically on the report. Anyway, there is often a reference, or 'tag', on the order paper when a recent report is relevant to a debate on, say, Europe or the economy. Chairmen and members of select committees are also regarded by the media as experts to be interviewed or quoted when their area of specialism comes up. However, committees could do more to publicize their findings – via executive summaries or press releases – among their own colleagues in Parliament.

Another frequently made criticism is that committees have inadequate resources and insufficient powers. Both points are exaggerated, as was accepted by both the Procedure Committee in 1990 and the Liaison Committee in 1997. The latter concluded (p. xiii) from the reports of the chairmen of individual committees that there is no demand from the departmental committees themselves for a massive increase in staff, nor would such an increase improve the output of committees either quantitatively or qualitatively. The real constraint on any substantial increase in activity by select committees is the inevitable limitation of the time of busy members. We support without reservation the view that much of the value of reports is that they are essentially member-driven, not staff-driven, and they should remain so.

In the American Congress, the large and highly qualified staffs are often the driving forces behind inquiries and reports, rather than the busy congressmen and, especially, senators. No one wants a position where members of the Commons are no longer asking questions and determining the shape of reports (even if the drafting is largely done by the clerks), though that is not a real danger in Britain in the foreseeable future. The present basis of combining small permanent staffs and outside specialist advisers (providing assistance much more cheaply than if working as commercial consultants) has generally worked well. Fears of moving too far in the American direction should not prevent some expansion in the size of permanent staffs and advisers. This would, anyway, be necessary if the committees take more seriously their role in regularly scrutinizing administration, expenditure and legislative proposals, let alone senior public appointments. The select committees as a whole are not expensive, costing nearly £4 million in the 1995–6 financial year, after excluding the cost of directly employed staff.

A related argument is how far the resources of the National Audit Office (NAO), which audits the accounts of central government departments and other public-sector bodies on behalf of the Public Accounts Committee, should be put at the disposal of other select committees. This would certainly help the departmental select committees if they are to spend more time looking into administration as well as policy. The main objection, and it is a strong one, is that the NAO is allowed access to all government files on the basis that it is auditing them rather than providing briefs for inquiries into policy. A widening in the NAO's remit would risk undermining its trusted and impartial role in providing analyses of how public money has been spent, not just on grounds of probity but also efficiency and effectiveness. Departments would be much more wary if they thought the NAO was looking for material for potentially damaging, and controversial, inquiries into current policy.

There is, however, scope for more co-operation between the Public Accounts Committee and the departmental select committees about the NAO's programme of inquiries. The Public Service Committee suggested in its report on ministerial accountability (p. lxiv) in July 1996 that the departmental select committees should have the power to request a memorandum from the NAO concerning any aspect of the economy, efficiency and effectiveness with which the department concerned has used its resources. In practice, many informal links have been developed, and the Liaison Committee in its February 1997 report reflected the worries of the Public Accounts Committee that the NAO's access to all papers in departments might be jeopardized if the relationship was formalized and, indeed, there is a statutory bar on the NAO questioning the merits of the policy objectives of any department. But the role of the NAO can, and should, be greater in helping a wide range of select committees.

On powers, there have been some detailed problems. The Public Service Committee in 1995–7 pushed for greater precision over the rights of committees in asking to see specific named civil servants, which had been blocked by the Thatcher government during the Defence Committee's inquiry in 1986 into leaks during the Westland affair. Ministers have been reluctant to surrender their ultimate discretion, even though they have said they will 'normally' put forward chief executives of executive agencies to give evidence on matters assigned to an agency. The so-called Osmotherly Rules governing the conduct of civil servants in front of select committees have never had any formal parliamentary status. They were internal government guidance like 'Questions of Procedure for Ministers'. The Commons achieved an important symbolic advance in passing a resolution in the dying days of the 1992–7 parliament laying down the conduct it expected of ministers and civil servants in relation to the House. But, in general, there is no real problem over formal powers, as opposed to a Whitehall culture of secrecy (much reduced but still existing in some departments) and an absence of political will. Because the majority on every select committee, in the 1997 parliament a large majority, comes from MPs on the government side, there is a reluctance to push differences with ministers over the provision of information and the like to the point of public confrontation.

A more pertinent criticism is the absence of adequate follow-up.

Short-termism is an occupational handicap not just of financial markets and journalists but also of politicians. Few committees sustain an interest in a subject and this allows government departments to provide evasive answers in their formal responses knowing that, in most cases, they will not be pressed on them. There are exceptions, notably the Public Service Committee and Home Affairs Committee, which have followed earlier inquiries. But the Procedure Committee's verdict in 1990 (p. xix) that select committees were more willing to challenge negative government replies or check on progress on the implementation of recommendations may be over-optimistic.

One of the central weaknesses of the departmental select committees is what is commonly perceived to be their strength: their ability to pick and choose their own subjects. The Procedure Committee report of October 1990 strongly defended (p. xiv) the right of individual committees to decide how much time to devote to scrutiny of expenditure, policy or administration according to their own political judgment and in the light of the special characteristics of the departments they monitor. 'We are therefore sceptical about the scope for, and the desirability of seeking to pressurize the departmentally-related Select Committees into giving a higher priority to one type of work as opposed to another.' The same resistance to having a duty imposed to report on this or that subject was evident in the end-of-parliament survey of select committees in February 1997. For instance, Sir Malcolm Thornton, the then chairman of the Education and Employment Committee, said (pp. 30–31) he was 'less convinced by the idea of placing a duty on committees to take regular evidence from the relevant chief executives [of Next Steps agencies] and chairmen [of non-departmental public bodies]'. In particular, 'Committees should retain the power to set their own agendas, responding to the current debate and helping to shape the agenda where appropriate.' Moreover, 'given the large number of such bodies, the committee might well take up a considerable amount of its time interviewing all chief executives during each session'. Sir Malcolm was also worried about the danger of staleness if MPs went through the motions of taking evidence from bodies that had nothing particularly new to say.

This approach is also defended privately by senior Clerks both on the grounds that it is up to the members of a particular committee to choose their lines of inquiry and because diversity is anyway desirable and provides examples of best practice. I am less sure. There are certainly merits in a variety of approach, and it would be impossible anyway to impose uniformity. But the committees are not autonomous bodies. They have a specific duty to report to the House on 'the expenditure, administration and policy' of the various bodies in their area and this should not be completely a matter for each individual committee. They are not doing their job effectively unless they report properly to the House on the public-expenditure decisions of the departments concerned and the plans of the associated executive agencies and non-departmental public bodies. This need not always involve evidence-taking sessions each year with every single agency or body since they are so many. It would be up to the committee's staff to sift through the latter's reports to see what was worth examining, though the chairmen and chief executives of major bodies should report regularly. The same point applies to the main utility regulators since they are not properly answerable to Parliament (as I argued in Chapter Four).

The Commons Clerks are always wary, and rightly so, about the instinct of reformers always to call for a strengthening of select committees. This is not just because of the constraints of the party battle but also because of the demands on the time of MPs themselves. There is a limit to what can be asked of members with extensive constituency and party commitments who see no obvious personal advantage in the largely unreported work of select committees. I also believe that the patchy record of committees reflects the patchy quality of their MPs, given that virtually all ambitious members want to serve on the government or opposition front benches. That balance has to change if select committees are to be revitalized.

The other main long-term area of complaint and debate is the way Parliament considers legislation. As Gavin Drewry pointed out (in Ryle and Richards, p. 126), 'Parliament's main legislative function lies largely in legitimization.' The main decisions are taken before Parliament sees a bill: 'Most bills are the products of hard bargaining in Whitehall, with Parliament being presented, in effect, with a *fait accompli*, too late to exert any real influence.' This has limited the impact of procedural changes. Successive governments have attempted to streamline procedures – for instance, taking the committee stages of most bills upstairs in smaller standing committees. That became a widespread practice after the Morrison changes of 1945–6, while from the later 1960s the committee stage of the Finance Bill was usually split in two with the most contentious proposals being debated on the floor of the House and the more detailed, technical provisions being considered upstairs. The end product has been highly unsatisfactory, leading to a hollow, adversarial process in which government and opposition confront each other and achieve little. Most amendments are made in response to the arguments of affected bodies and pressure groups. Governments use the committee and report stages of bills as an opportunity to work out and improve the details, not as a chance to listen or permit sustained scrutiny. As I discussed in Chapter One, the legislative process was the subject of a devastating and authoritative report by a Hansard Society Commission under the late Lord Rippon published in 1993. There have been some improvements, mainly in the pre-legislative stage of greater consultation over draft bills and clauses rather than in the legislative stage when a bill has been published. As Tony Newton pointed out in a Commons debate on procedure on 11 July 1996: 'A more structured planning of the programme and more bills published in advance in draft would make it possible for departmental select committees to contribute to the debate by taking evidence and bringing out reports.' He regarded this as a more promising development than the use of special standing committees, taking evidence between the second reading and the usual line-by-line standing committee stage. This is because there would be more time for properly considered scrutiny than in the 'relatively compressed' twenty-eight-day period in which a special standing committee can operate more like a select committee. Moreover, 'It is inevitably easier for ministers to respond to points emerging from such scrutiny before the bill is published.' This is convincing since the pre-legislative stage is when decisions are really taken.

The Jopling Committee (more formally the Select Committee on Sittings of the House) in 1991–2 recommended a number of sensible improvements to the way the House conducted its business, including fewer late nights, Wednesday morning sittings and ten constituency (that is, non-sitting) Fridays per session. Most controversially, the committee recommended (p. xxi) that timetable provisions should be applied 'to all stages of Government bills after second reading'. After nearly three years of wrangling, some of the ideas on timing of business were implemented, but it was only possible to agree to voluntary timetabling of legislation in committee, which worked reasonably well over the following two years.

The handling of legislation was chosen as the first priority for the Select Committee on Modernization. But the memorandum submitted by Ann Taylor, the Leader of the Commons, to the committee, underlined the tensions in the reform process. Governments, and chief whips, always want certainty about the passage of legislation and, with a secure Commons majority, they are entitled to do so. She called for a flexible approach to the means of achieving increased consultation about legislation, and this formed the basis of the committee's first report in July 1997. This appears sensible on paper, but the question is always who determines the flexibility. There is little dispute about her suggestions for improving consultation before bills are formally introduced. This would be via the publication of Green and White Papers, or draft clauses and entire bills in draft – building on changes introduced by Tony Newton. This is the key stage when bills can be improved before they become part of a highly public, adversarial process. There is also usually more time to have adequate consultations with affected bodies and inquiries by departmental select committees then. The problem is more what happens once a bill has been introduced, when there is usually less time for lengthy investigation. The suspicion is always that the government of the day will only decide to use the proposed procedures for consultation on less contentious measures or ones which cannot be introduced until a later session, and will use traditional methods to force through the more important and controversial items in its programme. Yet, while the main parties may not agree on the principle of such measures, these are often the bills most in need of detailed scrutiny and improvement. Indeed, even where the main parties disagree sharply over the principles of a bill, there is still scope to improve the details. The Blair government has suggested that there should be a wider range of opportunities for evidence-taking before a conventional line-by-line standing committee starts, and more use of the existing procedures for special standing committees. These have been used on only seven occasions since 1981, all involving less contentious bills. But unless it is the norm for all bills to be considered in this way – except where the House specifically decides otherwise – then the proposals may make little difference in practice.

A perennial problem has been the balance between the right of a government with a majority to have its way against the right of the opposition to have its say. The weapon of delay is largely meaningless and the Jopling reforms, referred to above, resulted in voluntary agreement on the timetabling of most legislation for the second half of the 1992–7 parliament (though the programme was generally light then). The Modernization Committee suggested (pp. xxii–xxiii) the possibility of programming legislation through arrangements which are more formal than the deals agreed through the usual channels (that is, the whips) but more flexible than the guillotine. This might allow more give and take so that opposition members could put forward amendments which would not be rejected automatically by ministers. Legislation might be considered in a more orderly manner with the abandonment of the current rule that a bill (other than a private measure) must complete its passage through Parliament in a single session or fall. Such a carry-over would allow more time for scrutiny.

Most of the focus is usually on primary legislation – that is full acts which have gone through all stages in Parliament. Less discussed, but often as important in practice, is the adequate treatment of secondary legislation, both statutory instruments and the increasing number of European directives and regulations (which I discussed in Chapter Two). This is a largely hidden area of parliamentary activity, despite the assiduous and largely unheralded work of the Statutory Instruments Committee and the Joint Committee of both Houses. The Procedure Committee in a report in June 1996 on 'Delegated Legislation' argued (p. ix) that 'There is too great a readiness in parliament to delegate wide legislative powers to ministers, and no lack of enthusiasm on their part to take such powers. The result is an excessive volume of delegated legislation.' It cannot, however, be avoided and the priority is to ensure that such delegated legislation receives adequate parliamentary scrutiny and that amendments and improvements can be made. The committee made a number of recommendations for improving procedures to allow more time for scrutiny and the creation of a sifting committee to identify which proposals required more debate, on the lines of the European scrutiny committees. The Commons has shown that it can act in this area. Following the Deregulation and Contracting Out Act of 1994, a special Deregulation Committee was created in 1995. This permitted detailed examination of deregulation proposals within a set sixty-day period, the exposure of flaws and problems which has allowed improvements to be made in draft orders. Almost every amendment recommended by the committee has been accepted.

Even if there remains much disagreement over the scope for constitutional change generally, there is wide agreement across the party spectrum on much of what needs to be done in the House of Commons, according to reports produced over the last few years by Tessa Keswick and Edward Heathcoat Amory (of the Centre for Policy Studies), Andrew Lansley and Richard Wilson (in a pamphlet published by the Conservative 2000 Foundation), Professor Philip Norton (a conservative critic of wholesale constitutional reform), a series of reports from Charter 88 (Power, 1996) and Democratic Audit (Dunleavy, 1995), and the Liberal Democrats (in a report heavily influenced by Michael Ryle, a former senior Clerk). They all agreed on the need to give select committees more powers, both in scrutinizing the executive and in examining legislation. Virtual unanimity exists both on the need for all bills to be examined either in special standing committees or by revamped super-committees and for the end of the sessional cut-off whereby bills automatically fall at the end of a session. The suggestion that the chairmen of select committees should be paid the same as ministers of state has been made in virtually identical language both from the right by Tessa Keswick and Edward Heathcoat Amory and by centre-left reformers from the Charter 88/Democratic Audit stable like Professor Patrick Dunleavy (1995). Extra payments for chairmen, they agree, are necessary to reflect the importance of the role of select committees in overall policy development. Most of these commentators have recognized that their ideas will add to the workload of members and have either favoured making the committees larger or reducing some of the other workload of members (even the apparently heretical idea that they should do less welfare casework in their constituencies).

Yet many of these reports have accepted that a cautious, incremental approach, like that apparently favoured by the Blair government, is not enough. For instance, a reduction both in the number of ministers and in the size of the Commons is favoured by many on the right, like Douglas Hurd, Tessa Keswick and Edward Heathcoat Amory, and Philip Norton, as well as by the Liberal Democrats. Keswick and Heathcoat Amory have argued for a 20 per cent reduction in the number of MPs (down to around 525 to 530) and a similar proportionate cut in the number of ministers (down to just over 70). Norton has talked (1997) of reducing the number of MPs to 500, and possibly fewer. For instance, if every member represented a constituency with an average size of 100,000 electors (as some nearly did before the 1997 boundary changes), there would be 436 members. The Liberal Democrats have proposed a reduction in the number of members of the Commons to about 450 and aiming for a limit of 10 per cent of members being paid as ministers.

These ideas, however, require a fundamental re-examination of the role of Parliament, both its place within the broader constitutional context and its internal workings and structure. Is the Diceyan doctrine of parliamentary supremacy any longer sustainable? Or is Parliament to be part of a more pluralist structure constrained by a bill of rights and with formally entrenched powers for local government, regional assemblies, etc.? Is it possible to reconcile the telling contrast, highlighted by Douglas Hurd (1997), that 'the legislative process should be measured and where necessary slowed. The executive process has to match the speed of the world in which we live'? If we want to preserve Parliament at the centre of our political system, does the balance with the executive need to be altered? If select committees are to live up to the hopes and ambitions of their supporters, does the present career structure of the Commons – dominated by frontbench ambitions – have to change?

CHAPTER TEN

Parliament and the Constitution

> This task of reviving or remaking the old checks and balances must be undertaken, not in a sweeping, blank-sheet fashion, but rather with a careful appreciation of practicalities; what will fit in with our parliamentary system, what MPs and public opinion will find fitting, what is consonant with national tradition and international obligation.
>
> Ferdinand Mount, *The British Constitution Now*, 1992

> Now that the din of constitutional argument is in the air, it cannot be said too strongly that an effective Parliament has to be central to any new constitutional settlement. A more robust Parliament would even make some elements of constitutional reform less pressing.
>
> Tony Wright, MP, and David Marquand, *Political Quarterly*, April–June 1996

If Parliament is to thrive in the next century, the intellectual strangle-hold that Dicey's doctrine of parliamentary sovereignty has had over the past century must be broken. Instead of providing an impregnable wall to protect Parliament the doctrine has left Parliament isolated as other sources of power have grown up outside the battlements and, indeed, have undermined them. Like it or not, Parliament is no longer the absolute and sole repository of power. So instead of pretending that it is, or merely bemoaning the challenges to its supremacy, it is necessary to think more creatively about Parliament's role in the constitution.

British politicians are, however, remarkably casual about the constitution. They are forever willing to strike attitudes, denouncing this or that political development as an infringement of some great constitutional principle. But they are reluctant to think about the constitution. As Nevil Johnson, hardly a constitutional radical, so vividly complained twenty years ago (1977, p. x), 'There has over a fairly long period been a retreat from constitutional ways of thinking in Britain.' Writing at the beginning of this decade, Ferdinand Mount argued (1992) that, 'We have deceived ourselves into thinking that this preference for pragmatism, for muddling through, is the age-old British way of doing things, when, in fact, it has really grown up only during the past 100 years and is a symptom of decadence rather than continuity.' That was exposed by the general sterility of the discussion of the constitution during much of the period of Tory rule from 1979 until 1997. On the one side, there was the almost Panglossian complacency of Tory ministers; on the other, there was the sweeping radicalism of Charter 88 and the fundamentalist reformers. The defenders of what they think is the status quo failed to recognize the extent to which the constitution has changed, and Parliament's place in it, as I have argued in this book.

The supremacy of Parliament is already being qualified by Britain's membership of the European Union, while British judges are already being influenced by the European Convention of Human Rights. But this is in a messy and unsatisfactory way, which is one of the main arguments for incorporation. It is not possible, if it ever was, to return to some neat model of a unitary state in which Parliament reigned supreme, untroubled by Europe, an activist judiciary, executive agencies, utility regulators, an assertive media, globalization, let alone by a bill of rights or a devolved Scottish Parliament. Parliamentary sovereignty has never been absolute in practice. It has been qualified by claims of the higher authority of the people since the Irish Home Rule arguments of the 1880s onwards over the use of the referendums, let alone by the introduction of universal suffrage after the First World War, while, more recently, some judicial activists have talked about a 'higher-order' law. Indeed, some Scots argue that parliamentary sovereignty is an English concept that has never been accepted north of the border. In a case brought against the Lord Advocate, the senior Scottish law officer in 1953, the Scottish Lord Justice Cooper ruled that the principle of parliamentary sovereignty had not been introduced in Scotland. Both the Claim of Right in 1988 and the Scottish Constitutional

Convention insisted that sovereignty belonged to the Scottish people. In a parallel argument, Robert Hazell, director of the Constitution Unit in its productive two-year life, has made the point (1997) that the United Kingdom has not been a unitary state in the way that Conservative defenders of the Union often claim. It has, rather, been what political scientists call a union state, combining distinct and different nations with different legal, educational and religious systems, separate administrative arrangements and, in the case of Northern Ireland for fifty years, legislative devolution too. So there is no neat system of a supreme Parliament under threat, but instead an already diverse structure.

The constitutional radicals are, however, wrong to exaggerate both the faults in the existing system and the significance of any changes. A written constitution or devolution are not instant answers to all the nation's ills. And I do not believe that there is general, or even very substantial, acceptance yet of the case for a wholesale transformation of Britain to a federal state (certainly not in England), or even to a written constitution, as in the USA. Changes in Britain are going to be asymmetrical and step-by-step. I also think that there is only likely to be a gradual shift away from the Diceyan approach to parliamentary sovereignty. As David Marquand wrote, complainingly, in 1988 (p. 242): 'The whole notion of federalism – the notion that state power should be divided between different tiers of government, each supreme in its own sphere – is alien. So is the central European view of democratic government as a process of consensus-building, based on power sharing between different social and political interests: the "consociational", as opposed to the majoritarian, conception of democracy.' That is one reason, among many, why Britain has been such an uneasy partner in the European Union.

But the gradualists – in which I include the Blair government – are at fault as well in appearing to suggest that a series of piecemeal changes can be carried out without having much wider implications. Scottish devolution is not solely a matter for those living north of the border. But the Labour leadership appears almost frightened of scaring people off if they talk about the broader constitutional picture. These doubts, which I expressed in *The Times* in July 1997, brought an immediate response from the Lord Chancellor himself. He argued that the interconnections had been thought through. Moreover, as soon as the Blair government was formed, the Prime Minister had set up a cabinet committee with responsibility for constitutional reform policy, 'for the very reason that we need to consider the whole picture and to ensure that our programme maintains its coherence'. Lord Irvine pointed out that he personally chaired three separate committees, on devolution, on freedom of information and on the incorporation of the European Convention, in order to ensure that the implications of each of the reforms are thought through and the linkages are got right. Freedom of information legislation must be consistent with the European Convention, while by legislating to ensure that those affected by administrative decisions are always given reasons, the Government aims to show that the convention is a basic floor of human rights, not a ceiling. We will see. The intention is there, but is the will? Can a generation of politicians so used to the executive mindset genuinely agree to changes that make their life harder? After all, the politicians and advisers at the top of the Blair government have succeeded by imposing tight discipline on their party rather than by permitting debate and dissent. There is a tension between their professed belief in decentralization and in changing the way that government is run and their everyday centralist instincts.

We are now at an unstable half-way stage. Change has occurred, and will occur even more rapidly over the next few years. Yet there is no clear intellectual framework. Important innovations are being grafted on to the traditional doctrine of parliamentary sovereignty. But it can no longer bear the weight. It would be better – is, indeed, vital – to think about Parliament's place in a more pluralist structure. I do not believe we should jump rapidly to a fully fledged federal system guaranteed by a written constitution. There is no demand for that, nor is it supported as an immediate answer by a major party. We are not going to have Home Rule all round in the foreseeable future and elected politicians will not grant judges the powers of the US Supreme Court. But we should aim to create, perhaps to re-create, a more formal system of checks and balances, given that the informal constraints and understandings of the past have disappeared. These checks would not be a threat to Parliament, but rather a guarantee of its future role in relation to other institutions. This should happen in a step-by-step way, rather than as a result of some big-bang transformation, which is neither necessary nor suits the British political character. Yet changes should be coherent and internally consistent rather than piecemeal.

For a start, we need to think about how constitutional changes occur and should be entrenched (where I, like everyone else, owe a big debt to the work of the Constitution Unit over the past few years). At present, in a classic Diceyan way, one Parliament could change the electoral system, only to have the changes amended by its successor. Provided the government of the day had a working majority in the Commons, the only hurdle would be the ability of the Lords to delay the measure for one session under the Parliament Act. The sole exception is that the Lords has an absolute veto on any measure to extend the life of the parliament. In one sense, as Robert Hazell has argued (1997), there are doubts whether within our parliamentary system at present, and with the doctrine of the sovereignty of Parliament, 'there can be any effective legal form of entrenchment.' What Westminster gives Westminster can give away. In the absolute sense that is true. But obstacles can be created to safeguard constitutional changes and, incidentally, protect against overhasty changes. There are various possible methods of entrenchment (as I discussed in Chapter Five), which should apply to key elements of the constitution such as changes in the voting system, establishment or abolition of any tier of government, and any bill of rights, as well as the maximum length of a parliament (whether or not fixed). Any proposal certified as being of 'first-class constitutional importance' by the Clerks of the House should fall into this category. It should be subject to a post-legislative referendum of those affected, while a reformed House of Lords (one largely based on election rather than inheritance or nomination) should have a special role as the guarantor of such entrenchment, linked to the use of referendums. The key question about the future of the House of Lords is less to do with its composition than with what powers it should have in relation to the House of Commons. Any doubts about interpretation of these entrenched provisions should be resolved by the law lords, or whatever name is given to the most senior appellate court.

A bill of rights, initially the European Convention of Human Rights, would of itself provide a powerful check and balance upon the will of the House of Commons. Much would depend on which version is chosen. I think Britain is unlikely to go down the road of the USA and create a Supreme Court with powers to strike down laws passed by the legislature whatever the views of elected politicians. That in itself has severe disadvantages, making the constitution inflexible and making nominations to the Supreme Court a matter of immense political importance. A more likely way forward for Britain is the acceptance that Parliament can, if necessary, override the courts' interpretation of the bill of rights after a ruling or by making clear in primary legislation its intention to override a provision in the bill of rights for some exceptional reasons such as national security. The New Zealand version of a largely interpretative role for the courts in saying whether or not a statute is consistent with the bill of rights has an obvious appeal to ministers, and to many judges. Elected politicians are wary of giving the judiciary the power to strike down an Act of Parliament. However, under the Canadian version, the courts can strike down laws subject to being overridden by the legislature – a 'notwithstanding' clause. Parliament would then have to make a specific and open decision when legislating about whether to override the bill of rights. That approach would still preserve parliamentary sovereignty since Parliament would itself have decided to give the courts this power to judge whether legislation is inconsistent and to provide remedies. Indeed, the existence of a let-out to allow Parliament to legislate 'notwithstanding' the convention would be weaker than Britain's current absolute obligations to treat European Union laws as superior to British laws, passed by Parliament, where they conflict.

Either the weaker or stronger approach to incorporation of the European Convention would still leave the courts, and in particular the law lords, in a special position in interpreting and safeguarding constitutional and other rights. This would inevitably push the top judges into a more public, and probably controversial, role, raising questions about their appointment. Consequently, there is a strong case for an independent advisory body such as a Judicial Appointments Commission to ensure greater transparency in the appointment of top judges. But if the senior judiciary takes on this expanded role, the law lords should no longer play an active part in the House of Lords as long as they are serving on its Appellate Committee.

Any new constitutional settlement must include the remaining prerogative powers of the Crown, or rather the Prime Minister and government of the day. The seventeenth-century revolution is in many ways incomplete. Parliament asserted its independence and sovereignty then. But the Crown/executive still retained, and retains, considerable powers which have only gradually, and not yet completely, been checked by Parliament and the courts since then. The extension of the franchise and rise of tightly disciplined parties removed the Crown's influence over the choice of ministers, but those ministers were able to exercise widespread discretion outside the direct control of Parliament. Revealingly, the main challenge to executive discretion in the past twenty years has come from the courts, rather than the legislature. But if we are moving towards a more formal system of checks and balances, these remaining prerogative powers are an anomaly. Inescapably, we are moving from being subjects of a remote, and in theory arbitrary, executive to becoming citizens with legally defined rights. High Tory romantics may regret this, but they should talk to judges about how far this change has already occurred. Even to mention the prerogative powers is to risk being accused of closet republicanism and being some-how unsound or maverick. That is nonsense. After all, much of the political debate in Britain for the three centuries up to the mid-nineteenth century was about the political power of the monarchy. The prerogative powers of the Crown should be a matter of political debate. Only some of these powers are any longer anything directly to do with the monarch. Most are exercised by the Prime Minister and other ministers in the name of the Crown.

The main residual direct constitutional powers of the monarch involve the appointment and dismissal of a prime minister and the granting of a dissolution of Parliament leading to a general election. These all involve the prime minister of the day going to Buckingham Palace for an audience with the monarch, in theory to seek permission or to be appointed. This is not the place to repeat the lengthy discussion on these issues by Professors Vernon Bogdanor and Peter Hennessy. In most cases, of course, there is no problem. The choice of prime minister is determined by the votes of the electorate and the decision on the timing of a general election does not place the monarch in a politically embarrassing situation. Indeed, the prime aim of the party leaders and the main official advisers is to avoid putting the monarch in a position of controversy, where he or she is seen to be favouring one side or another. But the issue is not entirely theoretical. Awkward situations involving the monarch have arisen in the past – for example, in 1910–11, 1923, 1940, 1957 and 1963 – and will no doubt do so again. But these did not compromise the impartiality of the monarchy because many of the discussions were conducted in secret and did not emerge until later. But not only is there now more criticism of the monarchy (largely for unrelated reasons to do with the private lives of the Queen's children) but it would be virtually impossible to keep consultations quiet in view of the extent of media coverage now – and quite right too. So these reserve constitutional-political powers need to be separated more from the person of the monarch himself or herself. I am, however, sceptical of suggestions of making the Speaker of the Commons responsible for asking this or that party leader to form a government when the decision is not clear-cut and no single party has an overall Commons majority. Not only is there no Speaker for a week after an election until the House has met, but this additional role would, in practice, risk undermining the non-partisan position of the Speaker, who would then have to deal with party leaders, both successful and aggrieved, on a day-to-day basis thereafter. It would be better if these residual powers were exercised by the monarch as an umpire distant from Parliament, but on the basis of advice of a group of elder states-men, both former prime ministers and leading public servants. This already happens informally to some extent, but these arrangements should be formalized with the identities of those involved being known and the broad principles under which they would operate made public beforehand. It is impossible to be too precise since, by definition, the rare occasions when the choice of prime minister is not clear-cut are likely to be inherently complicated. But greater transparency and public debate is desirable.

Moreover, any new government should be formally endorsed by the Commons, as, in effect, already happens with the vote at the end of the Queen's Speech debate. Similarly, a prime minister wanting to call a general election should have to obtain the approval of the Commons on a substantive motion naming polling day. Different arrangements would be necessary if we moved to fix-term parliaments; an early dissol-ution could not then be called by the prime minister of the day since that would defeat the purpose of having a fixed term. One trigger for an early election might be if the incumbent government fell and no alternative administration could be formed commanding a majority in the Commons. The theoretical right of the monarch to refuse a dissol-ution is impossible to exercise in practice since it would mean a direct confrontation with the prime minister. Under my suggestion, a prime minister whose party has just lost its overall majority in the Commons at a general election would not be allowed to seek an immediate replay in a second election unless he or she could win a vote in the House. By definition in these circumstances, the combined votes of the other parties could deny such a dissolution, forcing the prime minister to resign and giving another party leader the chance to form a government. This formula could still apply if we moved to a system of fixed-term parliaments where there could be a reserve power to call an earlier general election if the prime minister of the day obtained the approval of the Commons, though there might have to be some special trigger mechanism. None of these ideas would threaten the existence of the monarchy. Rather, by removing the risk of political controversy, they might make its survival more likely.

Much more important are the prerogative powers exercised by the prime minister and other ministers in the name of the Crown. These remain considerable, and have only gradually been limited by Parliament and particularly the courts. The executive is still able to act on its own authority in, for example, making appointments and ratifying treaties. But these powers should be subject to the scrutiny and approval of Parliament. On this, I agree with Tony Benn: patronage is the real source of power. Just as in finance and legislation where the Government puts proposals to Parliament to consider and approve, so major public appointments should have to be ratified by the Commons. As Andrew Marr has argued (1995, p. 338), if Parliament

> fails to be the centre of democratic legitimacy the heart of its function has been lost. The sprawling and insufficiently-accountable domestic state is therefore a matter for parliamentarians themselves. They must, above all else, reassert their authority over the patronage state based at Downing Street. If, as the theorists assert, Parliament really is sovereign, then there can be no reason why MPs should not agree that the heads of executive agencies, and of the big quangos, and of many other public bodies with real power over our lives, should be confirmed in their jobs by parliamentary committees, and hold them subject to parliamentary approval.

The initiative would remain with the executive. Only ministers could make nominations, but Parliament would have to consent after scrutiny by the relevant select committees. I would not include senior judges in this process to minimize partisan influence on the judiciary, but there should be a more transparent and open method of appointing them, as discussed earlier. Following the Nolan report, there are already improved procedures for openness in many public appointments but, welcome though these are, they are essentially administrative, not legislative. I discussed the various practical implications in Chapter Four and the safeguards needed to prevent abuse and not to deter high-quality people from putting themselves forward. The constitutional implications are clear. Bringing these prerogative powers within parliamentary control would strengthen the accountability of ministers, thus ensuring that MPs properly undertake one of their key roles.

This would be just one part of an attempt to ensure that these alternative centres of power are fully answerable to elected politicians – whether at Westminster or locally. The suggestion about the ratification of major public appointments by Parliament should be matched by a more systematic mechanism for ensuring the accountability of the various semi-detached public bodies, from the Bank of England, to executive agencies, non-departmental public bodies, NHS trusts and the plethora of education councils, to the BBC. This involves a different approach by select committees, which would not just be able to pick and choose what they investigate, but would have a duty to report to the House on the annual reports of these bodies and the expenditure plans of government departments, as well as examining major public appointments. Select committees should also be involved in considering proposals for legislation ahead of the finalization of drafts. This is a more important, since it is a more decisive, stage than the equally necessary task of making scrutiny of legislation by Parliament more deliberative through, for example, the use of special standing committees. I favour retaining the distinction between select and standing committees, though the former should have larger memberships to cope with the additional demands on them.

But these proposals raise both constitutional and practical implications. The two are related. Parliament cannot govern, and should not seek to do so itself. At the same time, the prime role of members of the Commons is either to sustain and form part of a government or to oppose it. This inevitably limits any idea of the Commons having a separate role in scrutinizing the Government. We do not have a formal separation of powers: indeed, the traditional Tory view, expressed by Douglas Hurd (1997) is that the function of the legislature is to sustain the executive and help it to make decisions in the national interest, rather than to check and make life difficult for the executive. There has always been an inherent contradiction in talk of members of select committees behaving in a non-partisan way, somehow detached from the parties to which they belong. Typically, these ambiguities have been fully explored by Enoch Powell. In the Commons debate in February 1979 on the Procedure Committee report which led to the establishment of the departmental select committees, Powell sought to correct some of the exaggerated claims of the reformers: 'In the last resort, it is allegiance to party as a condition of continuing and remaining effective in the House which is the lever by which governments overpower the House at their will from time to time. When we have perceived that, we notice that we are using the word "House" with a certain ambiguity. There are respects in which the House is a corporation: it is one of its attributes that it has a corporate character, and no one knows from one moment to the next when it will assume that corporate character . . . However, that is not the whole truth about the House. The House is not just a corporation, and simply to talk about the House *vis-à-vis* the Government is a totally inadequate description. The House comprises parties and, for most of the purposes of the House, its partisan character overrides its corporate character. If it did not, we could not be the continual, living and flexible expression of the will of those whom we represent.'

Powell was right to warn of the dangers of disappointment if you believe it is possible to redress the balance of power between government and the House of Commons. But that does mean it is impossible to lessen the influence of the executive over the legislature. British constitutional practice has never been a question of absolutes, but of a varying balance between the often conflicting pressures of sustaining an executive and holding it to account at the same time. That balance can, and should, be shifted within the overall constraints of party loyalties in a system where the executive is part of the legislature. That is also necessary for practical reasons. Parliament, or rather the House of Commons, cannot take on the strengthened role that I envisage unless the dominance of the executive is reduced. This dominance is behavioural as much as procedural. The problem is not just the ability of ministers to control business. That is inevitable when a party has an overall majority in the Commons, though more could be done procedurally to force ministers to explain themselves and obtain the approval of the legislature for their actions.

The more serious problem is behavioural. It goes back to an apparent paradox put forward by Norman St John Stevas in the debate on procedure in February 1979 when Powell also spoke. He said, 'We have a professional government and we still have an amateur legislature.' The same point that 'Parliament remains essentially an amateur body' has been made by Professor Philip Norton (1997). Its methods of scrutiny are not rigorous by the standards of the private sector, and, as Martin Summers has shown (1994), many, if not most, new members are unprepared for parliamentary work. This view of the Commons as 'amateur' may seem odd, even contrary, in a period when so much is written, usually disapprovingly, about the rise of the professional politician (in particular by myself, 1993). But the two statements are not incompatible. The growing generation of professional full-time politicians is primarily concerned with serving on the government or opposition front bench. They are keen to join the professional government, not become professional legislators. Few talented MPs enter the Commons with the ambition to remain backbenchers or serve on select committees for their whole time in the Commons. Even Frank Field, one of the most successful select committee chairmen, and on the back benches for most of his time in the Commons since 1979, admitted to me during the 1997 campaign how much he would like to be part of the Blair team – to which he was duly appointed two weeks later. This pattern of ambition has been shown by survey after survey of the ambitions of MPs as well as by the willingness of members to give up the chairmanships of prominent select committees to be middle-ranking or junior ministers, or in one case even a junior whip.

At present, around 89 out of 659 members of the Commons are ministers or whips, while between thirty and forty more are parliamentary private secretaries. They may not earn any more than their basic MP's salary but they have to be as loyal as fully paid ministers. And there are usually several more in party leadership posts. And the main opposition party usually shadows each ministerial post. Before the May 1997 election, Labour had a shadow team of more than a hundred. Even the much reduced Conservative opposition after then still had about sixty shadow spokesmen and whips. At a stroke, this accounts for nearly a third of the Commons, and many of its most talented

members. The remaining two-thirds include many who have been ministers or will be in future, as well as the mad, the bad and the odd.
Some long-serving backbenchers prove valuable members of select
committees, but the quality is very patchy with too many mediocre
members. Ex-ministers and future ministers are often among the most
effective members of select committees and are otherwise active in
holding ministers to account. But the future ministers often spend only
a short time on the back benches before either joining the government
or the opposition frontbench team. The cabinet and shadow cabinet
of summer 1997 spent just a year or two at the very most on a select
committee before eagerly joining their parties' front bench or becoming
a parliamentary private secretary. That was true of most of the Blair
cabinet and the Hague shadow cabinet. Only four members of the
former had spent more than a year or so on a departmental select
committee, reflecting the quick promotion of anyone of talent when
Labour was in opposition. By contrast, roughly two-fifths of the Hague
shadow cabinet had spent at least a couple of years on a departmental
select committee. That leaves select committees with patchy memberships: at the beginning of parliaments some talented new MPs who
disappear within a couple of years, but a hard core of former ministers
and a mixed bag of long-serving backbenchers. The departmental select
committees appointed in July 1997 were even patchier, in part because
of the extent of the Tory losses in the 1 May election. That removed
many ex-ministers from the running, and several of the former ministers
who were not on the Tory front bench chose not to serve on committees. This removed a valuable pool of experience. On the Labour side,
much of the talent had gone into the Government, so with a few exceptions the senior Labour members of select committees were not of the
highest quality. This provided a great opportunity for new members on
both sides, who took roughly two-fifths of the places. On past trends,
however, it is questionable how long some of them will serve before being
promoted on to the lowest rungs of the patronage ladder.

The magnet attraction of the front bench needs to be reduced. This
can be done in two ways: first, by reducing the number of ministers in
the Commons; and, second, by increasing the attractions of service on
select committees. All kinds of reasons can be advanced for the rise
from 33 to 86 in the number of ministers in the Commons since 1900:
the expansion of the welfare state, the growth in the complexity of

government involvement in society, the associated rise in the number of interest groups and Britain's membership of the European Union. All make big demands on the time of Whitehall departments. But it is not clear whether they require so many ministers. Many of the tasks performed by ministers who are MPs could equally well be undertaken by ministers who do not sit in the Commons, by special advisers or by senior civil servants. There is certainly a cachet about 'I've been to see the minister', even if one knows he or she is useless. It also suits civil servants to have ministers as public defenders of their department and its policies. In one sense, the large number of ministers ensures that civil servants are not seen publicly in a partisan light and is part of the price for a non-political civil service. But the balance is wrong. Of course, ministers are needed at the top of departments and to be accountable to the Commons, and, in a different way, to the Lords. But the balance is wrong, not least for its impact on the career patterns and focus of the Commons itself. Douglas Hurd has argued (1997) that junior ministers are 'one of the neglected assets of our parliamentary system. Several dozen of these able men and women would actually be more useful, and find a more rewarding role, leading the parliamentary efforts of their parties and helping to strengthen, for example, the performance of the select committees.' He has suggested that there should be a reduction in the number of ministers to match the reduction in the responsibilities of government itself.

The main reason for keeping the present number of ministers is to allow the Chief Whip – also known as Patronage Secretary – to dangle the bait of office in front of the ambitious and to have as big as possible a payroll vote as a ballast in the Commons. Many senior civil servants and ministers, or rather ex-ministers, privately accept the case for reducing the size of the executive. The Liberal Democrats, who have never tasted the pleasures of office, have suggested a maximum limit of 10 per cent of the size of the Commons being paid as ministers. At present, this would be 65 or 66, and the limit could even be ten to a dozen lower, especially if Scottish and Welsh devolution reduces the need for the present total of eight Scottish and Welsh Office ministers in the Commons. Even without such a painful reduction in paid opportunities, the number of MPs available for select-committee work could be increased if the total number of parliamentary private secretaries was halved by having only one per department.

This change in career patterns would only work if service as a back-bencher and on a select committee is made more attractive. This is partly a general question of restoring the role of the Commons and, more specifically, of giving select committees a more clearly defined responsibility and duty for improving accountability. A change in atti-tudes is needed – not some woolly well-intentioned bipartisanship but an acceptance that select committee and scrutiny work is as worthwhile as service on the front bench. A reduction in the size of front benches, and in the number of parliamentary private secretaries, would force the ambitious to focus on the committees as a way of making their names and exercising influence. At the same time, the party whips should be less eager to pluck out talented new members for promotion. There could also be more scope for a genuine two-way movement between ministerial office and chairmanship of, or senior post on, a select committee, rather than the latter being regarded as a consolation. This is apart from the problem – of former ministers leaving the House at the first election after they have ceased being ministers. In his valedic-tory report in February 1997 as chairman of the Liaison Committee (representing all select committees) before he retired from the Com-mons, Sir Terence Higgins, a long-serving committee chairman, argued (p. 3) that one of the strengths of the select-committee system has been

> the balance between new members who (particularly when their party is in government and they are not encouraged to speak on the floor of the House because it would delay the progress of business) are able to make their mark in a select committee. These need to be balanced by experienced members, particularly ex-ministers. It is very important that these senior members should be prepared to serve on select committees. Their experience is particu-larly important because they know how Government departments work from the inside.

The departmental select committees set up in July 1997 suffered because, by definition, there were relatively few ex-Labour ministers available to serve and many former Tory ones chose not to serve (with notable exceptions like Peter Brooke, Douglas Hogg and Virginia Bottomley).

The standing of select committees would be powerfully reinforced if their chairmen were paid. The Review Body on Senior Salaries (chaired by Sir Michael Perry, the former chairman of Unilever) discussed in its July 1996 report possible links between pay and a career structure in the House of Commons. The Review Body rejected any idea that length of service should be a factor in determining pay. It noted, however, from evidence submitted to it that some posts carrying additional responsibilities 'were worthy of financial remuneration. Some commented that to introduce remuneration for these responsibilities could provide progression for senior backbenchers and encourage ex-ministers to remain and use their experience for the benefit of the House.' The main offices referred to in evidence were the chairmen of the Public Accounts Committee and major select committees, and opposition frontbench spokesmen. Some witnesses suggested that the responsibilities of a major select committee chairman 'can require the same level of expertise as some junior ministerial posts'. A pay comparability exercise carried out for the Review Body by Hay Management Consultants also concluded that the responsibilities of this type of post were weightier than those of most backbenchers. There were differences about which posts should receive an additional payment: should it be just chairmen of major departmental select committees and scrutiny committees, or should it also include chairmen of standing committees who preside over the line-by-line consideration of bills? The Review Body noted that reform of the committee structure was already under discussion and recommended (p. 11) that it 'should consider further with the relevant Parliamentary authorities whether to make recommendations on the structure of additional remuneration for holders of certain positions of additional responsibility in the House'.

Nothing happened before the May 1997 general election, and, afterwards, Ann Taylor, the new Leader of the Commons, was distinctly unenthusiastic about the suggestion. This is wrong: of course there are difficulties in deciding which people in responsible parliamentary positions should be paid extra, and there are tricky questions about how committees are picked and chairmen chosen. Given the present practice of members of select committees being in effect nominated by the party managers – and then transmitted to the Committee of Selection – this would increase the already powerful patronage of the whips in all parties. I am sceptical of the suggestion by Labour MPs Graham Allen (1995) and Derek Fatchett (1994), and by Greg Power of Charter 88 (1996), that members of select committees should be elected by all

MPs. This would turn the process into a competition of ideological slates within parties, rather than producing well-qualified and talented committee members. Far better would be to return to the original conception of the Committee of Selection, which would make the choice and not merely rubber-stamp the choices of the party whips. It would be desirable if the whips were not on the committee, though they would naturally make their views known. Of course, the time is never right for a decision to pay some MPs more. There would always be a populist backlash in the more ignorant tabloids about greedy MPs. But the issue cannot be avoided. If Parliament wants to create a more diverse career structure, then the chairmen of select committees and others in similarly responsible positions should be paid more.

This question is symbolic of Parliament's willingness to change its attitudes, and to shift from being almost entirely an expression of party battles to adopting, as well, a more creative role. The constitutional changes that I outlined in the first half of the chapter set the context for a new place for Parliament in a more pluralist political system. But the procedural and behavioural changes I have discussed in the second half of the chapter are as important. The first provides a new role for Parliament; the second is intended to ensure that it fulfils that role.

CHAPTER ELEVEN

Conclusion – Ten Proposals for Reform

The challenges to the power, influence and relevance of Parliament are readily apparent. Some of these changes reflect social and economic forces beyond the control of any national government. Others are to do with institutional changes – relations with the European Union, the role and attitudes of the judiciary, and the organization of government itself. Parliament, and in particular the House of Commons, has responded slowly and inadequately. Following the May 1997 general election, there has been a renewed drive to modernize the House of Commons. Many of the ideas put forward by Ann Taylor, both in opposition and as Leader of the Commons, are sensible and the proposals in the first report from the Select Committee on Modernization are in the right direction. My doubts are on two, related, grounds. First, is there a real will at the top of the Blair government, where it counts, to allow the Commons to become a thorn in its side by questioning and scrutinizing? Or are the instincts of ministers, as I suspect, as executive-minded as that of their predecessors? And, second, does the analysis of what is wrong go far enough? Again, I am doubtful. Even senior parliamentarians seem reluctant to grasp the extent to which power and influence have gone elsewhere. In this chapter, I make ten specific proposals which would help.

1. Central features of the constitution should be formally entrenched. These would include, for example, changes in the voting system, establishment or abolition of any tier of government, any bill of rights as well as the maximum length of a parliament (whether or not fixed).

Any major constitutional proposal – those at present classified as of 'first-class constitutional importance' – should be subject to a post-legislative referendum of those affected. A permanent Electoral Commission would be established to administer such referendums and other aspects of the electoral system. A reformed House of Lords (one largely based on election rather than inheritance or nomination) should be the guarantor of such entrenchment.

2. The law lords, as the senior appellate court in the UK, would have the power to say whether a law was inconsistent with the European Convention of Human Rights, or a successor bill of rights, and to strike it down unless Parliament had specifically indicated its intention to override these rights. This would be similar to the Canadian approach, with an appropriate let-out clause if Parliament wanted to override the Convention or bill of rights. There might be provision for any ruling to be suspended for a defined period to allow the Government to say, and then for Parliament to decide, whether the Convention or bill of rights should be overridden. This would preserve parliamentary sovereignty in specific cases. But, as a necessary consequence, the law lords would have to accept that they could no longer play an active part in the legislative work of the House of Lords as long as they were serving on the Appellate Committee.

3. The remaining prerogative powers, exercised by ministers in the name of the Crown, should be subject to parliamentary control. Major public appointments made by the Government on behalf of the Crown would have to be approved by Parliament. Any nomination of a senior post (in effect, those requiring the personal approval of the prime minister) would first be considered by the relevant departmental select committee which would recommend whether there should be a debate and vote on the floor of the House on the appointment.

4. The number of paid ministers and whips serving in the Commons should be fixed at a maximum percentage of the total membership of the House. My preference would be an upper limit of 8 per cent, which would mean a maximum of 53 paid ministers and whips, down from 89 at present. This reduction would be easier to achieve once Scottish and Welsh devolution has been implemented. And there would be a further adjustment if the size of the Commons itself is reduced (see

proposal 10). The number of parliamentary private secretaries should also be limited to one per department.

5. The chairmen of select committees, and others in responsible parliamentary positions, should be paid an additional sum on top of their ordinary MP's salary. This might be around £10,000 to £15,000 for chairmen, on top of a backbencher's pay of £43,000 a year. This would be to enhance the standing of backbench and select committee work by comparison with the front benches.

6. Departmental select committees should have the duty, not the option, to report to the House every year on the expenditure programmes of the departments they monitor and the plans and reports of the leading executive agencies, non-departmental public bodies and regulators within their remit. This would be to ensure proper accountability of the new public sector, which has grown up outside the traditional Whitehall–Westminster network.

7. All legislation should go through a lengthy period of consultation to avoid the current frequent errors, and the amendments and amending bills now required. Governments should be obliged to publish consultative Green and White Papers and draft bills before any major legislation, and failure to do so could be grounds for delay by a reformed House of Lords. These proposals and drafts would be considered by departmental select committees or special select committees (depending on the weight of business in any area). This would be the main time for consultation. But, after publication and second reading, all bills would go to a special standing committee which could hear witnesses, unless the Government specifically sought the permission of the House for an accelerated procedure in exceptional circumstances. This would remove the discretion, and loopholes, in the proposals of the Select Committee on Modernization, and would force the Government to take responsibility for short-circuiting the procedures for greater consultation. All bills would be timetabled automatically with the arrangements being supervised by a business committee of the House chaired by one of the Deputy Speakers and excluding any party whips. The present annual cut-off for most legislation at the end of a session would disappear, but bills would have to become law within two years of being published or else fail.

8. Scrutiny of the heavy volume of European legislation should be strengthened, following the extension of the time for consideration of new proposals by national parliaments agreed at the Amsterdam summit. The European legislation committee should be given an enhanced standing and be integrated more with departmental select committees in considering future European legislative plans, as well as directives and regulations. The Westminster Parliament should also improve its contacts with the Strasbourg Parliament to increase awareness of what is on the agenda.

9. The post-Nolan procedures for regulating the personal conduct of MPs need to be strengthened after the cash-for-questions affair. Apart from the proposals to clarify the criminal law on the bribery and corruption of MPs, the House's self-regulatory procedures should also be reviewed. The post-Nolan rules on disclosure of outside interests should be tightened up so that members can no longer claim that their commercial activities have nothing to do with their being an MP when they obviously do. These rules also need to be enforced. The Parliamentary Commissioner for Standards should be able to initiate inquiries and publish his reports independent of the Standards and Privileges Committee so as to demonstrate his independence. The committee should operate more on a judicial basis with lawyers presenting the case against a member and defending him or her. The committee would still decide whether to act against a member and the full House would, as now, vote on what sanctions to apply.

10. The size of the House of Commons should be reduced and it should sit for less of the year. This may seem inconsistent with earlier proposals, which would increase the workload on many MPs, especially those active on select committees. But a reduction in the number of ministers in the Commons, plus decentralization of power to other elected bodies, and a less hurried timetable for legislation, should permit both a reduction in the number of members – say, from 659 to around 500 – and a changed pattern of sitting. The full House does not need to sit as often as it does. Many debates are poorly attended with no meaningful vote at the end. They could as easily be held in Grand Committees which any member could attend, as happens with Scottish and Welsh members in debates about their countries.

*   *   *

None of the above changes is an instant solution to the woes afflicting Parliament, but together and separately they address many of its current problems. They preserve parliamentary sovereignty in the absolute sense, but recognize the need for formal, and entrenched, checks and balances on the will of the current majority in the House of Commons. These proposals also offer MPs a chance to play a fuller and more satisfying role, both as potential and actual ministers and in scrutinizing the proposals and actions of ministers and other public bodies. Parliament would have a more modest role, alongside other institutions, but it would be reinvigorated, and still at the centre of the political system.

Bibliography

Adonis, Andrew, *Parliament Today*, Manchester, Manchester University Press, 1993

Allen, Graham, *Reinventing Democracy, Labour's Mission for the New Century*, London, Features Unlimited, 1995

Amery, L. S., *Thoughts on the Constitution*, Oxford University Press, 1947

Bagehot, Walter, *The English Constitution* (with an introduction by R. H. S. Crossman), London, Collins, Fontana Library, 1963

Ball, Stuart, and Seldon, Anthony, (eds), *The Heath Government 1970–74*, London, Longman, 1996

Blair, Tony, The Mais Lecture, City University, 22 May 1995

Blair, Tony, Speech at NewsCorp Leadership Conference, Hayman Island, Australia, 17 July 1995

Blair, Tony, interview with the *Scotsman*, 4 April 1997

Bogdanor, Vernon, *The People and the Party System, The referendum and electoral reform in British politics*, Cambridge, Cambridge University Press, 1981

Bogdanor, Vernon, *Politics and the Constitution, Essays on British Government*, Aldershot, Dartmouth, 1996

Bogdanor, Vernon, 'Ministerial Accountability', in special issue of *Parliamentary Affairs*, on the Scott Report, vol. 50, no. 1, January 1997

Bogdanor, Vernon, *Power and the People, A Guide to Constitutional Reform*, London, Victor Gollancz, 1997

Brazier, Rodney, *Ministers of the Crown*, Oxford, Clarendon Press, 1997

Brittan, Sir Leon, *Europe: The Europe We Need*, London, Hamish Hamilton, 1994

Butler, David; Adonis, Andrew; and Travers, Tony, *Failure in British Government, The Politics of the Poll Tax*, Oxford, Oxford University Press, 1994

Butt, Ronald, *The Power of Parliament*, London, Constable, 1967

Cockerell, Michael, *Live From Number 10 – The Inside Story of Prime Ministers and Television*, London, Faber and Faber, 1988

Constitution Unit, The, *Reform of the House of Lords*, 1996

Constitution Unit, The, *Scotland's Parliament, Fundamentals for a New Scotland Act*, 1996

Constitution Unit, The, *Delivering Constitutional Reform*, 1996
Constitution Unit, *Human Rights Legislation*, 1996
Cormack, Patrick, 'Restoring Faith in Parliament', *Journal of Legislative Studies*, vol. 2, no. 4, winter 1996
Cowley, Philip, '111 Not Out – the press and the 1995 Conservative leadership contest', *Talking Politics*, vol. 8, pp. 187–90, 1996
Crick, Bernard, *The Reform of Parliament*, London, Weidenfeld and Nicolson, 1964
Curtice, John, 'Is the Sun Shining on Tony Blair? The Electoral Influence of British Newspapers', *Harvard International Journal of Press/Politics*, vol. 2, no. 2, spring 1997
Deardourff, John, 'Coverage Drives Campaigns: Reflections on the Decline of Property Reporting', *Harvard International Journal of Press/Politics*, vol. 1, no. 2, spring 1996
Dicey, A. V., *Introduction to the Study of the Law of the Constitution*, 1885
Dicey, A. V., *England's Case against Home Rule*, 1886
Doig, Alan, 'Select Committee on Members' Interests', *Parliamentary Affairs*, vol. 47, no. 3, July 1994
Donaldson, Lord, 'Beware this Abuse', *Guardian*, 1 December 1995
Doolittle, I. G., *The City of London and Its Livery Companies*, London, Guildhall Library Publications, 1982
Donoughue, Bernard, and Jones, G. W., *Herbert Morrison, Portrait of a Politician*, London, Weidenfeld and Nicolson, 1973
Defence, Select Committee on, 1985–6, 'Westland plc, Government Response to the Third and Fourth Reports from the Defence Committee', Stationery Office, Command 9916
Dunleavy, Professor Patrick, 'Reinventing Parliament – making the Commons more effective', Joint Report by Charter 88 and Democratic Audit, 1995
European Legislation, Select Committee on, Twenty-seventh Report Session 1995–6, 'The Scrutiny of European Business', Stationery Office, House of Commons Paper 51–xvii.
European Legislation, Select Committee on, Twenty-eighth Report Session 1995–6, 'The Role of National Parliaments in the European Union', Stationery Office, House of Commons Paper 51–xxviii.
European Legislation, Select Committee on, Thirteenth Report 1996–7, 'The Draft Protocol on the Role of National Parliaments', Stationery Office, House of Commons Paper 36–xiii.
Fatchett, Derek, 'Reforming the Commons', Fabian Discussion Paper No. 19, Fabian Society, 1994
Flemming, John (chairman), 'The Report of the Commission on the Regulation of Privatised Utilities', Hansard Society and European Policy Forum, 1997
Fowler, Norman, *Ministers Decide*, London, Chapmans, 1991

Franklin, Bob, 'Changing Newspaper Reporting of Parliament', *Parliamentary Affairs*, vol. 49, no. 2, April 1996

Franks, Suzanne, and Vandermark, Adam, 'Televising Parliament: Five Years On', *Parliamentary Affairs*, vol. 48, no. 1, January 1995

Gordon, Richard, and Wilmot-Smith, Richard, *Human Rights in the United Kingdom*, Oxford, Clarendon Press, 1996

Greer, Ian, *One Man's Word: The Untold Story of the Cash-for-Questions Affair*, London, André Deutsch, 1997

Griffith, Professor John, and Ryle, Michael, *Parliament, Functions, Practice and Procedures*, London, Sweet and Maxwell, 1989

Griffith, Professor John, 'This Bill Should Have No Rights', *Spectator*, 15 February 1997

Hazell, Robert, 'Delivering Constitutional Reform', CIPFA/Times lecture, 14 July 1997

Heath, Sir Edward, 'Parliament Must Not Be Run by an Outsider', *Independent*, 20 May 1995

Hennessy, Peter, *The Hidden Wiring*, London, Victor Gollancz, 1995

Heseltine, Michael, *The Challenge of Europe: Can Britain Win?*, London, Weidenfeld & Nicolson, 1989

Hill, Andrew and Whichelow, Anthony, *What's Wrong with Parliament?*, London, Penguin, 1964

Hodder-Williams, Richard, *Judges and Politics in the Contemporary Age*, London, Bowderdean, 1996

Home Affairs Committee, Third Report 1995–6, 'Judicial Appointments Procedures', vol. 1, Stationery Office, House of Commons Paper 52–1

Home Office, 'Clarification of the law relating to the Bribery of Members of Parliament, A Discussion Paper', December 1996

Home Office, 'The Prevention of Corruption – Consolidation and Amendment of the Prevention of Corruption Acts 1889–1916: A Government Statement', June 1997

Hood Phillips, O., and Jackson, P., *Hood Phillips' Constitutional and Administrative Law*, London, Sweet and Maxwell, 1987

Howe, Geoffrey, *Conflict of Loyalty*, London, Macmillan, 1994

Hurd, Douglas, 'Is there still a role for MPs?', Royal Society of Arts, Wednesday, 29 January 1997

Hutton, Will, *The State We're In*, London, Jonathan Cape, 1995

Irvine of Lairg, Lord, interview in *New Statesman*, 6 December 1996

Irvine of Lairg, Lord, Keynote Address to the Conference on a Bill of Rights for the United Kingdom, University College, London, Friday, 4 July 1997

Irvine of Lairg, Lord, 'My Pivotal Role in the Constitutional Revolution', *The Times*, Saturday, 12 July 1997

Jenkins, Roy, *Gladstone*, London, Macmillan, 1995

Jenkins, Simon, *Accountable to None, The Tory Nationalization of Britain*,
    London, Hamish Hamilton, 1995
Johnson, Nevil, *In Search of the Constitution*, Oxford, 1977
Jones, Bill (ed.), *Politics UK*, London, Prentice Hall, third edition, 1997
Jones, Nicholas, *Soundbites and Spin Doctors*, London, Cassell, 1995
Jowell, Professor Jeffrey, 'Restraining the State: Politics, Principle and
    Judicial Review', The Sovereignty Seminar, Birkbeck College, March
    1997
Kavanagh, Dennis, and Seldon, Anthony (eds), *The Major Effect*, London,
    Macmillan, 1994
Keswick, Tessa, and Heathcoat Amory, Edward, *A Conservative Agenda,
    Proposals for a Fifth Term*, London, Centre for Policy Studies, 1996
Klug, Francesca; Starmer, Keir; and Weir, Stuart, *The Three Pillars of
    Liberty, Political Rights and Freedoms in the United Kingdom*, London,
    Routledge, 1996
Lansley, Andrew, and Wilson, Richard, *Conservatives and the Constitution*,
    London, The Conservative 2000 Foundation, 1997
Leicester, Graham, 'Westminster and Europe. Proposals for Change, The
    Role of National Parliaments in the European Union', The Hansard
    Society and the European Policy Forum, 1997
Leigh, David, and Vulliamy, Ed, *Sleaze, The Corruption of Parliament*,
    London, Fourth Estate, 1997
Lewis, Derek, *Hidden Agendas, Politics, Law and Disorder*, London, Hamish
    Hamilton, 1997
Liaison Committee, First Report, Session 1996–7, 'The Work of Select
    Committees', vols I and II, Stationery Office, House of Commons
    Paper 323–1 and 2
Liberal Democrats, 'A Parliament for the People, Proposals to Reform the
    House of Commons', Policy Paper 20, September 1996
Linton, Martin, 'Maybe the *Sun* won it after all', *British Journalism Review*,
    vol. 7, no. 2, 1996
Loveland, Ian, 'Parliamentary Sovereignty and the European Community:
    The Unfinished Revolution?', *Parliamentary Affairs*, vol. 49, no. 4,
    October 1996
Mancuso, Maureen, 'Ethical Attitudes of British MPs', *Parliamentary Affairs*,
    vol. 46, no. 2, April 1993
Mancuso, Maureen, *The Ethical World of British MPs*, Canada,
    McGill-Queen's University Press, 1995
Mann, Thomas, and Ornstein, Norman (eds), *Congress, the Press and the
    Public*, Washington DC, American Enterprise Institute and The
    Brookings Institution, 1994
Marquand, David, *The Unprincipled Society, New Demands and Old Politics*,
    London, Jonathan Cape, 1988
Marr, Andrew, *Ruling Britannia, The Failure and Future of British Democracy*,
    London, Michael Joseph, 1995

Marshall, Geoffrey (ed.), 'Ministerial Responsibility', in *Oxford Readings in Politics and Government*, Oxford, Oxford University Press, 1989

Marshall, Geoffrey, 'The Referendum: What, When, How?', *Parliamentary Affairs*, vol. 50, no. 2, April 1997

Mawhinney, Brian, 'Government, Politics and the Media', lecture at Manchester Business School, Wednesday, 28 February 1996

Members' Interests, Select Committee on, (the Strauss committee), 1969–70, Stationery Office, House of Commons Paper 57

Members' Interests (Declaration), Select Committee on, 1974–5, Stationery Office, House of Commons Paper 102

Members' Interests, Select Committee on, First Report 1989–90, Stationery Office, House of Commons Paper 135

Members' Interests, Select Committee on, First Report 1991–2, 'Registration and Declaration of Members' Financial Interests', Stationery Office, House of Commons Paper 326

Members' Interests, Register of, 31 January 1997, Stationery Office, House of Commons Paper 259

Modernization of the House of Commons, Select Committee on, First Report 1997–8, 'The Legislative Process', Stationery Office, House of Commons Paper 190

Mount, Ferdinand, *The British Constitution Now*, London, Heinemann, 1992

Mulgan, Geoff, *Politics in an Antipolitical Age*, Oxford, Polity Press, 1994

Mulgan, Geoff (ed.), *Life After Politics, New Thinking for the Twenty-first Century*, London, Fontana Press, 1997

Mulgan, Geoff, *Connexity, How to Live in a Connected World*, London, Chatto & Windus, 1997

Nolan, Lord, chairman of Committee on Standards in Public Life, First Report, 'Standards in Public Life', May 1995, Stationery Office, vols 1 and 2, Command 2850–1 and 2

Nolan, Lord, chairman of Committee on Standards in Public Life, Second Report, 'Standards in Public Life – Local Public Spending Bodies', May 1996, Stationery Office, vol. 1, Command 3270–1

Nolan, Lord, Radcliffe Lectures, Warwick University, November and December 1996

Norton, Philip, *Does Parliament Matter?*, London, Harvester Wheatsheaf, 1993

Norton, Philip, and Wood, David M., *Back from Westminster, British Members of Parliament and Their Constituents*, Kentucky, University Press of Kentucky, 1993

Norton, Philip, 'The United Kingdom: Political Conflict, Parliamentary Scrutiny', in 'National Parliaments and the European Union', *Journal of Legislative Studies*, vol. 1, no. 3, autumn 1995

Norton, Philip, 'Think, Minister . . .' *Reinvigorating Government in the UK*, London, Centre for Policy Studies, 1997

Pannick, David, *Judges*, Oxford, Oxford University Press, 1987

Parliamentary Commissioner for Administration, Select Committee on the, Second Report 1995–6, 'Open Government', Stationery Office, House of Commons Paper 84

Parliamentary Commissioner for Administration, Select Committee on the, First Special Report 1996–7, 'Government Response to the Second Report of 1995–96 on Open Government', Stationery Office, House of Commons Paper 75

Parliamentary Commissioner for Administration, 'Annual Report for 1996', Stationery Office, House of Commons Paper 386

Parliamentary Press Gallery, 'Partners in Parliament' – report of a working party on the state of the Press Gallery, July 1964

Pinto-Duschinsky, Michael, 'Tory troops are in worse state than feared', *The Times*, Friday, 6 June 1997

Power, Greg, *Reinventing Westminster: The MP's role and reform of the House of Commons*, London, Charter 88, 1996

Procedure, Select Committee on, First Report 1977–8, Stationery Office, House of Commons Paper 588

Procedure, Select Committee on, Fourth Report 1988–9, 'The Scrutiny of European Legislation', Stationery Office, House of Commons Paper 622

Procedure, Select Committee on, Second Report 1989–90, 'The Working of the Select Committee System', Stationery Office, House of Commons Paper 19

Procedure, Select Committee on, Seventh Report 1994–5, 'Prime Minister's Questions', Stationery Office, House of Commons Paper 555

Procedure, Select Committee on, Fourth Report 1995–6, 'Delegated Legislation', Stationery Office, House of Commons Paper 152

Procedure, Select Committee on, Third Report 1996–7, 'European Business', Stationery Office, House of Commons Paper 77

Public Accounts, Committee of, Eighth Report 1993–4, 'The Proper Conduct of Public Business', Stationery Office, House of Commons Paper 154

Public Accounts, Committee of, Sixteenth Report 1996–7, 'The Work of the Directors General of Telecommunications, Gas Supply, Water Services and Electricity Supply', Stationery Office, House of Commons Paper 89

Public Service Committee, Second Report 1995–6, 'Ministerial Accountability and Responsibility', Stationery Office, vols I, II and III, House of Commons Papers 313–i, ii and iii

Public Service Committee, First Special Report 1996–7, 'Government Response to the Second Report from the Committee (Session 1995–96) on Ministerial Accountability and Responsibility', Stationery Office, House of Commons Paper 67

Public Service Committee, Third Report 1996–7, 'The Citizen's Charter', Stationery Office, vols I and II, House of Commons Papers 78–1 and 11

Putnam, Robert, *The Strange Death of Civic America*, Prospect, March 1996

Referendums, Report of the Commission on the Conduct of Referendums, The Constitution Unit and Electoral Reform Society, 1996

Rhodes, Professor R. A. W., *Understanding Governance, Policy Networks, Governance, Reflexivity and Accountability*, Buckingham, Open University Press, 1997

Richardson, Professor Jeremy, 'The Market for Political Activism: Interest Groups as a Challenge to Political Parties', *Western European Politics*, January 1995

Riddell, Peter, 'Newspapers respond to changing nature of parliamentary democracy', *The Times*, Wednesday, 20 October 1993

Riddell, Peter, *Honest Opportunism – The Rise of the Career Politician*, London, Hamish Hamilton, 1993; in new expanded edition, London, Indigo, 1996

Riddell, Peter, 'State of the Parties', in Jones, Bill (ed.), *Politics UK*, London, Prentice Hall, third edition, 1997

Riddell, Peter, 'Our Ostrich MPs and the Constitution', *The Times*, Monday, 7 July 1997

Rippon, Lord (chairman), 'Making the Law', The Report of the Hansard Society Commission on 'The Legislative Process', London, The Hansard Society for Parliamentary Government, 1992

Robertson, Geoffrey, 'The DPP should act now – Does Neil Hamilton belong in Parliament or in jail?', *Guardian*, Tuesday, 8 April 1997

Rose, Professor Richard, and Davies, Phillip, *Inheritance in Public Policy: Change without Choice in Britain*, London, Yale University Press, 1995

Rozenberg, Joshua, *Trial of Strength, The Battle between Ministers and Judges over Who Makes the Law*, London, Richard Cohen Books, 1997

Ryle, Michael, and Richard, Peter G., *The Commons Under Scrutiny*, London, Routledge, 1988

Ryle, Michael, 'Disclosure of Financial Interests by MPs: The John Browne Affair', *Public Law*, pp. 313–22, Autumn 1990

Salmon, Lord (chairman), Royal Commission on *Standards of Conduct in Public Life*, 1976

Scott, Sir Richard (Lord Justice), 'Report of the Inquiry into the Export of Defence Equipment and Dual-Use Goods to Iraq and Related Prosecutions', Stationery Office, February 1996, House of Commons Paper 115

Scottish Constitutional Commission, *Further Steps: Towards a Scheme for Scotland's Parliament*, Edinburgh, 1994

Scottish Office, *Scotland's Parliament*, Stationery Office, Command 3658, July 1997

Seaton, Jean, and Pimlott, Ben (eds), *The Media in British Politics*, Aldershot, Avebury, 1987

Seaton, Jean, 'Sovereignty and the Media', The Sovereignty Seminar, Birkbeck College, May 1997

Sedley, Stephen (Mr Justice), 'The Common Law and the Constitution', *London Review of Books*, 8 May 1997

Seldon, Anthony, *Churchill's Indian Summer – The Conservative Government 1951–55*, London, Hodder and Stoughton, 1981

Senior Salaries, Review Body on, Report No. 38, 'Review of Parliamentary Pay and Allowances', Volume 1: Report, Stationery Office, Command 3330–1, July 1996

Seymour-Ure, Colin, 'The Media in Postwar British Politics', *Parliamentary Affairs*, vol. 47, no. 4, October 1994

Shell, Donald, and Beamish, David (eds), *The House of Lords at Work, A Study based on the 1988–89 Session*, Oxford, Clarendon Press, 1993

Sittings of the House, Select Committee on, Report 1991–2, vol. I, Stationery Office, House of Commons Paper 20–1

Socialist Commentary, 'Three Dozen Parliamentary Reforms, by one dozen parliamentary socialists', July 1964

Standards and Privileges, Committee on, First Report 1996–7, 'Complaint of Alleged Improper Pressure Brought to Bear on the Select Committee on Members' Interests in 1994', Stationery Office, House of Commons Paper 88

Standards and Privileges, Committee on, Fourth Report 1996–7, 'Complaint Against Mr Michael Howard', Stationery Office, House of Commons Paper 359

Standards and Privileges, Committee on, First Report 1997–8, 'Complaints from Mr Mohamed Al Fayed, The Guardian and Others against 25 Members and Former Members', Stationery Office, House of Commons Papers 30–1, 11 and 111

Standards in Public Life, Select Committee on, First Report 1994–5, Stationery Office, House of Commons Paper 637

Standards in Public Life, Select Committee on, Second Report 1994–5, Stationery Office, House of Commons Paper 816

Straw, Jack, 'Democracy on the Spike', *British Journalism Review*, vol. 4, no. 4, 1993

Study of Parliament Group, 'Specialist Committees in the British Parliament, The Experience of a Decade', *Political and Economic Planning*, vol. XLII, no. 564, June 1976

Summers, Martin, 'Repossessing the House: parliamentary audits and the constituent's charter', *Demos Quarterly*, issue 3, 1994

Trade and Industry Committee, First Report 1996–7, 'Energy Regulation', Stationery Office, House of Commons Paper 50–1

Trade and Industry Committee, Third Report 1996–7,

'Telecommunications Regulation', Stationery Office, House of Commons Paper 254

Tunstall, Jeremy, *Newspaper Power, The New National Press in Britain*, Oxford, Clarendon Press, 1996

Walsh, Kenneth T., *Feeding the Beast, The White House Versus the Press*, New York, Random House, 1996

Weir, Stuart, 'Questions of Democratic Accountability', *Parliamentary Affairs*, vol. 48, no. 2, April 1995

Weir, Stuart, and Hall, Wendy, *EGO TRIP: Extra-governmental Organisations in the UK, and their Accountability*, Essex University, Charter 88 Trust/Human Rights Centre, 1994

Weir, Stuart, and Wright, Tony, 'Power to the Backbenches? – Restoring the balance between Government and Parliament', A Report on a Democratic Audit poll of backbench MPs, Democratic Audit Paper No. 9

Wolf, Martin, 'Far from Powerless', *Financial Times*, 13 May 1997

Woodhouse, Diana, 'Politicians and the Judiciary', *Parliamentary Affairs*, vol. 48, no. 3, July 1995

Woodhouse, Diana, 'Politicians and the Judges', *Parliamentary Affairs*, vol. 49, no. 3, July 1996

World Bank, 'World Development Report 1997: The State in a Changing World', Oxford University Press for the World Bank, 1997

Wright, Tony, 'Beyond the Patronage State', Fabian Pamphlet 569, London, Fabian Society, 1995

Wright, Tony, and Marquand, David, 'Commentary – Reinventing Parliament', *Political Quarterly*, vol. 67, no. 2, April–June 1996

Index